# A BLINK IN TIME

# A BLINK IN TIME

*Tales from GoAnna*

**KELLIE NISSEN**

**Published by Write Angles Press**

Copyright © 2024 Kellie Nissen

All rights reserved. No part of this book may be reproduced by any mechanical, photographic, or electronic processes, or in the form of a phonographic recording. Nor may it be stored in a retrieval system, transmitted or otherwise be copied for any public or private use other than for 'fair use' - as brief quotations embodied in articles and reviews, without prior written permission of the author.

ISBN:   (Print) 978-0-6459237-0-4
        (eBook) 978-0-6459237-1-1

 A catalogue record for this book is available from the National Library of Australia

Cover and inside pages design by Claire McGregor (https://clairemcgregor.com.au)
Back cover photograph by Mel Thornberry (https://melthornberryphotography.com/)
Author photograph by Gray Tham (https://www.simplygray.com.au)
Editing by Kaaren Sutcliffe (https://kaarensutcliffe.com.au/)
Illustrations by Dani Vittz (https://danivittz.com.au)

Disclaimer

The author has endeavoured to ensure the information contained within this book is correct (or was correct at the time of publication) but takes no responsibility for any error, omission or defect herein.

# Dedication

There are too many individuals to whom I wish to dedicate this book and I can't possibly single people out. I'm sure, too, that each of the twenty-two women whose stories you are soon to read would have people they'd like to dedicate their stories to – in which case, this section would be another book.

In Australia, fifty-seven people a day are diagnosed with breast cancer. Nine people pass away every day from causes related to breast cancer. *A Blink in Time: Tales from GoAnna* is dedicated to all of you – to everyone who has been touched, in some way, by breast cancer.

I learned a new Japanese word at the start of 2024: OU-BAI-TOU-RI.

桜梅桃李

Each syllable is a flower – cherry blossom, Japanese apricot, peach blossom and the Japanese plum. Each of these flowers are appreciated for their beauty but more so for their unique qualities.

*Oubaitouri* means to bloom in one's own time and to embrace one's unique style. For me, this is the essence of *GoAnna*.

# Contents

| | |
|---|---|
| **Foreword: Kerrie Griffin OAM** | **1** |
| **Author's Note** | **6** |
|    On memory | 6 |
|    On the book's structure | 7 |
|    Where does the name GoAnna come from? | 7 |
| **Glossary of Terms** | **9** |
|    Dragon Boating Terms | 9 |
|    Medical Terms | 11 |
| **Prologue** | **19** |
| **Sunrise Paddle** | **21** |
| **The Coach** | **23** |
|    Jenny's Story: You Will Be You Again | 26 |
| **Bench 1 – Left** | **34** |
|    Clare's Story: Just a Chapter in My Book | 37 |
| **Bench 1 – Right** | **50** |
|    Elly's Story: Keeping Things Normal | 52 |
| **Bench 2 – Left** | **60** |
|    Megan's Story: Cactus | 62 |
| **Bench 2 – Right** | **76** |
|    Anne's Story: A Ride You Can't Get Off | 78 |
| **Bench 3 – Left** | **86** |
|    Kathy's Story: Beautiful Trauma | 88 |
| **Bench 3 – Right** | **97** |
|    April's Story: A Process to Go Through | 99 |
| **Bench 4 – Left** | **113** |
|    Joan's Story: Been There. Done That. | 116 |
| **Bench 4 – Right** | **122** |
|    Amanda's Story: Just Make Them Even | 125 |
| **Bench 5 – Left** | **140** |
|    Marion's Story: No Room for Complacency | 143 |
| **Bench 5 – Right** | **151** |
|    Nadine's Story: Your Own Emotional Roller-Coaster | 153 |

| | |
|---|---|
| **Bench 6 – Left** | **158** |
| Denise's Story: Live in the Now | 161 |
| **Bench 6 – Right** | **167** |
| Katherine's Story: No Time for This – I'm Booked on a Dragon Boat | 170 |
| **Bench 7 – Left** | **185** |
| Janet's Story: A Bit of a Detour | 187 |
| **Bench 7 – Right** | **196** |
| Deb's Story: This Too Will Pass | 198 |
| **Bench 8 – Left** | **210** |
| Anita's Story: But I Don't Have Cancer, Do I? | 213 |
| **Bench 8 – Right** | **223** |
| Sugar's Story: An Awakening | 225 |
| **Bench 9 – Left** | **239** |
| Nat's Story: If You Didn't Laugh, You'd Cry | 241 |
| **Bench 9 – Right** | **262** |
| Joanne's Story: Let the Games Begin | 264 |
| **Bench 10 – Left** | **273** |
| Che's Story: Always Go Forwards | 275 |
| **Bench 10 – Right** | **285** |
| Gillian's Story: Not Without Me … | 287 |
| **The Sweep** | **303** |
| Lyndall's Story: It Was Tough But I Was Tougher | 306 |
| **End of Session** | **315** |
| **Epilogue** | **317** |
| **Appreciation** | **318** |
| **A Little Bit of History** | **320** |
| Dragons Abreast Australia (DAA) | 320 |
| Dragons Abreast Canberra (DAC) | 320 |
| Paddling with Anna | 321 |
| **Where to Find More Info** | **323** |
| Breast cancer support | 323 |
| Dragons Abreast (dragon boating for breast cancer survivors and supporters) | 324 |
| Dragon Boating (in general) | 324 |
| Other references | 324 |

# Foreword: Kerrie Griffin OAM

*When the heart weeps for what it has lost,
the soul laughs for what it has found.*

~ A Sufi saying and motto of Dragons Abreast Canberra ~

I am humbled and delighted to share these feisty tales of the lived experience. Here are recurring themes of the immediacy at the time of a breast cancer diagnosis. Themes include no family history, being on a roller-coaster, struggles with 'scanxiety' and frustration about not knowing your options and the need to be your own advocate as well as maintaining a good sense of humour. Somehow, the chemo brain fog leads to beautiful trauma and a greater appreciation of family, friends, nature and life.

Breast cancer does not discriminate, and you find people from eclectic and diverse backgrounds bonding in the Dragons Abreast Canberra dragon boat. These kindred spirits are stronger together as they raise awareness about breast cancer in the community. But they don't talk about the lived experience of breast cancer because they are focused on their technique, timing and the surrounding nature, which is good for the soul. However, if you do need advice you instantly have this excellent resource to point you in the right direction. The Dragons Abreast Australia tagline is appropriately: *Connect. Move. Live.*

Professor Don McKenzie's 1996 groundbreaking Canadian research promoting the benefits of dragon boating resistance skills for women living with breast cancer was the catalyst for starting Dragons Abreast

Australia in 1998, not long after the launch of the Breast Cancer Network Australia (BCNA) at Parliament House in Canberra in October 1998. *Exercise is medicine* wasn't embraced until 2010 by clinicians' research but is now widely promoted globally.

In 1999, I had a melanoma removed and that episode was finished. In 2001, I was diagnosed with breast cancer and I felt like I was on a roller-coaster. Unfortunately, at that time, psychosocial treatment was a distant dream in the future. In 2015, my older sister, Lesley Thomas, was diagnosed with breast cancer and I appreciated the enormous improvements in multidisciplinary care, targeted therapies, new drugs and protocols. There's still much work to do, especially in the field of metastatic cancer to help those managing a recurrence. Those vital improvements are the result of lobbying by BCNA and Dragons Abreast Australia.

BCNA works to ensure that Australians affected by breast cancer receive the very best support, information, treatment and care appropriate to their individual needs. BCNA provides free resources for those with early and metastatic breast cancer. BCNA is represented by the Pink Lady silhouette, symbolic of its focus on the women diagnosed with breast cancer and all those around them. *What you don't know until you do* is a fantastic and relevant new BCNA podcast series.

Every cloud has a silver lining, and my family and friends are very supportive. I found my tribe in Dragons Abreast Canberra and feel extremely privileged to be a member. Paddles up!

*Foreword: Kerrie Griffin OAM*

In the words of Anna Wellings-Booth OAM, founder of Dragons Abreast Canberra,

> *May the great dragon continue to blow us gently towards further adventures – living life to the full and making every moment count.*

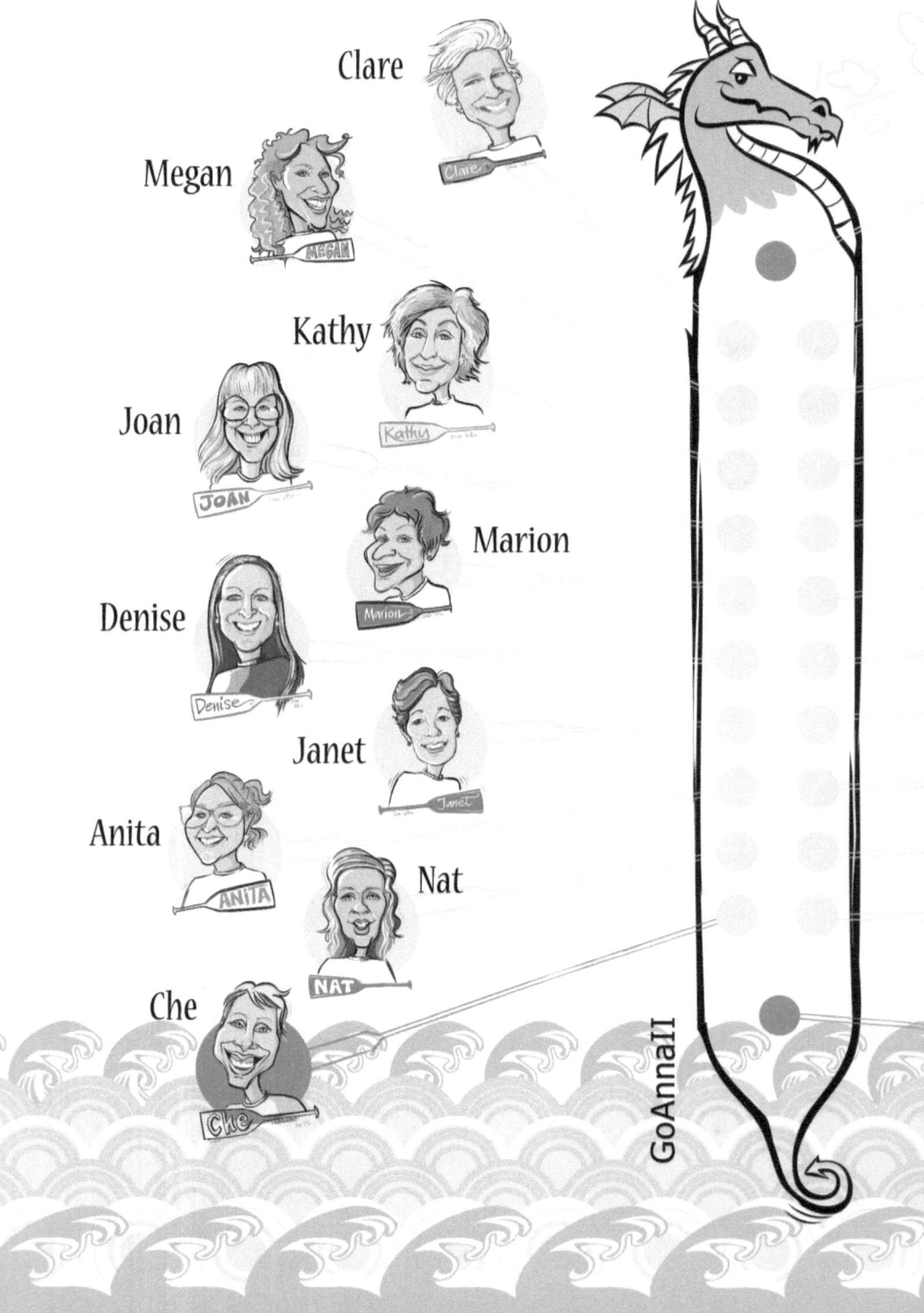

 Jenny

 Elly

 Anne

 April

 Amanda

 Nadine

 Katherine

 Deb

 Sugar

 Joanne

 Gillian

 Lyndall

# Author's Note

The idea for this book presented itself while I was writing my memoir, *What Cancer Said – And what I said back*. I wanted to support some of my experiences and emotions with 'short, punchy anecdotes' from 'a few' of the ladies I paddled with in Dragons Abreast Canberra (DAC).

I put the call out, expecting to hear back from four or five people.

Twenty-two DAC members got back to me. That's a full crew. I could certainly run with that.

I interviewed them. The way they opened their hearts and shared their stories with me was humbling. They were all talking about the same core event – breast cancer – but every single story was different. Devastating. Poignant. Funny. Heartwarming.

Following the interviews, I set about scanning through the transcripts to 'pick out the gold' – select those short quotes I could use in my book. This was when I realised — every part of every one of their stories was 'the gold'.

I couldn't dissect the stories, extract the good bits and discard the rest. It wasn't my place to choose what was worthy of being shared and what wasn't. I had to honour each story. In its entirety.

And so, *A Blink in Time: Tales from GoAnna* was born.

## On memory

You will still find pieces of gold from these twenty-two wonderful women in *What Cancer Said,* but in this book you will find each Pink Lady's story in full, in their voice, as it was told to me.

Their stories are how they remember them – but memory is a funny thing. Sometimes, for whatever reason, it's accurate down to the last detail. Often, it's prompted by notes we have kept. Usually, it distorts over time.

*Author's Note*

Perspectives can be different too. The memories those of us who had breast cancer have about particular happenings can often be quite different from those of the people around us. You may notice this in two of the stories – Jenny's and Nadine's. They are both 'supporter' members of DAC and I interviewed them to obtain the supporter perspective. Jenny talks about her sister Lyndall's diagnosis and recovery, and Nadine talks about her experiences with her mother, Marion.

Nobody – the person who experienced the breast cancer or the supporter – is hiding anything or deliberately bending the truth; it's just the way our memories work.

## On the book's structure

While *A Blink in Time* was written to honour the twenty-two women who shared their stories with me, I also wanted to acknowledge the other thing that brings us all together. Not breast cancer – that's a given – but dragon boating.

I wanted to give you a taste of what dragon boating means and is for us, as members of Dragons Abreast Canberra.

Ideally, I'd love you to come down to Grevillea Park, on the shores of Lake Burley Griffin in Canberra, one morning and join us for a training session, but I know that's not practical for everyone. So, the next best thing I can offer is to take you with us through narrative.

In between each of the twenty-two stories is a short narrative, introducing each Pink Lady and giving you a taste of our training sessions. You'll get to experience a bit of everything – warm-up, drills, racing and endurance, as well as the shenanigans, laughter and playful moments that make up a training session for us.

## Where does the name *GoAnna* come from?

Dragons Abreast Canberra own two dragon boats, a ten-seater called *Gecko* and a twenty-seater named *GoAnna II*.

Founded in 1999, the DAC members went by various names, including *The Allsorts* – taken from the popular Licorice Allsorts lollies, because 'all sorts of people are diagnosed with breast cancer'. In 2004, the decision was made to compete under the club name, *Tickled Pink*, a name that stayed with the team until 2012 when it was officially changed to *GoAnna* in honour of the club's founder, Anna Wellings-Booth OAM. However, the team had been incorporating the cry 'Go Anna' into their cheers for years before this.

The story goes that, while the team was out paddling, Anna's friends would often see her in the boat, seated in her usual position – Bench 5 on the left – and call, "Go, Anna!" from the shore. The cry, and then the name, stuck and is a fitting tribute to an amazing woman.

You can read more about Anna in the appendix, which also contains information about dragon boating and our overarching association, Dragons Abreast Australia.

I invite you to close your eyes for a moment and imagine you are out on the lake with us, feeling yourself surging forward with the breeze ruffling your hair. Then, open your eyes and enjoy the stories from twenty-two wonderful, resilient women.

We welcome you aboard *GoAnna*.

# Glossary of Terms

## Dragon Boating Terms

**AusDBF**
The Australian Dragon Boat Federation is the sport's governing body in Australia.

**Coach**
Each team has at least one coach. Coaches must be accredited and can either be a survivor or a supporter member. Coaches sometimes also have a role as a sweep or drummer.

**DAA**
Dragons Abreast Australia is the national association – a charity and run by volunteers – that oversees all Dragons Abreast affiliated clubs across Australia.

**DAC**
Dragons Abreast Canberra is a dragon boating club for breast cancer survivors and supporters based in Canberra — with the team name *GoAnna*.

**DBACT**
Dragon Boat ACT is the governing body of the sport of dragon boating in the Australian Capital Territory.

**Drummer**
The drummer sits at the front of the boat, facing the crew. They work with the sweep to communicate instructions to the paddlers and beat the drum to set the pace in conjunction with the strokes. (Alternative name: caller)

**Engine room**
The middle section of the boat is referred to as the engine room. In a standard boat, there are eight paddlers, or four benches, in this section. These paddlers provide the 'power' in the boat.

## Gunnel
Also known as the gunwale, the gunnel refers to the sides of the boat.

## IBCPC
The International Breast Cancer Paddlers' Commission is the international overarching organisation responsible for encouraging the establishment of breast cancer dragon boat teams. Among other events, the IBCPC coordinates the international survivors' regatta held approximately every four years.

## Kashgar Cup
Awarded annually to the Dragons Abreast Canberra member who has made an extraordinary contribution to the work of Dragons Abreast Canberra.

## Pacers
The first three benches of a standard boat, these six paddlers are made up of the two strokes (in Bench 1) who set the pace, and the next four paddlers who match the pace of the strokes. Pacers are also known as 'fronts'.

## Paddler
Dragon boat crew members are referred to as 'paddlers' (because we 'paddle' forwards, we don't row backwards).

## PFD
Personal flotation device, also known as a life jacket.

## Rookie Award
An award presented to a paddler who joined Dragons Abreast Canberra in the preceding paddling season from September to September, and who has shown improvement in paddling skills and persistence in attending training sessions.

## Small boat
Often referred to as a '10s' boat, the small boat takes a maximum of ten paddlers, plus the sweep and a drummer.

## Standard boat
Often referred to as a '20s' boat, the standard boat takes a maximum of twenty paddlers, plus the sweep and a drummer.

### Stroke
The two paddlers seated in Bench 1 at the front of the boat are known as the 'strokes'. The strokes set the pace and level of power as called for by the sweep, helped by the drummer.

### Supporter
In a Dragons Abreast team, supporter members are paddling members who have not had breast cancer. They most often become members to support a family member or friend who is a breast cancer survivor.

### Survivor
A Dragons Abreast team is mainly made up of 'survivor' members, people who have had a diagnosis of breast cancer.

### Sweep
The sweep, also known as the 'steer' or the 'steersperson', stands at the back of the boat and controls the sweep oar. The sweep is responsible for steering the boat, giving commands and keeping the crew members safe. The sweep determines whether conditions are safe for paddling, and works with the coach to plan and deliver training sessions.

### Trimmers
The six paddlers seated in the last three benches of a standard boat are referred to as the trimmers. Also known as the 'rockets' or the 'backs'.

## Medical Terms

The following cancer-related medical terms is not a complete list but covers the terms mentioned by the twenty-two women in their stories. They are listed here to reduce repetition in the stories.

### Arimidex
Arimidex is an aromatase inhibitor, prescribed to women who have entered menopause. The tablet medication reduces the amount of oestrogen made by the body, with the aim of slowing or stopping the growth of cancer. It is usually taken for five years or so once other treatments are finished.

### Aromatase inhibitors (AIs)
Medication that helps reduce the amount of oestrogen that is made in the body. Types include Anastrozole and Letrozole. These are taken after

surgery or radiation is completed and only prescribed to postmenopausal women.

**Breast care nurse**
A breast care nurse is a Registered Nurse who specialises in the care of people with breast cancer. The program is funded and managed by the McGrath Foundation, in memory of Jane McGrath (wife of cricketer Glenn McGrath), who died from breast cancer.

**Breast expander**
Commonly known as a 'tissue expander', an expander is used to stretch the skin and tissue after a mastectomy, to make room for a breast implant.

**Breast implant**
After a mastectomy, women can opt for a breast reconstruction where a saline or silicone breast implant may be used to rebuild the breast.

**BreastScreen ACT**
This organisation is the national breast cancer screening program and operates in every state of Australia, providing women over 40, who have not been previously diagnosed with breast cancer, with a free mammogram every two years.

**Chemotherapy**
Also referred to as 'chemo', chemotherapy is the use of anti-cancer drugs to destroy cancer cells. It may be used before or after surgery and radiation therapy. Chemo is often delivered intravenously, although some tablet forms are becoming available.

**Clear margins**
An area of healthy cells around the cancer that has been removed.

**Craniotomy**
An operation to open the skull to access the brain for surgical repair.

**Docetaxel**
Also known as 'Taxotere', Docetaxel is a chemotherapy drug. It is used to treat primary breast cancer that has not spread beyond the breast or lymph nodes, often in combination with other chemo drugs.

**DCIS (Ductal carcinoma in situ)**
DCIS is when the abnormal (cancer) cells are contained in the milk ducts and have not spread.

## Encapsulation
An encapsulated breast implant is a condition in which thick scar tissue forms around a breast implant, causing it to become hard and often painful.

## Endone
A strong opioid medication commonly prescribed for pain.

## ER+ (Oestrogen Receptor positive)
Cancer cells that have receptors that allow them to use the hormone oestrogen to grow.

## ER/PR+
Cancer cells that use both oestrogen and progesterone to grow.

## Gamma Knife surgery
A highly precise form of radiation, Gamma Knife is non-invasive and used to treat various brain conditions, including malignant or benign tumours.

## Herceptin
A HER2 inhibitor targeted therapy that works against Human Epidermal growth factor Receptor 2-positive (HER2+) breast cancers.

## HER2
Human Epidermal growth factor Receptor-2: a healthy protein in normal amounts.

## HER2-negative (HER2-)
Breast cancer with a normal amount of HER2 protein.

## HER2-positive (HER2+)
Breast cancers that have a higher-than-normal amount of the protein called HER2 on the surface of the cancer cells.

## Invasive Ductal Carcinoma (IDC)
Cancer that started in the milk ducts and spread to other parts of the breast. It is the most common form of breast cancer, accounting for 80 per cent of diagnoses.

## Letrozole
Letrozole is one of the aromatase inhibitor medications that may be prescribed to treat breast cancer in postmenopausal women. It is

often used for women who have had other cancer treatments, such as Tamoxifen.

**Lobular carcinoma**
Lobular cancer starts in the milk-producing glands of the breast. This type of cancer tends to form a 'thickening' rather than a 'lump'. Lobular carcinoma may be 'in situ' (contained) or 'invasive' (spreading into the breast tissue). Invasive lobular carcinoma is the second most common form of breast cancer.

**Lumpectomy**
Surgery to remove cancer from the breast, where the cancer or other abnormal tissue is removed along with a small amount of healthy surrounding tissue. The rest of the breast remains intact.

**Lymphoedema**
A swelling of the arm, hand or chest wall caused by fluid build-up following the removal of lymph nodes during breast cancer surgery. Not all women will develop lymphoedema after breast cancer surgery.

**Mastectomy**
Surgery to remove the whole breast or the majority of the breast tissue and nipple; undertaken to treat or prevent breast cancer.

**Metastatic breast cancer**
Commonly shortened to 'mets', this is breast cancer that has spread to another part of the body, most commonly the brain, bones, liver or lungs. This can occur quite some time, many years, after the initial diagnosis and treatment.

**Neoadjuvant therapy**
Neoadjuvant therapy is often recommended to reduce the size of the tumour before surgery. The treatment starts several months before surgery and may involve chemotherapy, targeted therapy or hormone-blocking therapy.

**Neutropenia**
A condition in which you have a low number of neutrophils (white blood cells) and are therefore more susceptible to infections. This is carefully monitored during chemotherapy and radiation therapy.

*Glossary of Terms*

**PBS (Pharmaceutical Benefits Scheme)**
An Australian Government initiative whereby the government subsidises the cost of medicine for many (but not all) medical conditions.

**PR+ (Progesterone Receptor positive)**
The cancer cells have receptors that allow them to use the progesterone hormone to grow.

**Radiation therapy**
Also called radiotherapy, this treatment uses X-rays to destroy or injure cancer cells so they cannot multiply.

**Sentinel lymph node biopsy**
A surgical approach to identify and remove the sentinel lymph node to determine if the cancer has spread, and if so, how far.

**Tamoxifen**
A drug used to treat breast cancer in both premenopausal women and postmenopausal women, as well as some men. This tablet is often taken for five or more years.

**Taxol**
The brand name for Paclitaxel; a chemotherapy drug given as a drip into a vein.

**Treatment team**
The collective term for the group of medical professionals people with breast cancer usually see. The team includes the GP, surgeon, medical oncologist, breast care nurse and radiation oncologist.

**Triple negative breast cancer (TNBC)**
An aggressive and fast-growing cancer that does not have any of the three receptors commonly found in breast cancer cells – the oestrogen, progesterone and HER2 receptors. This cancer is one of the most difficult to treat.

**Zoladex**
A type of hormone therapy used to treat breast cancer in premenopausal women and given as an injection into the abdomen.

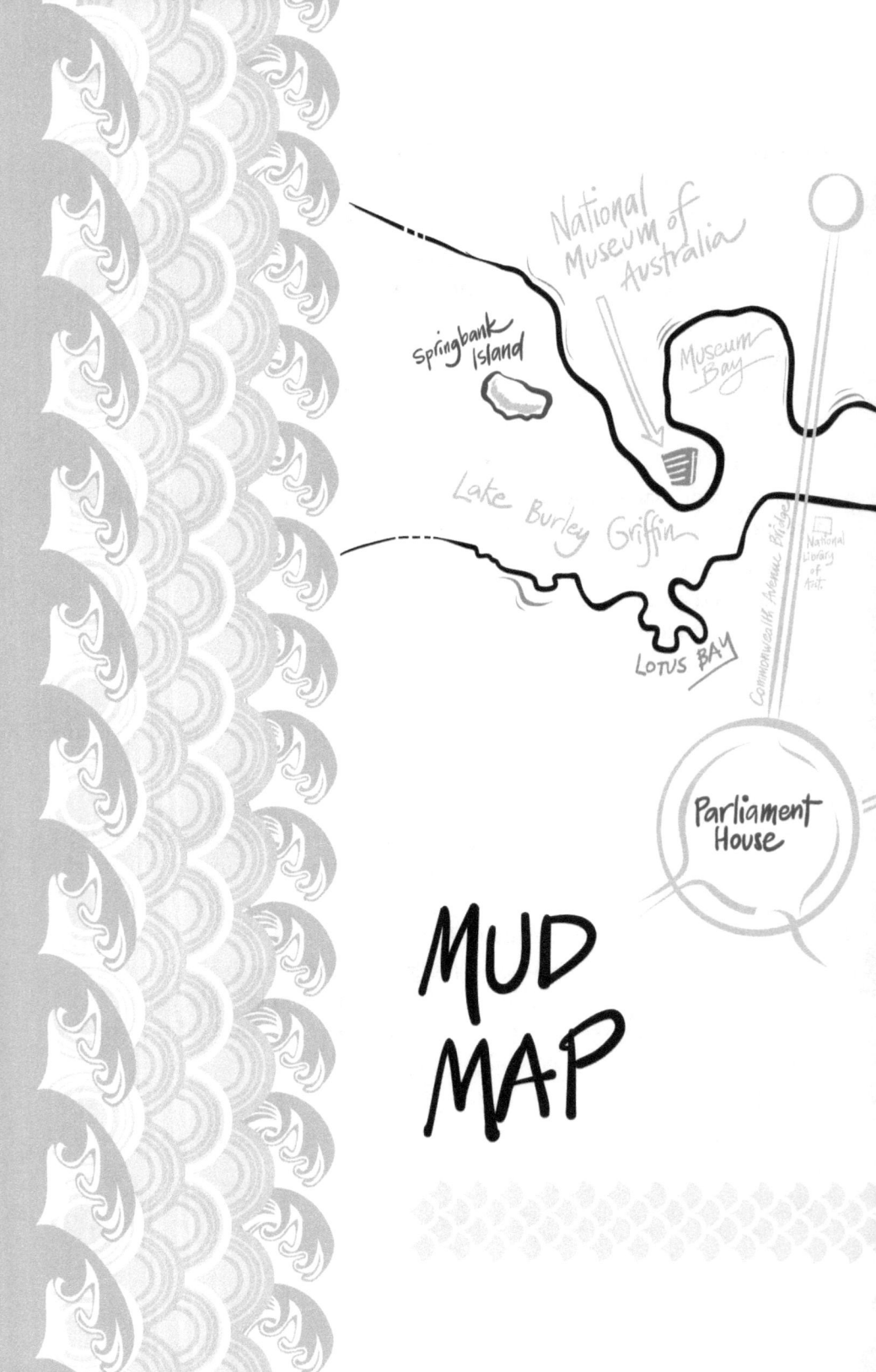

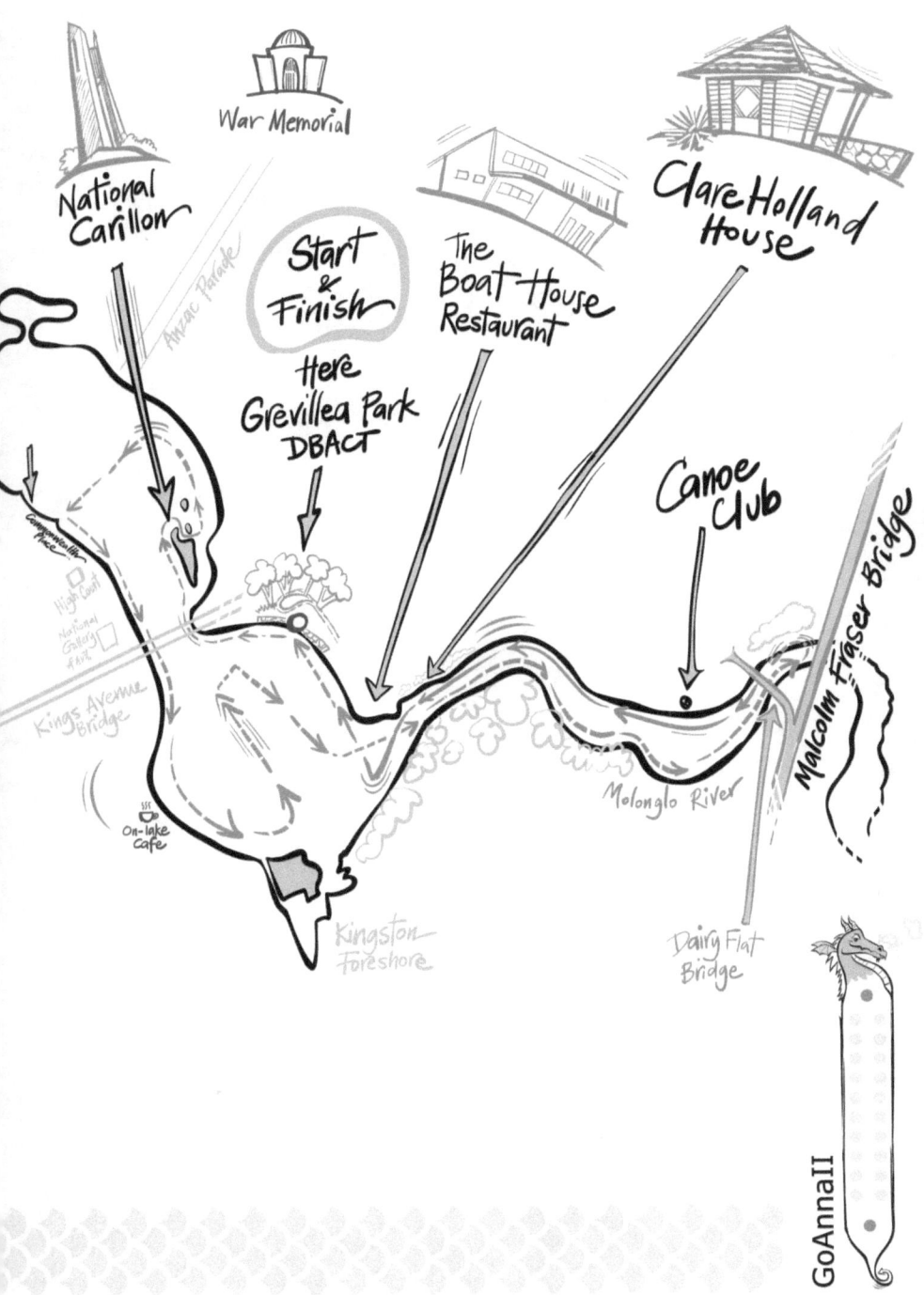

Kellie Nissen

# Prologue

An eerie mist hovers over the lake in the stillness of early morning. Beyond the dark, the sun hovers, yet to warm and melt the shimmering crystals that cover the sparse clumps of grass – sparkling like stars on a clear night as they catch tiny rays of light.

Heads and tails stored safely in the shed, drums silent and still – the dragon boats sleep. Tucked up in their blue marine canvas nightgowns, they sit atop their tyre beds in two neat rows, and wait. All present and accounted for – except one. Empty tyres, nightgown neatly folded and cast to one side, trolley-tracks winding their way to the shore.

Listen. Watch.

Kellie Nissen

# Sunrise Paddle

Out on the lake, a long silhouette emerges from the mist. The call of the sweep cuts through the dawn silence and, if one stops breathing momentarily, the plink and swoosh-pop of twenty paddles – working as one – form a rhythmic time stamp on the day.

Light sweeps the lake and dims. A car door slams. And another. The crunch of footsteps across crystal grass.

"I see she has them out early."

A murmur of agreement while we peer at the dragon skimming over the water. The Auroras – Australian representatives – committed to frosty training as they prepare for the world titles.

"They look good."

And they do. But so do we.

We are GoAnna. Dragons Abreast Canberra. DAC. The Pink Ladies. We are paddlers. Team mates. Friends. We train all year round – the heat of summer through to the frost of winter when we rug up, crack sheets of ice off the boat before heading out into the bracing freeze. We have been through more than icy noses and chilled fingertips. That chill will wear off once we get out on the water, blowing 'smoke' through our nostrils and mouths – like fire from a dragon's breath.

A badge of honour worn with pride, we were the second Dragons Abreast club to form in Australia; now, we are the oldest, longest-running club in the country.

We are here for many reasons – competition, fitness, connection, rehabilitation, fun. Whenever we can we train, socialise, gather, compete in local regattas, interstate competitions and international regattas – Canada, Italy, New Zealand. We'll be in France in 2026. Bring it on.

All women paddlers, today we range in age from 78 to 42. We are single, married, separated. We have children, grandchildren. We are nurses, teachers, scientists, public servants – retired, semi-retired, working fulltime, part-time, volunteers.

Kellie Nissen

We don't discriminate.

Neither does breast cancer.

We all have our goals, our limitations, our frustrations, our successes and our joys. We are many. But on the water we are one.

*GoAnna!*

# The Coach

A few of us routinely arrive early to take photos. Enjoy the morning silence. Get a park – even at this time of the morning, especially with the Auroras out training.

With the help of a few extra people, we were able to get our boat dressed and down to the water where she now sits, wedged on a submerged tyre up against the pontoon. Her tail held high, head upright, her eyes impatiently seeking her crew.

*GoAnna II.*

The boat wears her name on her flank with pride. Painted pink scales travel the length of her spine, down to her tail – erect and ready. Eyes bright. The silver ball in her mouth gleams, catching the headlamp worn by our sweep, Lyndall.

"Will we put the drum on today?" she asks.

Lyndall's sister, Jenny, nods. One of the team's coaches, she's also a drummer. Having the sisters top and tail the boat is something special.

There's a regatta coming up, so the full kit-out comes as no surprise. It's all part of the training.

Keys jingle and clink as we toss them into 'the pink bag'. Nobody wants their car keys sinking to the bottom of Lake Burley Griffin should there be a mishap.

"Are we good?" Lyndall calls us all over and reads names from a list. "We're all here, and we're right on time. Let's warm up, then."

Twenty-two women, clad in hot pink life jackets and an assortment of footwear, form a circle on the grass near the sandy shore. Jenny runs us through our warm-up drills.

Star jumps, squats, skis.

Figure eights, chicken wings and boxing moves.

"Who's stroking today?" she asks once the warm-up is done.

The strokes. The two paddlers that sit in the first bench. Set the pace and timing. Inside arms rising nice and high so the rest of us can follow their movements.

Elly and Clare look at each other. They raise their hands.

"Unless someone else wants to …" Clare says. We all know full well that nobody does.

"Excellent," Jenny says. "Everyone else line up behind them."

Lyndall walks down the line, checking with her sweep's eye for how the weight will balance in the boat – right and left, front and back. "I think we're good. Let's load."

A smattering of chatter threatens to turn into something bigger. "Quietly," Jenny says, an edge of authority in her voice.

We snap to attention, ready to enter our dragon's domain. Lyndall stands tall and straight up the back, sweep oar in hand. Once we are loaded, sitting with our hips against the gunnel, and Jenny is perched aloft the drummer seat, Lyndall calls, "Ready to backset."

As one, we all place our paddle blades behind us, ready to reverse the boat out.

"Attention. Go."

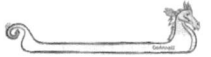

*The Coach*

**Name:** Jenny Milward-Bason
**Joined DAC:** 2018 as a supporter for sister Lyndall
**Favourite boat position:** drummer
**Best DAC moment:** going to Florence in 2018 for the IBCPC regatta
**Bucket list:** to walk a section of the Camino Trail

Kellie Nissen

# Jenny's Story: You Will Be You Again

> *Lyndall called and asked if I would come in
> with her to the screening clinic. I didn't know
> anything at this stage. I was completely in the dark.*

"I'm getting some test results," Lyndall said, "for the biopsy I had. Would you come with me?"

This was the first I'd heard of this test and I knew nothing about biopsies, but with Mum's breast cancer experience, I thought, 'Well, this could go badly.'

We went in, both of us sort of expecting – hoping – it would be nothing, that it might be a storm in a teacup. The practitioner started talking to us both, going through the results and the tests. I was sitting there listening and all I could think was, 'Oh, my God.'

I burst into tears.

There I was, the 'support' person, crying – and Lyndall was the one who was calm and trying to make me feel okay. It was the wrong way around.

There was no control over my reaction; the news took me completely by surprise. I didn't know how this journey was going to go, particularly with Lyndall's husband John, who was a bit all over the place. We could never predict how he was going to react.

Once I'd finally pulled myself together, I went with her, a few days later, to her first appointment with the surgeon. John was with us as well, but he was a mess; my recollection is that he wasn't in the room for part of it.

Anyway, the surgeon was talking about the options Lyndall had and I was sitting there thinking, 'I'm not going to say anything. It's not my decision.' As far as I was concerned, my role was to listen with an open mind and try to remember everything that was said.

Lyndall looked okay on the surface, but I know there was shock there. There had to be. I didn't think she would necessarily hear everything that was said – or the way it was said – and John didn't process information in the way that was needed.

I was there for most of the consultation but left the room and waited outside when John came back in so it could be just the two of them.

Lyndall was, I think, in two minds about what to do. "I'm going to have to think about it," she said when she came out. "Work out what the best way forward is."

"Look, we're going to run into Christmas," I said. "The doctor said if you want to start the process before Christmas, you'll have to make a fast decision." I thought that was a good thing in a way because Lyndall is the sort of person who normally weighs up every single pro and con before making a decision. Whereas, if I were in her place, I would have said yes or no straight away. No mulling it over. I like a time constraint when making decisions, Lyndall, not so much.

Her medical team decided on a lumpectomy; Lyndall decided to have the lumpectomy before Christmas.

I thought it was probably the best option, given the size of the lump and where it was.

Lyndall managed to get in for her surgery right before the Christmas shutdown. I was around for most of the surgery side of things; helping her get over that. John was more on board after this. When she was about to start chemo in the new year, he became extremely protective. I'd turn up to visit and he'd say, "No, she's sleeping." I felt pushed away by him during a lot of her chemo treatment.

The other thing I was concerned about was that Lyndall had decided to go back to work all through her chemo. I understood the theory behind her decision, but I wasn't sure about her energy levels — even though knew I was basing this on our mum's experience, and their situations were quite different.

*I wasn't so much worried about whether she could do the work, but what the pressure might do to her health as well as how much support she was going to need with her boys, who were still quite young.*

The worry I had about Lyndall's health was compounded by not being able to see her. I was working quite hard myself, plus doing all the other family stuff that Lyndall would normally have done; she had no energy for it.

Lyndall did come to my granddaughter's first birthday. It was on the weekend, a Saturday brunch at home, and when she turned up I said, "What are you doing here?" She must have been well into her chemo by that stage, perhaps close to her fifth round, and she looked terrible.

I thought, 'How could I not know this?' She looked so unwell. I let her sit down for a while and then got somebody to come and pick her up to take her home.

After she left, I turned to my ex and said, "How I could be so disconnected from this? How could I be so not in the picture?"

That's what I needed to start pushing to see her more and be more involved. But it was hard work. I was also concerned because, towards the end of her chemo, I didn't think she was doing so well with her energy levels at work. She thought she was, but she wasn't. She wasn't bouncing back. I started taking her boys for her every so often. They were amazing throughout this but they all needed a break. I'd take them shopping and a few other places, just to take the pressure off Lyndall.

I did what I could, but I felt I was on the edge.

When the radiation treatments started, I was a little more aware of what was happening – the draining effect it had on her, the inability to eat or drink much and how she was so tired all the time.

I became the nagging voice. "You should take some time off work," I'd say.

She'd argue back, "We're really busy at the moment."

I'd counter-argue. "They can do without you for a few days. Just rest. It's important."

Definitely the nagging sister.

In the end, she did take some time off, probably more days than she'd planned because there was no way she could keep going. I think she managed better with the chemo than the radiation, to be honest. Most of the time, she seemed to bounce back after the chemo but with the radiation, she kept getting more and more tired.

On the whole though, after every treatment she had a slower recovery; more symptoms, more illness, more everything. It was hard to watch. I learned a lot about the whole process and what people go through.

After her radiation finished, they put her on Tamoxifen.

Oh. My. God.

---

*That medication brought out her 'crazy'.*

---

I don't know what she was feeling on the inside, but everybody on the outside was stunned. We were all like, 'Oh my God, she's crazy.' She was so unpredictable. Not the calm lady we knew; not at all. We'd have these disagreements. I doubt Lyndall remembers, but I'd open my mouth and get snapped at.

She was always fighting her weight because of the medication. I remember thinking, 'Oh, this is the first time you've been in my shoes.' It affected her memory too. I felt like she was turning into me there for a bit.

I'd try to reassure her. "Look, it's okay," I said. "It's the medication. There's nothing you can do about it except put up with it."

She did try to get back to being as 'normal' as possible, even when she was on Tamoxifen. The first time Lyndall decided she was ready to be 'normal', she wanted to go on a bushwalk with the club we were with.

On the day of the walk, I rang her up to check.

"Yes, we're going," she said. "I'm going on this bushwalk."

I rang the lady who was organising it all. "Lyndall wants to come," I said. "Can we take it down a notch? Perhaps something flat to start with because she's not going to cope with hills. She's not eating properly. She has no energy. She's still wearing a cap because her hair is only starting to grow back."

The group were great. Very supportive.

Off we went. Lyndall looked like marshmallow-person; obviously must have been feeling the cold. She's walking along and I was watching her get more and more wobbly-looking. After about two kilometres, I could tell she was absolutely knackered. We could all see it, so everyone turned around and went back – we didn't want her to fall over.

In some way, I'm sure she felt like she'd succeeded in doing something, but for us, we all felt really concerned she wasn't ready. It was a slow build back into fitness for her.

She doesn't talk about it much but I knew she was pretty pleased with how the treatment went, pleased with the results and how the scar looked. I think that really gave her a boost. She came back to being her normal self, probably over the next six months or so. Still a bit crazy, like menopause symptoms, I suppose – the hot sweats and that sort of stuff. Her symptoms were fast-tracked compared to when I went through menopause. Mine took years and years, whereas she was getting it all in one year. It was hard, I know, but I couldn't help thinking how unfair that was because I was still in the middle of it while she was going through it. I think she coped amazingly well.

---

*One day, she said, "I'm going dragon boating. I'm going to do that."*

---

"You're going to do what?" I said. I had no idea how she'd found out about this.

"I'm going to try dragon boating with Dragons Abreast."

I don't know where, but I'd heard of Dragons Abreast. Perhaps someone at work had mentioned it? Anyway, I went along with her and she was so happy! My granddaughter was there and was cheering from the shore. When Lyndall got off the boat at the end of the session, you couldn't wipe that smile from her face. All she wanted to do was talk about it and show me the stroke and how to hold the paddle.

I was so excited for her. She loved it so much. It was such a gift for her to be with other people who had gone through what she'd experienced, and for her to see how it's not the end of the road.

Lyndall bought a paddle pretty quickly – not long after that first session – and my ex and I got her a PFD and some DAC shirts and a jacket. Her first paddle was in November and by January she'd joined and was competing in regattas. She was always talking about it, trying to get me to come along and get on the boat. "You'll love it," she'd say. "You'll have a great time."

"But, I'm not a breast cancer survivor."

"So? We have supporters in the boat too."

"Really?" I hadn't known that.

That's when she knew she'd got me. "Yeah, you can come along as a supporter. You'll love it." She looked at me – doing the hard sell. "And it would be good for you."

That last comment got me because I'd stopped doing most of my regular fitness activities, apart from bushwalking.

*So, there I was, finally doing my first paddle on a cold and miserable May morning in 2017.*

I finally agreed because Lyndall was having such a great time. I'd seen her on the water several times and she couldn't stop talking about it. She made dragon boating sound like fun; made it sound like something I could do.

To join, I had to fill out a declaration stating that I swore allegiance to breast cancer awareness goals … or something like that. Then Lyndall kitted me out and suddenly, I was sitting in the boat.

Talk about being a slow learner. I think Lyndall picked it all up quite quickly — but not me. At times, I felt our coach was a little impatient because I wasn't a survivor so therefore I 'must not have any issues'. I had lots of other injuries, though. A range of health conditions and chronic asthma. At the time, my asthma was quite out of control; I ended up getting pneumonia during my first year of paddling and had to stop for several months. When I was healthy enough to get back on the boat, I found myself at a regatta, lining up to do the two-kilometre race.

Two kilometres! That's around fifteen minutes of non-stop paddling – after not having paddled for several months and getting over pneumonia.

I nearly died … but I made it! I didn't stop.

As a supporter, you often feel like you've got to give a little more because you're the lucky one. It's a pressure you put on yourself; it doesn't usually come from the other paddlers. We have a funny mix in our club. We have many people who are quite fit and very competitive paddlers.

Then we have others, like me, who aren't so fit or have health issues – but we love it just as much and want to do our best. For the team, it's all about being as one. Supporting each other with fitness and confidence and listening to the grumbles.

Not long after I joined, the coordinator of the DAC committee found out I was an accountant. "How would you like to be our treasurer?" she asked.

"I'm not a survivor," I said.

"That's okay," she said. "You don't need to be a survivor to be the treasurer."

I told her I'd give it a year and see how I went.

I'm still the treasurer.

---

*Being in the boat and paddling as a supporter, rather than a survivor, has been interesting. If I'm honest, I don't even like the word 'survivor'. I feel it needs to be something more positive. Sure, initially you've survived breast cancer but afterwards, you're thriving.*

---

Lyndall is a perfect case in point. She's a survivor, sure, but she has absolutely thrived in Dragons Abreast. The club has given her so much.

And me, too.

It's been fantastic to be on the boat with a whole lot of women who supported Lyndall when she was going through that hard time, trying to get herself back. Regain her independence.

Meeting so many women with all their different diagnoses and treatments. Listening to what they've all gone through, and how it's so different for everyone. Some have dealt with quite radical and traumatic treatments, and others less so. This experience has made me look at breast cancer in a new way.

I've had a couple of scares over the past few years. I've had biopsies and that sort of thing. I'm always aware and I hold my breath after every scan, until I get the results.

I was fed up with the number of tests I was being put through at one stage, and ended up putting my foot down. "That's it. You haven't found anything. There's nothing to find."

But I still go back the next time in case there is something to find. I have my test every year and I'm supposed to have an ultrasound every other year. I haven't had one for three years now but I really should because I've got dense breasts, which make cancer harder to pick up with a check or mammogram alone. I know things now that I wouldn't know if I wasn't part of the breast cancer community.

I'm very vigilant about checking. Not only feeling for lumps – it's not always a lump – but checking for things that look funny or odd, like the whole orange peel dimpled skin analogy. Those sort of things.

Oddly enough, I've found I'm no longer scared of the breast cancer itself. I am, however, scared about not knowing either way.

---

*A diagnosis is scary, but it doesn't scare me anymore.*

---

I don't think I'd be as uncertain as I was before because I now have a much better idea of what's out there for support. Lyndall didn't have this. She had to find out for herself – like many people do – in bits and pieces.

This whole experience changed me and the way I view things, even though I didn't have breast cancer myself. I understand the importance of being able to get your health back. I see the amazing resilience of human beings. All the time, you hear people say, "Oh, my God, I don't know how you manage that. I don't know how you can cope with that."

Resilience. You just do.

As humans, we are knocked down and we pick ourselves up. I'm not saying it's easy. I'm not saying it's quick. But we do. I've seen it. I'm still seeing it.

So many people lose themselves at some point but I feel, strongly, that most people can and will come back from that.

You do not have to lose who you are.

Kellie Nissen

# Bench 1 – Left

"Easy!"

We stop back-paddling, our paddles hovering just over the water. Waiting, silent, we inhale the cool air, our noses and fingertips tingling. The only sound is the push-pull-plunk of the sweep oar as Lyndall manoeuvres the boat into a better position, facing Kings Avenue Bridge.

The National Carillon peeks over the top of the bridge, shrouded in shadow and early morning light. Magical. This is why we're here.

"Numbering off from the front," calls Lyndall. We wobble slightly. "Paddles flat. Hips to gunnel."

Paddle blades rest flat on the lake's surface and steady the boat.

"One," Jenny calls from the drummer's perch.

Clare, then Elly, stroking from Bench 1, continue the count.

"Two."

"Three."

Numbers tumble backwards, like ripples, down the boat. Not missing a beat.

"Twenty-two." Lyndall finishes the count. "Twenty-two on board. In the unlikely event of a capsize, let go of your paddle. Hand above your head, swim to the surface. Account for your buddy. The back bench will look after me. Front bench will look after Jenny."

We all nod at our bench buddy – I've got your back.

"We'll number off and find—"

"Twenty-two," we chorus.

"Then we'll swim to shore, number off again, where we'll find—"

"Twenty-three," Katherine calls before anyone else gets in.

"Ohhh-kaaaay," Lyndall says.

"We have to bring *GoAnna* with us," Katherine says, putting on her serious teacher voice. "Can't leave her behind."

Indeed! We feel *GoAnna* shift beneath us. Pleased. Perhaps having a chuckle too. Katherine always makes us laugh. Can't be serious all the time, now.

"Warm-up paddle to the bridge," Lyndall calls. "Strokes – a steady pace."

Clare – lead stroke – raises her hand in acknowledgement.

"Are you ready?" The whole crew snaps to the ready position, leaning forward, arms poised in an A-frame.

"Attention!" We lean a little further forward. A collective exhale.

"Go!"

In unison, twenty paddles, acting as the claws of the dragon, slice into the water and pull back, propelling the boat forward in a smooth movement.

Again.

Again.

Again.

Nineteen paddlers following Clare's lead.

Kellie Nissen

**Name:** Clare Purcell
**Initial diagnosis:** 2012, invasive lobular carcinoma
**Age at diagnosis:** 51
**Job at diagnosis:** Registered Nurse
**Job now:** retired
**Joined DAC:** 2013
**Favourite boat position:** stroke
**Best thing about DAC:** the celebration of life
**Natural highs:** competing internationally and doing well in all regattas
**Proudest moment:** watching my children – Daniel, Erin and Amy – evolve into amazing humans; becoming the proud Kaki (gran) of Ziggy and Shirley
**Famous for:** my shoe collection when my children were teenagers; now it's mainly dragon boat shoes in my wardrobe

# Clare's Story: Just a Chapter in My Book

*From the minute I walked into my
oncologist's office, we had a good rapport.
He said, "How are you?" and I said, "Fucking awful."
I guessed he was used to that because he didn't blink an eye.*

I didn't have a lump – it was more of a thickening. So, I decided there was nothing wrong and went on with my life.

It was denial, for sure.

But it was more than just denial. I had lots of family things happening. My mum had not long passed away and there were other issues I was contending with.

I had no time, and definitely not the emotional capacity to cope with anything else at that point, so I put it to the side. Rightly or wrongly, that's what I did.

Every day, I would walk past BreastScreen four, five, maybe six times. I worked in the same building, as a nurse, and I would look at their clinic and think, 'Yep. That's what I've got to do.'

But I didn't.

For many months, I kept passing by and thinking the same thing.

Then one day I said to myself, 'Shit! It's a new year. I've got to deal with this.' I went in and had a mammogram.

*I had a very big tumour. Eight centimetres. Massive.*

There's not a lot I can recall from that time. I must have blocked things out, but I know I went through a period of harsh critiquing of myself and how I handled things. That was in 2012, and even now I still think, 'Geez, what if I'd got onto it earlier?'

So many what if questions.

But, when it boils down to it, I know that given everything else that was going on, I wouldn't have survived dealing with this as well– not emotionally. It was a bad period in my life so I guess, in a way, my mind was looking after my body; telling me what to do and when. I have to believe this.

Of course, the diagnosis was then in January — when everything slows down or shuts down. Not the greatest timing. I rang several doctors and couldn't get in, so decided to take a chance and walk into a breast surgeon's rooms. With my results in hand, I marched up to the surgeon's office and gave the paperwork to the receptionist. "Can you get me an appointment?"

She nodded. "We'll ring you back," she said. "He'll triage you."

A few days later, I was in.

---

*"I can't operate on you. It's too big."*

---

Nobody wants to hear those words.

He rang and made an appointment for me with the oncologist and an hour later, I was sitting in front of him, just having told him I was fucking awful.

It was the truth.

A straight-shooter, he said things as they were. "It's too big. It can't be operated on so we're going to have to start you on neoadjuvant therapy to try and reduce it."

I can't remember what I said at the time – I've blocked a lot of it out – but it must have been along the lines of berating myself for not having come in earlier because he said, "Don't worry about it. You can't change it. You're here now."

He started me straight away on Zoladex injections and daily Letrozole tablets. This threw me into a full-on medically-induced menopause in a matter of days. One day I was peri-menopausal, the next I was menopausal.

The oncologist wanted to see me a few days after commencing treatment to check that I wasn't going mad with the hot flushes and everything that goes with menopause.

I was fine.

At that point, I was more than happy to accept whatever treatment was necessary. I found the side effects to be comforting. I know that sounds strange but it's true. It meant the drugs were doing their job. They were switching off oestrogen production.

To get my head together, I took a week off work. When I went back I threw myself into it –right up until the day before my surgery, about seven months later.

A lot of people continue working through their treatment to maintain normality or to stop themselves dwelling on everything. Work was busy and I'd taken on some managerial responsibilities. It was a good decision for me to work. It gave me purpose and kept me occupied.

I didn't want my diagnosis to become whispers in the work corridors or a pity fest. I didn't want it announced at a team meeting.

I didn't want to be an agenda item in a meeting.

As it turned out, I called everyone into my office, one by one. It was a bit dramatic, looking back. Methodically, I told them what had happened – that I'd been diagnosed and was on treatment but that I'd be at work.

Most people responded well.

A few of us cried.

Some of the men had what I thought of as the funniest responses.

"What's your prognosis?" one said.

"How long have you got?" said another.

*Different people deal with news like this in different ways.*

The hardest part was telling my kids, Daniel, Erin and Amy. They were all adults, but it was still extremely hard. Seeing the looks of shock and pain on their faces – that was difficult. Were they wondering if I was going to die? I don't know. It was just horrible. And I really didn't have much that I was able to tell them. I knew that it was going to be a long process from diagnosis to surgery. There were so many unknowns.

The worst was ringing my son Daniel in New York. To be so far away was very hard for him. He wanted to come home. As desperately as I would have loved that, it really wasn't viable. He had to work. He had his life in the US. "There's no point," I told him, "because I'm not actually having surgery yet." I made a deal with Daniel that as soon as my treatments were finished, I would visit him in New York.

My children and my husband, Greg, were my support team. Everyone needs a cheer squad in the hard times. My friends at work – especially Alicia and Kate – were also in my cheer squad. They are the ones who rally around and laugh and cry with you.

My first surgery didn't happen until seven months after that mammogram. That's over half a year of being a bit of a guinea pig, because the therapy I was on was fairly new. I had regular MRI scans to check the progress of the treatment. I knew I was the subject of multidisciplinary meetings, so I didn't feel forgotten. I was seeing my medical oncologist at least every four weeks.

My medical team wanted to see how much my tumour had shrunk in response to those therapies. I was grateful to be living in a country where cancer research was in the forefront.

It was scary to be told I would not be operated on for months. And I didn't know how many months. It all came down to my response to the therapy. The anxiety and worry I felt about leaving the tumour in place for so long was real and ever-present. However, despite this I was able to settle into my life of work, drug therapy, specialist's appointments and MRIs. I had a small metal marker inserted near the tumour so progress via MRI could be tracked more easily.

Finally, I received a phone call from my oncologist while I was at work. "They're going to operate on you in two days," he said.

All I could say was, "Okay. Thank you." There was no time to think about it.

So many months since I'd noticed the thickening. Another seven months of therapy. Then two days until surgery.

Game on!

On my last day at work, I was rushing to get there and I had a fall. I ended up in Emergency to rule out a foot fracture. With the aid of crutches, I got to work. There was no way I was going to miss my lunch that my workmates had planned. It turned out to be a day full of much love and laughter. Alicia, my colleague and good friend, pushed me to lunch in a wheelchair that had a flat tyre. The trip was such a hoot. Without my friends from work the lead-up time to the surgery would have been so much worse.

It was surgery day and the therapies had worked. The tumour had shrunk to an operable size — small enough to only require a lumpectomy.

I got both good and bad news following the surgery. The lymph nodes were clear but they didn't get clear margins around the tumour – so I had to go back for a second surgery.

They didn't get clear margins from that one either.

I didn't want to keep doing this, so I decided the best course of treatment was a mastectomy.

The surgeon agreed. He was probably going to suggest it anyway.

Prior to the mastectomy, I decided I wanted to have some form of breast reconstruction. After considerable thought, research and advice from my surgeon, I settled upon an immediate reconstruction using a breast implant, rather than using my own tissue, fat and skin, which is more invasive. My reasoning was simple – extensive surgery and recovery was daunting, and even though an implant would come with its own issues, it seemed like the most straightforward path for me.

Radiation can occasionally cause encapsulation, where the scar tissue forms a tight, constricting capsule around the implant. I was aware of this but considered the risks to be small.

Unfortunately, my implant did become encapsulated. It was painful.

After discussion with my surgeon, I agreed to the removal of the implant so a tissue expander could be inserted. A tissue expander is like a breast implant with one big difference – there is a port on the expander, enabling the surgeon to introduce sterile saline at intervals to expand the pocket in the breast. It sounded okay but it also meant another surgery.

Three expansions later, I was ready for the expander to be removed and my second implant inserted, although it was with some trepidation that I was admitted to hospital for the surgery. Of course, while I prayed for success, I was acutely aware that the implant may encapsulate again.

Sadly, that's how it played out and I had no choice but to have surgery number six in my breast cancer journey.

This time, the decision was the simplest one I'd made – remove the implant and call it a day. I had tried hard but it simply wasn't meant to be.

It took me a while to work out how to dress to look even. My lopsidedness didn't faze me. I learned that horizontal stripes are not your friend and adjusted to life with one breast. Eventually, I was fitted for an external breast prosthesis and the rest, as they say, is history.

Even though I had initially wrestled with the thought of not having two breasts – especially at night when I was alone with my thoughts and fears – I came to a realisation that my femininity and self-esteem were not aligned with the number of breasts I had. I am worth so much more than what the media, beauty and fashion icons have us believe. I am still a woman. I can still feel pretty. I can still wear nice clothes – not to mention the beautiful mastectomy lingerie you can get these days. I can function as an important member of the community.

And I do.

I took time off from work when I had surgery, returning as soon as I could after each one. I worked throughout radiation therapy as well. I never really slowed down. It was almost like I had something to prove to the world.

---

*If I take too much sick leave –*
*it's like an admission that I'm sick. I'm not sick.*

---

That's how I dealt with it.

Also, if I'd taken sick leave, I would have been home by myself. None of my kids lived at home anymore and Greg was at work. I'd have had too much time to think! Those days felt long and lonely.

The thoughtfulness of my good friend and boss, Kate, made my return to work easier. I didn't feel the need to have to explain to her if I was having a bad day. I look back on it now as just an unspoken understanding. Some days I would be managing well. Other days, not so much. Without a doubt, my recovery had its up and downs. And so many of these down days I kept to myself.

The days I did stay home, even picking up a book was out of the question. It would have taken too much brain power and concentration to read! All I could do was watch TV.

Funeral ads.

They were everywhere. Every ad break.

Maybe I was just more aware of them but they really bugged me.

Then, one day, the phone rang. "Hello," the person at the other end of the line said. "Can we offer you funeral insurance?"

It wasn't one of my best days and it got to me. Let's just say I was 'firm' in my response. There are moments when you're influenced, almost triggered, by things that are out of your control. Sure, I could have turned off the TV but I needed something to do.

I mentioned the phone call to my surgeon and he said, "Yes – that's what they do. They target people." It's unbelievable.

Another thing I found quite funny – though I'm not sure it was at the time – just before I was due to have surgery, every time I watched TV, all I saw were voluptuous women with their boobs hanging out. I remember thinking it wasn't fair; I was going to be losing mine soon and I didn't want to watch these people flaunting themselves. It probably wasn't even that bad; I was just hyper-aware.

*Any show of cleavage was like adding insult to injury at that time.*

So, work was the best place for me with my cheer squad – my second family.

After one of my surgeries, I got some flowers from work. The message was simple and resonated with me: You are Bold and Beautiful.

Yep. That summed it up.

I remember at one stage during my radiation the doctors thought I had an infection brewing. Rather than staying in hospital, I had the 'hospital in the home' nurses visit me at home to give me antibiotics through the cannula I had in my arm.

"I'm going to come back to work," I said to Kate.

With the cannula.

Seconds after I said that, I realised: 'You can't do that. You work with vulnerable people. How would that look, sitting there at work with a cannula in my arm?' But that's where my thinking was – I'm fine; I'll come to work.

When I was at work though, it was like therapy. I was lucky enough to share an office with Alicia. We had some laughs. Lots of laughs.

I'd always shut the door of the office if I had to make a phone call to my oncologist or the breast care team. Countless times I remember whacking my top up so Alicia could check a dressing. Nothing was out of bounds for us. One time, Alicia was sitting there while I was on the phone to the breast care nurse. The nurse was telling me about sexual lubricant. Nothing was a secret.

There were other moments I look back on and laugh about.

Radiation burns your skin and it can get itchy and sore, rubbing against tight clothing. I was driving home from work and it was hot in the car and I was sore. I didn't think twice; I started pulling off my bra while I was stopped at the lights. I had one hand on the steering wheel and was pulling my bra strap down over the hand, then the whole bra out from under my top.

I looked to the side and there was a person in the car next to me, staring. Shocked. I wasn't worried – you do what you have to do, sometimes. I'm just lucky it wasn't a police car next to me.

There was also the time Alicia and I went to Melbourne for a work conference. It was a day trip – only three days after I'd finished radiation treatment. The plane trip home should have taken one hour, but four hours later we were still in transit with nothing to eat but a packet of twisties between us. Sitting next to Alicia on the plane, I was telling her all I wanted to do was rip off my bra and get home to bed. I'm not sure of my exact words and I had no idea how loud I was talking but the man next to Alicia had a funny sort of perplexed grin on his face. He must have heard every word. I don't think we explained. We were happy to leave it all up to his imagination.

---

*There were moments of great kindness, too, from strangers. They're the ones that stay with you.*

---

At some point early on, perhaps not long after my diagnosis when I was still beating myself up about everything, it was bucketing rain – sort of matched my mood. Anyway, I'd parked and was walking across the road to work. No umbrella. Soaking wet and completely bedraggled. I was standing at the lights and I must have looked terrible. This guy came up beside me, covered me with his umbrella then walked with me across the road. I looked at him and thought, 'Oh my God, you just made my day.'

It's kindnesses like that you never forget. He had no idea what I was going through but somehow, I felt he knew.

Another time, Greg and I decided to go away so we flew up to Mooloolaba for the week. Wandering through the markets, we came across a woman selling little Christian charms and I found myself asking her if she had one for the patron saint of cancer patients. I had no idea if there was a patron saint for that but thought I'd ask.

There was! St Peregrine.

She showed me the charm. "Does a family member have cancer?" she asked.

"No," I said. "I do."

She gave it to me for free. "I want you to have this."

I'll never forget that; I wore that charm for a long time. I still have it.

---

*Unlike many others, I didn't need to have chemotherapy.*

---

My oncologist flagged this with me early on, right after my diagnosis. "I don't think you'll need chemo," he said. "But we'll wait until after your surgery to make that decision."

I didn't really think much about it until after the surgery when it was raised again. "You won't need it," he said.

My radiation oncologist had also said as much.

"Right," I said. "Okay."

"Now, don't go home and worry about not having chemo," he added before I left.

"No, no. I won't," I said.

Of course, I did. I went straight home and worried about it. That I should have it. So, I went back later and said, "Are you sure?"

He nodded. "Honestly," he said, "I wouldn't do anything."

Eventually, I overcame that worry. You have to trust your medical team.

Still, it hits me when I hear everybody else's stories. 'Crap,' I think, 'our cancer sounds similar. They had chemo and I didn't.' At the end of the day, though, you have to trust. One thing I learned very early on in my diagnosis was to trust my team. My surgeon, medical oncologist, radiation oncologist, breast radiologist – I called them my team because that's what they were. They were working for me, to give me the best possible treatment, to keep me alive. Literally, my life was in their hands. I had to trust in their knowledge and skill.

Seeing little rays of light at the end of each treatment tunnel is always good. After my surgery, I felt pretty good emotionally. Not confident but relieved – that it hadn't gone into my lymph nodes.

It's the little things that mean the most. Kate had candles burning at work on the day of my surgery. She told me that when Greg rang her to tell her the result of the surgery, her family erupted into cheers.

Then, finishing radiation, I was back to feeling fearful. You're in there almost every day for more than a month. It becomes routine. A backup. The staff are your support. Then, when they said I was finished, there was this void. Like I'd been cut loose.

I hadn't been cut loose, of course. I was still seeing the surgeon, the radiation oncologist and the medical oncologist on a regular basis – but not having to go into the radiation unit every day; it took a bit of getting used to.

As the years go on, the specialists drop off. First the radiation oncologist, then the surgeon, and finally the medical oncologist.

---

*They were all so wonderful and caring.
It was hard. Like cutting the apron strings
and going out in the big scary world alone.
I will be forever grateful to my team. I hope they realise.*

---

It's a long time to be in treatment and you'd think that I'd be celebrating at 'the end'. For me, though, what I've found is that the further away I am from that surgery date, the more anxious I am when I go to have tests. The yearly mammogram and MRI is stressful. Going to my doctor is stressful – even if it's not related to breast cancer. Everything is magnified.

I finished treatment about two years ago. For a little more than ten years, I was on Letrozole and on my last oncology appointment, I was told I could stop.

"I'd rather not," I said.

"You've got to weigh it up," was the reply. "You'll be doing more harm than good, particularly to your bones, if you stay on it."

It's a real psychological barrier – to have been on a drug for so long and then, when you come off it, all you can think is 'Holy shit.' It's not a good feeling.

It was like being abandoned. Taken off the medication and discharged from my last standing specialist. I was on my own.

Greg and I left the oncologist's office and went up to reception to pay. "When do you need to see doctor again?" the receptionist asked.

"I don't," I said. It felt weird. After ten years, I didn't make a follow-up appointment.

People in the waiting room started saying things like, "Oh, that's so good."

I turned around. I didn't know who they were but it was real. It felt good.

That night, I messaged a few people – family, friends – and told them: 'Hey, I'm free now.'

At the same time, a deep fear was rising in me. I didn't want to finish treatment.

---

*The last words I said to my oncologist before I left were, "If any experimental treatments come up, count me in."*

My breast radiologist, the last specialist in my team, retired two years ago. That was hard, but I was so happy for him. The work he had done to further breast cancer research was amazing. He understood how anxiety-provoking my yearly MRI and mammogram were. He was always there at the conclusion of the appointment to give me the result and allay my fears. Apparently, he did this for all his breast cancer ladies.

I remember telling him that, even in retirement, he would have to come back in once a year just to see me. Of course, I was joking. Or was I?

The fear is real.

It's always with me. Every now and then my mind switches over and I start with the 'should haves'. I should have gone for the mammogram earlier. I should have insisted on having chemo. I should have exercised more; looked after my body. Blah, blah, blah.

I still find it hard to be part of conversations about cancer; those conversations that force me to think about my own mortality. I got off Facebook for that reason. I found it confronting and difficult to have everything seem to focus on breast cancer. I needed change. I needed a new perspective. I needed to move forward.

I know that I can't forget about my cancer, but gosh it's good to put it to the side and, even for a short while, not to give it any thought.

I've found that I need to look after my emotional wellbeing, and sometimes that means I need to create some space, just for me. I feel stupid – the anxiety about medical appointments and conversations – but I have to look after myself and do whatever works.

But I do take pride in the fact that I have grown in this respect also. I love to lend my support, even if it is just a listening ear to friends and family – my brother and sister who have recently had their own cancer diagnoses. It's the least I can do.

The support I have found from all my Dragons Abreast buddies has been immeasurable. I have learned to roll with the punches and be thankful for my life as it is today. Life is a gift, and I don't take any of it for granted.

My two beautiful grandchildren, Ziggy and Shirley, have a way of keeping me young and they have given me a new zest for life. I plan to love all our future adventures, and there will be lots.

I did something a few years ago I never thought I'd do – an interview, on film, and for the *Woman's Day* magazine. It was for BreastScreen Australia. A room in my house got changed into a studio. They did my hair, my make-up – everything. I found it quite cathartic, to be honest. Just talking. I hear a lot of people say that their diagnosis, their cancer, made them a better person. That it was good in that respect and that they wouldn't change a thing.

Not me. I wouldn't wish that diagnosis on anyone. Does that make me different? I don't know. I do know that everyone who takes a ride on the breast cancer roller-coaster has different experiences. There is no right or wrong way to feel.

As I was talking during my interview, I surprised myself. I hadn't prepared – I was just talking – but then I heard myself say, "Breast cancer was a chapter of my life. That's all. It's not the whole story. My diagnosis was a chapter in my book and my story is continuing."

It's true.

I plan on having a lot more chapters in my book.

# Bench 1 – Right

Ten strokes in and the chatter erupts, rising and falling in time with each stroke.

Elly and Clare are busy catching up on grandchild antics. As they swap their grandmotherly joys, their stroke rate increases. The crew behind keeps pace and, before we know it, we're under the bridge.

"Steady," Lyndall calls.

Some paddlers stop – those at the back of the boat, closer to Lyndall. Those closer to the front keep going. The boat slows – less paddles pulling it along. Eventually, those still paddling realise what's happening and pull their paddles in, until it's only the two strokes still working at it. The rest of us sit with smug grins on our faces.

Jenny clears her throat. "Steady," she repeats Lyndall's command.

Clare looks up. Then back. "Oopsie." She gives Elly a nudge. "We were a bit distracted."

"I thought I was getting weak," Elly says.

We all know she could've kept going.

*Bench 1 – Right*

**Name:** Elly McGinness
**Initial diagnosis:** 2011, Oestrogen Receptor positive (ER+)
**Age at diagnosis:** 61
**Job at diagnosis:** Registered Nurse
**Job now:** retired
**Joined DAC:** 2012
**Favourite boat position:** stroke
**Most memorable moment with DAC:** participating in the IBCPC regatta in Florence, Italy (2018)
**Natural highs:** anytime I'm on a cruise

Kellie Nissen

# Elly's Story: Keeping Things Normal

*There's nothing I can do about it so just accept it. That's what I told myself. But I was scared, deep down; I was afraid. I wasn't prepared for this, but I had to be.*

In 2011, on 15 January, I woke up bright and early to get ready for dragon boating training. Before I got out of bed, for some reason, I put my hand on my breast.

There was a lump.

I have fibrocystic disease but this wasn't the same; it was bigger. But I had to get to training so I tucked the thought of the lump away and continued to get ready.

At the time, I was paddling with a different team but one of the ladies I knew had just been through everything with breast cancer. When I saw her at training, I didn't think twice. I took her aside and said, "I've got this lump."

Her response was as direct as my statement. "Get it seen to straight away."

That afternoon, I went to a health centre and spoke to one of the doctors. He didn't like the look of it and recommended I get a mammogram and ultrasound as soon as possible.

That was Saturday.

On Monday, I was lying on the table at the imaging centre; mammogram complete, ultrasound done and about to have a fine needle aspiration. They thought it was just a cyst, hence the fine needle aspiration rather than a core biopsy.

They thought wrong.

On Wednesday, I was back for the core biopsy.

The next day, my doctor rang. "You need to come in," he said. "We need to have a talk."

I knew then.

> *Once you get that diagnosis, it's all systems go.*
> *Doctors. Specialists. Forms. Scans. Tests. Go, go, go.*

The timing couldn't have been worse – my husband Peter and I were booked on a cruise with my sister and brother-in-law. We were due to leave the following Monday. However, as it turned out, I couldn't get in to see the surgeon for another two weeks – so in that respect, the timing was in my favour.

We went on the cruise.

Peter was the only one who 'knew', which made things interesting. He bought me this beautiful bracelet from one of the shops on the boat – just because – and he was on guard a lot of the time. "Be careful," he'd say.

If that bracelet and his attentiveness didn't make my sister suspicious, then my purchase of a lovely mohair beanie and scarf certainly did.

"It's January," she said. "What are you buying that for?"

"Oh, you know what winter's like in Canberra," I said. "I'm just preparing."

It was the truth – I was preparing.

When I eventually saw the surgeon, she gave me the option of having a lumpectomy or a mastectomy. I was fully prepared to have a mastectomy but she surprised me.

"I think a lumpectomy would be better," she said, "but go away and have a think about it."

I didn't want to think about it. The thing is you have to put your trust in the specialists.

> *"If I was your mum, what would you recommend?"*

She reiterated she thought a lumpectomy would be enough. So, that's what it was to be – on 10 March. Yes, nearly two months after I first found that lump.

On the way home from that appointment, all I could think of was an image of an apple with a bite taken out. That's a lumpectomy. In my defence, you're really not thinking straight at that point.

Now that the surgery date was sorted, it was time to tell the rest of the family. My kids were grown up, so we got them all together to talk to the them about it.

My daughter Heather was furious. "Why are you waiting so long?"

"There's no places available any sooner," I said. The surgery date was out of my hands, obviously, and she knew that.

"They said it's quick-growing," Heather said. I knew it was emotion speaking. "I think you should go to Sydney. Or Melbourne."

She was right in one sense; it was quick-growing. I'd had a mammogram the previous October and had the all-clear. Three months was all it took to be big enough to find. At that time, they said it was just over one centimetre. By the time I had surgery, two months later, it was four. That's quick-growing.

As far as the surgery went, there was nothing we could do about it. I didn't want to travel out of Canberra for this – away from family. In my head, I knew I had to accept it.

I started chemotherapy three weeks after surgery. Actually, it was after the second surgery a month later – they didn't get clear enough margins from the first. It was annoying but what could I do about it? It happens; it's quite common. What helped me through waiting for that second surgery was the fact that my first grandchild was born three days after my first surgery. I left the hospital and went straight over for cuddles. She kept my mind off things.

## *Nobody sails through chemo!*

Chemo isn't fun for anybody and I certainly didn't sail through it. I did end up with neutropenia – diminished white blood cells – from the chemo drugs. Once that was detected, I was given Neulasta, which is an injection to stimulate reproduction of the cells.

I was a Registered Nurse at the time and was still working part-time. I worked the whole way through my treatment – determined to keep everything as normal as I possibly could.

My work was enjoyable and kept my mind off what was going on inside my body. The week after my chemo treatment, I'd take a couple of days off but for the other two weeks, I was fine. I'd go into work with my beanie or turban on. Just a normal day and a normal week.

Normality was what I needed. Plus, my boss and the other staff were very supportive – and you need that, too. Even our conversations were normal. I'd say, "Well, I'm going to go and have some chemo and then I'll be back." And they'd say, "Yeah. Fine. See you then." Normal.

---

*That's how I looked at things.*
*Just get it done but live life pretty normally.*

---

Of course, normality is hard to sustain when your hair starts falling out. However, I dealt with this the same way as I dealt with every other step – just do it.

Before I started chemo, I took myself off to the wig library; that's like a book library but with wigs. Looking at all the different lengths and colours, I couldn't decide. Luckily, my younger son worked in the physio department just down the corridor from the wig library so I rang him and said, "Can you come and tell me which one I should get?"

We narrowed it down to three or four, and he took photos and sent them to my other kids who then had a family conference about which wig Mum should get.

I ended up going with the one they suggested; one a bit lighter than my hair colour and not quite the same style but that was fine – except for my mother.

Mum had dementia and I never told her about the breast cancer because I would have had to tell her again every time I saw her. And it would have upset her every time. The thing was, she realised there was something different about my hair, right from the first time I went in with my new wig.

"Oh, you've changed your hair," she said. "I don't like it. Go back to what you had before."

I thought quickly. "I will but, look, it cost me a bit of money to get this new hairstyle so I'll leave it for a while and then go back to how it was before. Okay?"

That seemed to satisfy her.

Mum died less than twelve months later, in April of 2012.

She never knew about my breast cancer. I was sort of sad that I couldn't talk to my mother about it – about what I was going through. I had great support from the rest of my family. My mother-in-law was wonderful – she always asked how I was even though she wasn't well herself – but it would have been nice to talk to my mum about it.

I hated that wig, you know. It was uncomfortable. At home, I just wore a beanie or the turban, but I needed to look normal for my mum.

*I can't remember ever thinking, 'Why me?'*

I must have gone through different emotions, but I can't remember. There was a lot going on with the chemo and issues associated with that, but I just kept going. I had radiotherapy for seven weeks too, but that was a breeze after chemo. I worked through that as well and was lucky to be able to make the daily appointments around my work schedule. Being able to talk to some of the dragon boating ladies and going along to Bosom Buddies seminars and BCNA events was great. I think I was pretty proactive when it came to keeping informed and it was good to know I wasn't alone.

On 25 November, I had my post-radiotherapy check and was given the all-clear. It was a huge relief. It was over. Peter was funny. "Okay, well, you've done all that now," he said. "Back to normal."

Well, normal meant a bit of a holiday.

A good friend of mine had an apartment in Queenstown in New Zealand and told me I was to go over there after everything and stay for as long as I liked. So, we did – we stayed for two weeks.

*It was such a good feeling to be
done with it all – I just did silly things.*

I did the jet boat thing over the rapids.
We went on a helicopter ride.
I did para-gliding.
I did the Skyline Luge.
I did the thing through the trees – the Zipline.

I thought, I'm going to do everything. I've been through so much other stuff, I'm going to do it all. It was like an acknowledgement that I was at the end of it all. I was finished. It was great.

The following year, that's when it dawned on me. It was tough. I was back at work but it wasn't the same for some reason. Then my mother died and, maybe because I felt I hadn't had the support from work when this was happening, I decided to take three months off. It was time out. I hadn't taken the time the year before, but now I needed it.

My mother-in-law died, too, in that period.

When I went back to work, I remember thinking, 'I don't want to be here anymore.' I'd be driving in and I'd be crying. I'm not a crier but I'd be crying all the way in. And then I'd get there and turn the tears off until I left at the end of the day – and I'd start crying again on the way home.

My oncologist thought my emotions might have been related to the anti-hormone drugs I was on. "They'll give you sore joints," he said. "It's not a particularly good quality of life – and it could account for the emotion you're experiencing." He took me off that drug and put me on Tamoxifen. I was still crying, so he took me off that and put me back on the Letrozole.

There was a lot of emotion; things I hadn't felt during the previous year. It was like it had all been bottled up and saved for now.

I didn't know what was going on but I knew I had to change. Work was something I could control. I wasn't enjoying it anymore so I gave notice and finished at the end of the year. I guess this experience was a combination of so many things – the cancer, my mum, my mother-in-law. In 2011, it was all about getting through it and 2012 was the emotional year. I'd been on autopilot and then I wasn't — and I wanted to look after myself.

It's been a long road.

In November 2016, my oncologist told me I could come off the drugs. I'd been on them for five years but I'd heard some people had to stay on for another five years. "Shouldn't I be staying on them?" I asked.

"No," he said. "The benefit for you would be negligible." Plus all of these drugs have an increasing level of toxicity. He explained that it was a balancing act between possible benefits and potential harm. "My recommendation is that you don't continue."

So, that was it – for the drugs and the active treatment, anyway.

"We have to celebrate, Mum," Heather said. "I'll organise a picnic."

I thought it would just be family but she'd invited a lot of people, it was a really large picnic. I was surprised. It was such a lovely way to celebrate the tail end of the previous five years.

Dragon boating kept me going throughout all of this.

Initially, I joined Dragons Abreast for social events and for interstate and overseas 'survivor regattas'. But I stayed with my original team for local and national competitions. Plus, I was in the state team. I was doing it all. Eventually, though, it became too much timewise, so I decided to paddle mainly with Dragons Abreast.

One of the best things about being with a group of people like this is the support. We don't sit there and talk about symptoms and so on but the support is there if you need it.

And you do need it – even after treatment is done. The next year. And the next. Every year when it comes time for the mammogram.

*The fear is always there. And the tension. It's still there.*

Lying on that table while they do the ultrasound – I hate it when they turn the screen away. I don't understand what it shows but I don't like not being able to see it. Especially when they're going over and over the same spot. That fear – the tension – it never goes away. Never gets less.

And every little niggle, every headache, every little something or other – you worry. When someone on our team has something going on – a sore hip or whatever – you worry. It's always there. All the time. In the back of your mind.

I don't think you ever get over it.

I don't think it's something where you can say, 'Oh yeah, that's done. It's finished.' Every year, you're going back to get the mammogram. It's a constant reminder.

There's always that chance.

And that's what you can't help thinking about.

It changes you, for sure. And, for me anyway, it was all about a reassessment of life. Of my life.

And it was about fighting. The fight to keep things normal. Because that's how I got through it.

# Bench 2 – Left

"Have a drink," Lyndall calls. "A quick one. Rowers are coming up."

A shaft of light falls between the two bridges, star-like twinkles top the murky brown. In the middle of summer, the bridges provide a good respite from the sun. Today, however, the shade is icy.

"Brrrr," Megan says. As if it heard her discomfort, the current complies by pushing the boat gently out into the sun.

"Paddles up!"

A flurry of activity ensues as we tuck away our drink bottles and lift our paddles into the ready position.

"Attention. Go."

Ten strokes and we've ducked around the bend and out of the path of the rowers – a swarm of them gliding past, their focus intent on where they've been, not where they're going. Lyndall turns us into the wake of their coaching dinghy and, with paddles flat, we ride out the bumps.

"That was close," Megan says. "I could've reached out and touched them."

"Capsize drills. Dodgems with rowers. What next?" Gillian says. Cheery and joking, yet the high pitch of apprehension is mixed in.

We don't blame her. Anything can happen but for the most part, we're safe. Good sweeps and a responsive team ensure that.

"Dragon boating is an extreme sport!" Clare calls from the front. "Lucky for us we have a paramedic on board."

"A multi-award-winning paramedic, no less," Jenny says.

Megan shakes her head. "They weren't anything."

**Name:** Megan Davis

**Initial diagnosis:** 2019, ductal carcinoma in situ

**Age at diagnosis:** 50

**Job at diagnosis:** Ambulance manager and intensive care paramedic

**Job now:** Emergency services executive

**Joined DAC:** 2019

**Favourite boat position:** stroke

**Most memorable moment with DAC:** participating in my first international regatta in New Zealand in 2023

**Proudest moment:** being awarded the Ambulance Services Medal on the Queen's Birthday Honours List in 2019 and having my three children with me at Government House when I was presented with the medal by the Governor-General

Kellie Nissen

# Megan's Story: Cactus

> *"What we really need you to do is
> have your free 'welcome to fifty' mammogram."*

When I turned 50, I started getting significant perimenopause symptoms – anxiety, hot flushes that would go for hours, agitation – the works. They were so bad, I felt like I couldn't function at work.

I ended up speaking to a girlfriend about it. "Go to the menopause clinic," she said. "Have a chat with them."

I booked in and had a chat with one of the doctors at the clinic and we went through all my symptoms. She agreed with me. "These symptoms are quite huge," she said, "compared to what most people go through." She outlined all the different things I could do, including hormone replacement therapy and all the rest.

"I think I'll try the hormone replacement therapy," I said.

"Because you're having such a bad time," she said, "we'll start you on it but what we really need you to do is have that mammogram."

Welcome to fifty.

I was like, right, okay. Yep. Sure. No worries. And away I went.

I was extremely busy at work. As a single mum, I was also extremely busy with my kids. We didn't have any history of breast cancer, or any cancer, in my family. So, I put it to the side. And kept putting it to the side until I went for another appointment with the doctor.

"Have you had your mammogram yet?" she asked.

I hadn't.

"I'll have to stop giving you the hormones if you don't go and get a mammogram."

That stopped me.

"The treatment doesn't cause cancer," she explained, "but if you were prone to cancer, it could accelerate it."

That made me book in for my mammogram.

Honestly, I thought there was nothing to worry about. I'd be fine. Off I went to the breast screening clinic.

About two weeks later, I discovered a missed call on my phone. I was in Brisbane at the time, just for the day. For a meeting. At lunchtime, I rang back.

It was a nurse from the breast screen clinic. Apparently, one of my breasts was not behaving and they'd noticed something that was an anomaly. I needed to make another appointment as soon as possible for further testing and screening.

After that phone call, I went back into the meeting and didn't think about it again until I was at the airport. A friend of mine had gifted me a free Qantas Lounge entry. I was so relieved to sit in the lounge area, where it was quiet and away from the general crowd.

While I was sitting there, I rang my daughter to let her know I was on my way home; she hadn't spent much time away from me at that point, and was staying with my stepson and his wife for the night, so I was just checking in with her. I didn't say anything about the lunchtime phone call.

Then I rang my baby sister. "The weirdest thing has happened," I said and explained the phone call.

"I'm sure it's nothing," she said. "It'll be something they can explain away. We've got no history, no-one's ever had breast cancer so it's going to be fine."

Finally, I boarded the flight – it was the last one out of Brisbane that night. As I waited for the plane to take off, back home to Canberra, I was so tired. I started thinking: Oh my God, what does this all mean?

I hadn't even considered breast cancer as a possibility.

And yet, here I was.

*Those thoughts sort of niggled for a bit but I tried to dismiss them. They'd already booked me in – for eight days' time. I was acting in a higher position, was busy running my team and had lots of other stuff going on. I had to put it out of my head.*

When I'd made the appointment for those extra tests, they told me to make sure I scheduled the whole day to be there. "We can't say how long it's going to take."

I couldn't believe it. As if it was going to take a whole day – really! I was convinced they were going to do another mammogram and say, "You're fine. Nothing to see here." So, I didn't bother taking the day off work.

I worked from the waiting room. In hindsight, that was pretty stupid but I was managing so much at the time. I was on the phone to the coroner's office and solicitors; I couldn't afford the time.

The waiting room started as a group of about twelve or fifteen women. All of us were sitting there in our special gowns, just waiting. One by one, they cycled us through to get our mammograms.

After the mammograms, about a third of the women disappeared. The rest of us had to go on to have an ultrasound.

More waiting.

There I was, typing away on my laptop while women were getting called into a room, coming out again after a bit, getting dressed and leaving with relieved looks on their faces.

Then it was my turn.

After the ultrasound, I was told to sit back in the waiting room to wait for a doctor to review it. By this stage, another five or so women had left and there was just a few of us in the waiting room.

I was called back inside. "We've seen something we'd like to biopsy." Apparently, they couldn't rule it out so needed to biopsy it that afternoon. "Take an hour. Go and find something to eat and settle down for a bit. Then come back and we'll do the biopsy."

Three of us were in the same boat – all of us coming back for a biopsy that afternoon. I was the last on the list.

I wandered off. I didn't get lunch because I was too busy with work, plus I was on call.

---

*This whole time, I was still dismissing it all.*
*It simply wasn't an option that anything would be wrong.*

---

When it was my turn for the biopsy, they wanted me to sit up at the mammogram machine to have it. They started to inject stuff into me and the nurses were chatting away to me when I suddenly realised I couldn't breathe.

I couldn't breathe. I couldn't talk. Being a paramedic, I instantly wondered if I was having an anaphylactic reaction. All these thoughts were running through my head: I'm going to die; who's going to tell my kids; I haven't even told my family I'm here. My mum didn't know. My sister didn't know. Nobody knew because I'd downplayed it so much.

Never in my life have I passed out, but I did that day. Sitting there in that chair, all those thoughts, not being able to breathe – I passed out.

It was only short but when I sort of came to, I could hear voices saying, "She's gone. She's passed out."

Then I heard the doctor saying, "I've got to get this biopsy."

They couldn't get me down because I was 'stuck' in the mammogram machine, so they just finished doing the biopsy.

Finally, they finished and got me out to lie down. My blood pressure was right up. One of the nurses was lovely. She gave me a cup of Yorkshire tea, her favourite, and, in her beautiful English accent, said to me, "Did you actually have lunch when you went out?"

"No, I didn't," I admitted. "I forgot. Actually, I was busy."

"Right," she said, "Let's feed you."

She was so nice. They all were, but they wouldn't let me go home by myself. Someone had to come to pick me up – tricky, because I hadn't told anyone where I was. I ended up ringing my best friend. "I'm at the breast clinic," I said and explained the whole thing.

My friend was so cranky with me — but she came and picked me up anyway.

I had the work car with me because I was on call that night. "You'll have to follow me," I said to her. "I have to drive the work car home." I didn't give her a choice.

My kids were at home when we got there. They were sort of looking at me, probably thinking it was all a bit bizarre – my best friend was there, she was putting the kettle on and chatting away. "Nothing to see here. Mum's just been a bit busy ..." Blah, blah, blah – just settling us all in for the night.

Kellie Nissen

---
*I remember realising at this point
that this could actually be something, after all.*
---

It was more than just nothing. I'd seen all those other women go in and then leave with relieved smiles on their faces, yet I was still there at the end. I suddenly thought: maybe this isn't okay. It was time to stop dismissing it.

I was called back in to the BreastScreen clinic a few days later. By that time, I'd told my baby sister who lives down the coast, so she came up to be with me for the day. It was a Friday before a long weekend, around Easter and Anzac Day. Somehow, they'd managed to squeeze me in.

In the morning, I went to work because I wanted it to feel like a normal day. I took the afternoon off, met up with my sister, had some lunch and then we went to the appointment together.

We sat in the waiting room, not saying much. Then, the door opened and the doctor and a nurse came out. Now, I used to be an oncology nurse, so when I saw the nurse looking at me, I thought, 'I've been that nurse and I've had that look on my face.'

I grabbed my sister's hand and we wandered in and sat on the couch. On the table in front of us was a box of tissues. I stared at them and all I could think about was how I knew they were going to tell me I had cancer. I knew what was coming.

I was right.

They'd found cancer – but it was so deep in my breast, there was no way I would have felt it – not for a long time. Not until it was absolutely nasty. I couldn't believe it; they'd caught it nice and early, which was great.

Finally, the doctor asked if had any questions.

"I have two sisters and a 12-year-old daughter," I said. "How is this going to affect them? How will this play out in their lives?"

They talked about this for a bit. Next to me, my sister had tears running down her face but I was in clinical mode. I wanted to know what I was facing and what I needed to do to get rid of it. "I just want it gone," I said.

The whole time we were there, there was this little voice in my head still saying, 'Surely this can't be happening to me? How unfair is this? Sure, I was a smoker in my young days, but I haven't smoked for a very long time. I look after myself. I'm a single mum. I'm a paramedic. I was an oncology nurse. Why me? Why now?'

Looking back, it sounds so self-centred to be thinking like that but, at the same time, I was trying to work out how I would navigate it all. How would I get my kids through it? I had no family in Canberra. I was still acting in a higher-level role. What on earth was going to happen and what would it mean for my future, and the future of my kids?

---

*It's funny how your logic works. The first weekend after I got the diagnosis, I woke up and all I wanted to do was declutter my house. If this is it, I thought, if this is my demise, I don't want the kids having to go through all my crap when I'm done. I decluttered the entire house. It was something I could control.*

---

The other weird thing that happened after my diagnosis was that all those awful menopause symptoms went away. It was like they'd never been there. Like my body was trying to send me a message. I don't normally believe in all of that – but still … I don't usually talk about those things.

I usually keep most things to myself.

Obviously, I had to tell my family, though, and that was hard. I needed all the facts first. I needed to pick my time.

I'd told my younger sister because she was there with me. She was the one who rang Mum after the diagnosis because I couldn't. Saying it out loud would have made it real, but I felt Mum needed to know.

Then there were my kids.

My daughter, my youngest, had just turned twelve. My eldest son was twenty; he was at university in Melbourne and my middle son was in Year 12.

It took me a while to figure out how to tell them. I didn't tell them straight away; I needed to know what I was facing and what the way forward was first. My kids and I are really close; we've been through a lot together so I didn't want them to worry before I knew everything and could tell them properly.

I ended up having a chat to my ex-husband first. "I need you to be aware," I said, "because you're part of their support structure." But I asked him not to tell anyone else because I felt that was up to me.

He asked when I was going to tell the kids.

"Tonight," I said.

Whenever I had something important to discuss with my kids, we'd go to my bedroom and sit on my bed. I've got lots of pillows all over it, so we could each hug something while we were talking, making it a safe space and special.

I'd given a lot of thought to what I'd say and talked to my sister about how to do it. I was concerned about my daughter, being so young but was also worried about my 18-year-old because he has ASD and I didn't know how he would react.

My sister found a book online, written by a woman in England about telling her young kids that she had cancer. It broke the steps down and seemed to me to be a nice, safe way of talking about it – so that was the approach I decided to use. Careful explanation, not too many big or emotional words. Nothing that might scare them. Not too many medical terms.

"The doctors found a lump in my breast," I said. "They believe it's cancer."

My son was amazing. He said, "I don't like the word cancer. I can't use that word."

"What word would you prefer?" I asked.

He thought for a bit. "Cactus," he said.

---

*So, from then on, we referred to my cancer as cactus.*

---

I tried to downplay everything for them. "I have to have an operation and some treatment," I said, "and I'll be fine." I didn't want to give them any fear that they were going to lose me.

It's interesting how different people respond.

My GP was a breast cancer survivor herself and sometimes it felt like she was spending more time telling me her story than listening to me and supporting me. I found that a bit difficult, to be honest.

I don't think I was quite myself. Normally, I love hearing about people. I'm a people person. But I remember thinking: this is about me; I don't give a shit about what you've been through. I didn't actually say that, of course, but that's how I felt.

However, my GP did put me on to a great surgeon. She was so reassuring, very capable, and came across as being very competent.

---

*You do need to have faith in the person who's going to be taking to your breast with a knife. You need to know they're going to do a decent job.*

---

One of the things that really hit me, though, was how, suddenly, everything is on display. If you've been through childbirth, you're aware that nothing's sacred but it doesn't take long for your body to become yours again. Whereas, with breast cancer, it felt like I had to pop my boobs out to everybody. Every man and his dog wanted to take a look.

For me, who's always been a modest person, that aspect of things was really difficult. I'd try and tell myself: you're a medical person. You look at people's bits all the time and you've never judged them; you've always been respectful. These people have the same philosophy as you. Deal with it. But it was hard.

My surgeon had a lovely registrar with her for a while at the start. This registrar said to me, "It's been so wonderful to meet you, but I'm moving out of this rotation shortly. I won't be there for your surgery. I would have loved to have followed you all the way through."

I was disappointed too because I'd felt a connection with her as well.

Anyway, the week before my surgery was scheduled, I was in Melbourne on a business trip. I didn't know it at the time, but this registrar happened to be in the airport at the same time and saw me there with my work colleagues. She was on the same plane home to

Canberra. On the day of my surgery, she came up to see me and said, "I've managed to extend for a month so I could continue on and be with you through this process."

I was really pleased.

"I saw you in Melbourne last week," she said, and told me where. "I nearly came up to say hello and then suddenly remembered I was your doctor. It would have been totally unprofessional, but can I say you looked like you were having a really good time so I hope you were – before having to come here today for this."

That was bizarre but lovely – those funny little connections that happen along the way.

My sister had made the trip back to be with me during my surgery. She was with me in the waiting room, which was great because I don't think I could have sat there on my own.

My mum also came to help me look after the kids. She'd arrived about two days before my surgery but I don't think she was coping with it all. She didn't want to be part of the hospital stuff; didn't want to visit me there. Neither did my son, which was to be expected, but my daughter had said that she really wanted to visit me in hospital after the surgery. I think she needed to see I was okay, and that was important for her.

In the end, though, Mum put the kibosh on that because the surgery took longer than they'd expected. I was in recovery a lot longer than I should have been and everyone was starting to get concerned.

By the time I got out of recovery, around eight o'clock at night, Mum decided it was too late to visit. Of course, I wasn't aware of any of this but heard later that my daughter was absolutely devastated.

My sister was great, as always. After she was sure I was settled, she went back to my place and woke my daughter up. "I've seen Mum," she said to her. "She's okay." She brought her in to see me the next day.

To be honest, I was upset. I was frustrated that Mum hadn't taken notice when I'd said, "Whatever happens, someone needs to bring her in to see me so she knows I'm okay." I was also disappointed and hurt that Mum didn't come and see me. She made so many excuses about why she couldn't come; she was busy getting dinner and doing this and doing that. I do my life on my own all the time, but this was a time I really,

really needed that little bit of extra TLC. I struggled with the fact that she wasn't there. My sister was, of course, but she had a young family of her own – everyone needs their mum, you know.

Mum was doing her best under the circumstances. She's never been good with medical stuff, and I could tell she wasn't coping. She was a bit short with the kids, and with me. All I wanted to do after my surgery was lie on the couch wrapped in my blanket and watch Netflix. I was in pain. I was sore all over and it felt like I'd been assaulted. I had — my body had been assaulted by the surgery. I also had that terrible, post-anaesthetic brain fog.

I was allowed to lay around for a day, then Mum said, "Okay, we've got to jolly you up. Now. You've got to get up. You've got to get dressed."

My reaction was like a little kid. "No. I don't want to."

She didn't cope with that at all and ended up calling in reinforcements – my aunt, her sister, from Brisbane. Admittedly, my aunt did calm Mum down a bit, but then they'd gang up on me and try to rally me up and around.

I just needed to heal – physically and mentally.

I'd make a real effort to get up and be present for the kids when they came home from school because I wanted to make it as normal as possible for them. In between times, after they'd gone to school and before they arrived home, I would collapse in a heap and let it all go.

The weekend after my surgery was the Queen's Birthday long weekend and I was getting a medal on the Queen's Birthday Honours List. So, on the Monday when all the awards were announced, I had people ringing me – the Chief Minister, the Minister for Emergency Services, the Commissioner – and no-one knew. So, I'm standing there, on the phone, wearing my dressing gown and trying to talk to all of these high-level people. I had to try and sound really excited and humbled and grateful, which I absolutely was, but I was also thinking 'My boobs are so sore'.

Once I recovered from my surgery and before I started radiotherapy, I drove down to Melbourne with the kids to see my oldest son. He'd wanted to be with me and to be there for his brother and sister – he's such an empathetic young man – but I'd told him to stay at uni. So, it was nice for all of us to have that week to catch up.

Kellie Nissen

---
*The other thing I did that week
was pick up a flyer about dragon boating.*

---

I'd gone into Colleen's to get a bra-fitting and on the counter was a flyer about Dragons Abreast.

I remember thinking that I'd just navigated breast surgery, was about to have radiotherapy and, by all accounts, was going to survive this. I'd always wanted to do something a little outside the box but never felt confident to do anything. I'm not much of a water person but dragon boating was something I'd always wanted to try. I also thought it would be a great way of getting fit and meeting other women who'd had similar experiences, or could at least identify with what I'd been through. At that particular point in time, it was exactly what I needed. I was already feeling brave and thought I could continue being brave and give dragon boating a go. I put the flyer on my fridge and promised myself I'd give it a go after my radiotherapy was done.

I hadn't told a lot of people at work what was going on. Obviously, though, I had to tell my immediate supervisors and a few others. During my radiotherapy treatment, my chief officer in particular was great. He said, "You just focus on what you need to do."

The whole time I was having my radiotherapy, I worked. Often, I'd have a half day at work, then go and have my radiotherapy. I wanted everything to feel normal. There was a lot of work I could sink my teeth into and that I really enjoyed, plus I was working with some amazing people. It was something I needed to do.

Radiotherapy, for the most part, went well. As I've mentioned, I'd originally been an oncology nurse but that was before I became a paramedic, and I've been a paramedic for twenty-six years so things were a bit different back then. One of the differences was, as I discovered, the whole 'tattoo' thing. Back in my day, we'd mark people up with what we call a 'Sharpie' pen now – like a permanent marker. I had no clue about these tattoos they give you these days.

I was in the rooms, having been measured up and all that, and then this trainee comes over. "I'm going to do your tattoos," she said.

"Sorry? My what?" I replied. What I really wanted to say was that I didn't want some trainee giving me my tattoos but I didn't.

There were three. The one in the middle of my chest is not quite in the middle – it's a little off centre. To this day, sometimes when I get out of the shower, my eyes are drawn to this off-centre tattoo. It's funny.

Towards the end of the radiotherapy, I became quite sick. Lots of nausea, all my skin started breaking down. Being a redhead, I was terribly burnt and ended up having to take about three weeks off. I was so unwell, and I couldn't eat.

Apparently, the way everything was lined up, the radiation was just nicking the top of my liver. I was miserable so I took personal leave and went back into my cocoon, staying at home and healing. No-one at work knew why, which is what I preferred. I've struggled with that decision since then, not telling many people. However, being in a male-oriented career, I've had to work hard to get to where I am today in management. I didn't want the fact that I had breast cancer to be something people used as a negative against me. I certainly didn't want people not asking me to do something because they thought I wouldn't cope.

I'm a very strong person and I'm very capable. Cancer doesn't define who I am or what I can do so, to this day, not many people know that I'm a breast cancer survivor.

The people I've told know about it because it felt right at the time. I've recently supported a colleague whose sister has aggressive, nasty breast cancer. "I'm a breast cancer survivor," I told her, "so, if there's anything you need, anything I can do to support you, let me know." That's all I say.

*It's not that I'm ashamed of it.*
*It's just that I don't want people to judge me for it.*

I didn't finish my treatment till the end of August or early September and I met some amazing people in that time. You do, when you're all sitting in that waiting room, day after day. I heard some incredible stories. Humbling stories. And people are just lovely.

One day, an older man was sitting next to me. He turned to me and burst into tears.

I said, "Are you okay? Do you need something?"

"I'm just looking at you and how young you are and how much of your life you've still got ahead of you," he said. "And I think it's horrible that you're here and going through all of this. I'm an old man and I've lived my life and as much as this is horrible for me, I've just realised that I've had a good life."

On another occasion, I met a lady there. She was picking up her husband, who was having his very last treatment. They lived down the coast so it was a long way to come every week. Anyway, she'd brought a beautiful bunch of coastal flowers from her garden to give to the nurses. I was sitting there in my blue hospital gown, feeling really unwell and not overly chatty. She sat next to me and started picking off petals and laying them on my lap. Each one she picked off, she explained how special it was to her, where they were in her garden and the meaning of each one. She didn't expect me to say anything.

When her husband came out, she wandered off. I gathered up all the petals and carefully brought them home and popped them in a bowl of water. They lasted a while that way, floating in the water, and I'd look at them and think how amazing some people are.

Without even knowing it, they'd both made such a difference to my day.

Then, of course, the light at the end of my treatment tunnel was dragon boating. That flyer was still on my fridge. It was a good thing I'd waited, considering the burns I ended up with and it just so happened that their 'Come and Try' coincided with the end of my treatment and was happening, thankfully, after I'd started feeling better.

I took my kids with me that first day. "You've got to sit here and watch," I told them. I suppose I was a bit nervous but once I got in that boat and we got started, I wanted to shout out, "Oh my God, this is amazing!" I loved it.

I think one of the hardest things for me going through the whole breast cancer thing was waking up in the middle of the night, particularly when I wasn't well, and having no-one to reach over to.

I felt really alone and really isolated.

*I was very cranky with the universe that this was my lot. Sure, give me cancer. Fine. But do you have to give me cancer when I'm single? And when I'm a single mum! I'm trying my hardest to be everything for everyone but no-one is there for me.*

I still reflect on that a lot.

Throughout the entire process, I've had some amazing assistance and support from close friends. I'd open the door and there would be a meal sitting on the front step for the kids and me because I'd mentioned I didn't feel like cooking. Flowers would get delivered and balloons and all sorts of beautiful things. Little care packages here and there. It was lovely and, in a way, I guess helped me start to accept that this was now my life. I'd had cancer. I'd had 'the big C' and it was going to be something that was part of me forever.

But I still wasn't going to let it define me.

I'd still keep giving the best I could to my family, to my work and to everything else.

There is that apprehension every year when I go in for my mammogram. I feel so vulnerable. I often think: Oh, God. I didn't know about it last time. I couldn't feel it last time. Where else could I have cancer that I don't know about?

I haven't. So far, so good. Everything's come back clear.

I know how lucky I've been and I'm getting there – just getting on with things.

At the risk of oversharing, last year I had a brief relationship with a guy. Having had breast cancer, having had the surgery and even though I've got a beautiful scar, just knowing that no-one had seen it in an intimate way before, it was a bit confronting.

I did tell him I was a breast cancer survivor but I was still feeling quite nervous about it all and then, suddenly, out of the blue, I just decided I was going to make a game out of it.

"I had to get three tattoos when I had my radiotherapy," I said to him. "I'll tell you where two of them are but you've got to find the third."

I'm learning to embrace it. Life is too short and too precious not to.

# Bench 2 – Right

With rowers disappearing into the mist, we have a few minutes until the next lot come out of nowhere.

Jenny – coaching today as well as drumming – calls for a ladder drill. "It's all about intensity and power," she says, "not pace."

We settle ourselves in for a long drill. Hips pressed to the side of the boat – the gunnel – feet firmly planted, eyes focused on our two strokes.

"Twenty strokes to get us moving again, then settle in for fifty strokes at sixty per cent power …" Jenny continues explaining the drill, which involves continuing the same twenty then fifty pattern, but increasing the power by ten per cent each time until we reach ninety per cent. At that point, we shift and go 'down the ladder'. It's not an easy drill but done properly, it makes you really focus on your technique.

Jenny looks down the boat. "Got it?" she says.

Everyone nods, but we also know we don't have to remember it all because Jenny and Lyndall will keep the instructions coming.

"Power, not pace," Anne says, to clarify. Probably also hoping what most of us are hoping – that our two energiser-bunny strokes don't get carried away. It's easy enough to do – though not necessarily fun to follow.

**Name:** Anne Baynes
**Initial diagnosis:** 2010
**Age at diagnosis:** 48
**Job at diagnosis:** Registered Nurse
**Job now:** Registered Nurse
**Joined DAC:** 2011
**Favourite boat position:** anywhere except sweep; stroking gets the best views
**Memorable DAC moment:** paddling to (former) Governor-General Quentin Bryce's residence and having morning tea with her
**Claim to fame:** being able to milk a cow by hand

Kellie Nissen

# Anne's Story: A Ride You Can't Get Off

*I wasn't in a hurry because I've had many breast lumps before and they were always just hormonal, so I wasn't concerned.*

About twelve years ago, I felt a lump in my breast. Not unusual for me, I'd had a few before with no issues. I went to my GP, but this time she wanted an ultrasound and a mammogram.

I still wasn't concerned; I got the request form and booked in with a private imaging company.

On the day I went to have the scans, the clinic reception staff said, "You're only booked in for an ultrasound; we can't do the mammogram."

That was frustrating, but what could I do?

In the ultrasound room, it's quite dark and you can't really see what they're doing but you can feel it. You sort of know something's going on when the sonographer is having a look around and keeps going back to the same area on your breast. They never say anything. This is exactly what happened to me. Then the ultrasonographer said, "I need to go and chat to someone," and left the room.

When she came back, a doctor was with her and he had a look, too. "There's a lump there that we want to biopsy," he said and biopsied it straight away.

As I got up to leave, I said, "How do I get my mammogram?"

"You'll have to go back to your GP and get another request form."

I waited till I knew the results were back from the biopsy and then went to my GP.

The results were negative.

I was happy with that but my GP was only moderately happy. "I'll give you another form so you can book for a mammogram."

At that stage, I was not at all concerned, in fact, I waited two or three months because I'd had that negative ultrasound result. I decided to go to a different imaging company because I was frustrated with the service

I received at the first one. I got the mammogram done and went back to the imaging company a week later to pick up the results.

*They'd lost the mammogram and the results.*

They couldn't find them. I remember standing at the desk and saying, "I'll wait until you find them."

They were running around and making phone calls but still couldn't find them. Finally, after about half an hour, someone came over to explain. "We had to send the mammogram to another radiographer to look at so we don't physically have it or the results here."

That's when I thought something was probably going on.

They told me they'd send the results straight to my GP – so I went home still not knowing anything.

Two or three days later, when I was at work, I had a missed call – I can't take calls at work. I rang back when I was driving home.

"You better pull over to the side of the road," my GP said.

The results had come back positive. I had breast cancer.

I didn't understand. "I had a negative fine needle biopsy!"

"It was blood-stained," my GP explained. "It may have caused a false negative result."

"What now?" I asked. I was so frustrated. Although I'm a health professional too, I was really disappointed in the whole process – not getting the original booking right, telling me they couldn't do the mammogram and ultrasound on the same day, a false negative biopsy, mammograms getting lost – it wasn't good.

"You'll need to go back and have another mammogram and core biopsy to confirm."

I think I was probably in denial at the time – I suspect I had worked out what the diagnosis was, and that would have increased my frustration at the system. Letting it go would have been easier – things like that happen, especially in big pathology or imaging centres.

The other thing that played on my mind was the time delay between having a negative result and going back for the mammogram. A voice in my head was saying, 'If you'd hurried, if you'd got to it more quickly, maybe it might have been different.'

Probably not, though. I know that.

---

*This time, the core biopsy results came back as positive and the real roller-coaster ride started.*

---

I had great faith in my GP. She booked me in quickly to a really nice surgeon, who happened to be a good friend of hers. My GP rang me at 5:30 pm and advised the second mammogram and core biopsy confirmed breast cancer and an hour later, I was on my way to see the surgeon who had agreed to stay back late.

My daughters were still in high school so I rang a friend to pick them up – usually I would have done that. Then, I rang my partner and asked him to come with me. He was always really supportive.

All this time, I was still in denial – sort of shocked and surprised by the results. I kept telling myself it was just a little lump. They'd remove it and everything would be fine. Maybe a bit of radiation or something.

The surgeon brought me crashing to earth. "There are three lumps," he said. "It'll be a mastectomy."

His words really threw me. I hadn't expected that at all.

The surgeon gave me some options and said I could take a couple of days to think about it.

I don't think I broke the news to my daughters very well. When I walked in with my partner that evening, they said, "Why didn't you pick us up?"

"I've got breast cancer," I answered. It was spur of the moment. In hindsight, I should have thought about a better way of telling them. I was still in shock myself. As it turned out, being teenagers, they were both busy with their own lives and while they did talk about it with me a bit, I think they mainly internalised it. Perhaps they talked about it with each other, or other friends. They didn't want to burden me, I guess.

By the time of my next appointment, the surgeon had come up with a plan – a mastectomy and chemotherapy. "I'm unsure whether you'll need radiotherapy," he said. "If it was my wife, I'd say not to go with the radiotherapy but I'll write you a referral for a radiation oncologist anyway."

If he was telling me he wouldn't recommend radiation for his wife, then I was happy to go with that. There was still the mastectomy and chemotherapy to get through; still so much of the endless roller-coaster ride to come. A ride you simply can't get off when you want to.

At that stage, I finally started to trust the process. I realised I had to let the system do its thing; I had to go with it.

My surgery was booked for a couple of weeks later. Very quick. In that time, I talked to a radiation oncologist and also had the pre-chemotherapy talk. Throughout this, I was still going to work. I didn't tell anyone at work until I had to; it's just the way I am. I keep things fairly internal.

I did tell my nursing supervisor and my medical director, of course, but it wasn't until just before the surgery that I sent out an email to everyone else: *Sorry. I'm on leave for the next few weeks as I've got cancer.*

Just like that.

I didn't want any sympathy because I think I'd just have cried.

---

*I wanted to pretend everything was normal.*
*I was still in denial, I suppose. I don't know.*

---

On the day of the surgery, I had to have a Sentinel Lymph Node Biopsy. This is to check to see if the cancer has spread into the lymph nodes. Basically, they inject some dye into your breast a few hours prior to surgery and then leave you to massage it so it goes through to your lymph nodes.

It felt really strange.

There I was, lying there on my own, massaging this breast I was about to lose. All I could think was that my body was letting me down. It was such an unusual feeling.

At some point while I was waiting to go into surgery, a nun came and spoke to me. Although she gave me the option of talking to her or not, I felt pretty powerless lying in the bed with this person I didn't know offering counselling. I'm not a particularly religious person but, even so, I didn't want to have any counselling prior to the treatment. It felt odd and difficult to say I didn't want to talk to her.

The other thing I personally found a bit odd was this bag of goodies I'd been given beforehand. I wasn't concerned with the pamphlets and information, or even the little stuffed breast, but there was a survey in with everything. It said something about university ethics but the gist of it was that they'd found that people who have breast surgery and chemotherapy often end up with some sort of temporary deficit in their thinking. They wanted to do a pre- and post-treatment survey to test this theory. All I could think was: so, I'm having surgery and chemo and now you're telling me I'm going to go crazy?

I didn't do it.

It felt inappropriate. Sure, they want to recruit people for their research but they'd chosen completely the wrong time.

My surgery went according to plan. I was home in three or four days – with my drains. The breast care nurses that come to see you are truly wonderful. I also made myself go for a walk every day. Each day, I'd go a bit further. I recall walking up Mount Majura – two drains hanging at my side. I kept telling myself I could do this; that I had to do this. I wanted to get back to normal as quickly as possible.

Once everything healed and the drains were out, it was straight onto the chemotherapy. Six cycles of three weeks each.

For me, the first week of the cycle was really difficult with all the side effects. The second week was when I felt pretty average. Then in my third week, I was back to normal. My surgeon had told me I could go back to work to keep my mind off things. I'd have a week off straight after chemotherapy. I'd go back to work for a couple of weeks and then do it all again.

That first week at work was pretty tough. I was tired. Being a nurse in an outpatient clinic, I would see lots of patients, one after another. There were a couple of occasions when I thought I was going to faint and I was just hoping I'd get through the appointment. I'd try to act normally, although a few times one of my work colleagues asked, "Do you want to have a couple of appointments off?"

"No, no," I'd say.

I'd make it through that week and then the next week was fine. Back to normal with no issues.

However, with each chemo cycle, I was becoming less robust and by cycle six, I was thinking: If there are any more cycles after this, I'm refusing to do them. I felt like I couldn't do it anymore.

It was important to me, though, to be quite independent throughout it all. I didn't want to be treated differently. I'd go in to have my chemotherapy and I often wasn't feeling great but then I'd look around and see people much worse than myself. I felt like I was one of the lucky ones.

I kept on making myself walk, too. I'd walk to the hospital to get the chemo. Walking was how I got through my treatment. It gave me something to challenge myself.

Sleeping was the worst – or not sleeping – especially in that first week after the chemo. And the nausea. I didn't want to ring up the community nurses in the middle of the night to have them come and give me an anti-nausea injection because I didn't want to make a fuss, so I'd just do it myself.

*I didn't want to be a burden on anyone.*

Joining Dragons Abreast was the best thing for me. I loved it as a support group. We didn't sit around talking about breast cancer. It was all about the paddling, but it was great knowing you could ask another paddler if you had a question.

The thing was, though, I was highly self-conscious at first when wearing the paddling uniform T-shirt. I felt like I was broadcasting to the world that I'd had breast cancer. It was probably four or five months before I stopped worrying about wearing my Dragons Abreast T-shirt out in public. I guess I didn't want people knowing I'd had cancer and feeling sorry for me.

It was the same with the turban option when I'd lost my hair – I didn't want that at all. I opted for a wig instead. Now, I wonder why anyone else would care and why I was embarrassed about it, but that's just how it was. People said they really liked my hair when I had my wig on. A couple of people didn't know it was a wig. "It's better than my normal hair, is it?" I'd say.

After the chemo, I didn't have radiation. Right at the start, the surgeon had said he didn't think I'd need it. I did speak to the radiation oncologist again; she had me booked in and told me all the pros and cons.

"If we were in different places," I said to her, "and you were sitting here, would you go ahead with radiation?"

"No," she said.

So, I didn't.

---

*Right after the main treatment ended, I was in this state of hyper-awareness. I wanted to do everything right and it felt like my whole world had changed, when, in fact, it hadn't.*

---

It took me about a year to get over surgery and treatment and realise that not a lot had changed but that I had become more aware of a few things.

Lymphoedema, for example. The risk of swelling in your arm due to flying or carrying a backpack. Going into a shop and seeing a beautiful shirt, then realising the cut was a little low for me to wear. All the things you never really think of until this happens.

But I don't feel like I'm missing out. Yes, my life has changed – but it hasn't. I'd even say that having cancer has given me opportunities I'd never have had otherwise.

I love bushwalking and I go for five-day hikes. I fly somewhere and forget my compression sleeve – and it's okay. Dragon boating has introduced me to the most awesome group of women, taken me to Florence to compete in an international Dragons Abreast competition, taken me on a 60 km dragon boat marathon on the Ord River in WA and even a paddle and morning tea at the Governor-General's residence.

It's all a long way behind me now. After three or four years, I stopped thinking about it much. Every now and then, I'll be in the shower and look down and get a bit of surprise.

I went through the airport the other day and the security pulled me over after I went through the X-ray machine, because they thought I was hiding something in my bra.

"I'm not," I said.

A female security guard gave me a very firm pat-down on my breast and was a little surprised, I think.

"There's nothing there," I said.

Every now and then that sort of stuff comes up and you just have to laugh about it. There's no point getting upset or angry.

Kellie Nissen

# Bench 3 – Left

Two ladder drills down and Lyndall finally calls it. "Easy."

"That was anything but easy," Denise quips. "I thought we were never going to stop."

But that's what training is all about.

"Remember what our coach used to say all the time?" Kathy says. "Train hard. Race easy."

Wise words indeed. A short race of 200 metres is over in less than a minute; 500 metres in three-ish minutes. Even including the paddle out to the start line, the forward and back as the starter lines us up, the race itself and the return to shore, it's all over in around 15 minutes. A training session, however, is at least forty-five minutes, and often longer.

"I love racing," Kathy adds. "That adrenaline rush at the start is amazing." She's lost in the moment.

Most of us on board love regattas. Love racing. The whole team pulling together, the drum marking time, the drummer and the sweep both screaming calls and motivation. Then, the triumph at the end when we've crossed the line. The three cheers for us and then the other boats before the cool-down paddle back to shore.

"That's why I'm here," Kathy says. "That's what I love."

*Bench 3 – Left*

**Name:** Kathy
**Initial diagnosis:** 2016, multifocal invasive lobular (ER/PR+, HER2-negative), invasive ductal
**Age at diagnosis:** 48
**Job at diagnosis:** Registered Nurse
**Job now:** Registered Nurse
**Joined DAC:** 2017
**Favourite boat position:** drummer, stroke, trimmer
**Memorable DAC moments:** my first international regatta in Florence, Flowers on the Water
**Best thing about DAC:** my team sisters
**Claim to fame:** 0.05 second reaction time when driving a race car

Kellie Nissen

# Kathy's Story: Beautiful Trauma

> *Having a job where I worked with people*
> *who were going through breast cancer surgery,*
> *I was quite matter-of-fact. I knew what the*
> *process was and being part of the medical industry,*
> *I also knew which surgeon I wanted.*

I was diagnosed in 2016.

The first indication I had was when my husband felt the lump. But, having polycystic breasts, it felt like just another cyst. It wasn't anything like how it was 'supposed' to feel or look like, so I wasn't particularly worried.

I went into work but we were overstaffed and I wasn't required. I came home and thought, 'Oh, I'll make an appointment to see the GP about it.' My GP sent me off for a mammogram and ultrasound – I usually had these yearly but had missed the previous one.

While I was there, the radiographer mentioned that my nipple was somewhat inverted. I hadn't been looking at my breasts like we're supposed to when we check them so I'd never noticed.

It was inverted and there was dimpling.

Something was detected in the ultrasound but they weren't too concerned. I went back to my GP when the report came through. "It says to do an MRI, if concerned," my GP said. "Let's just do it."

The MRI was still inconclusive so I ended up going for a biopsy. I'd already dropped my scans off to my GP and as I walked in, he said, "Who's your surgeon?"

That's when I knew it was more than likely going to be breast cancer, but there was no shock because I already suspected it.

> *The dimpling. The orange peel skin. The inverted*
> *nipple. The lump. Yeah, I knew it was breast cancer.*

I made an appointment with the surgeon but couldn't get in for a few weeks. When I told the radiologist, he said, "I've got to call him today, anyway. I'll see about getting you a much earlier appointment."

"Oh, no," I said. "It's okay." But he did it anyway and got me in much sooner.

The ball had started rolling.

The biggest thing for me was considering my children and how they would react. When I knew I was going for surgery, we wanted to tell all three of them together. One of them was at ADFA, the other two were at home. We couldn't make it happen, though, so we told the two that lived at home.

My youngest's reaction was quite surprising given he's the more emotional, sentimental child of the three. He said, "Well, can I get back and do my homework now?"

We said, "Okay, but don't tell your brother yet." We told my eldest son a few days later. That went okay, too.

The hardest people to tell were my parents. I didn't know that would be so difficult. My parents don't live in Canberra and I didn't want them to be alone when I told them on the phone, so I rang my eldest brother, who lived near them. "Can you arrange to be at Mum and Dad's when I tell them?" I asked. And he was.

---

*My mum has always been quite pragmatic and both Mum and Dad were fine when I told them, especially given they had my brother there.*

---

Mum pretty much dropped everything when I had surgery and treatment. She came down and took us all under her wing, so to speak. One issue we had was that my husband was studying at the same time. He was doing a Master's in one year – a very intense course – and he needed to go overseas as well. We were fortunate to have support from both my parents.

I had some close friends who were there for me as well. If I needed anything at all, they were just a phone call away. They were really good to me; they gave me the space I needed while being there at the same time.

There were a few who tried to cocoon me, but I'm quite a private person, so when I told a few people at work I asked them not to tell anyone. I don't like sympathy. I don't like being the focus of attention. They respected that.

What I have subsequently learned, however, is that there are two types of people. There are the people who are supportive – they're the ones you want in your inner circle. Then, there are the people who you have to help in order for them to get through what you're going through. These are the people you want in your outer circle.

Having had that experience, and coming to that realisation, was useful in the present role I'm in, when I have to counsel people.

> *You don't need the needy people. You just need the supportive ones. It's important to remember that.*

There's another group of people who somehow put themselves in your situation and if you don't react the way they think they would, they can get defensive. It's like they're upset with you for not dealing with things the way they think they would.

The thing is, everyone is individual but not everyone realises that. In the end, I found the best way would be to listen, not react and then just park it and limit my interactions with these people as much as I could.

I found it hard when I went back to work because there seemed to be quite a few people who thought I shouldn't be at work – that I wasn't ready or wasn't well enough. It's such an individual thing, though. For some people, work can be a great distraction. For others, it can give you back a sense of normality after having several months of everything being thrown up in the air or turned upside down.

At the end of the day, it's your choice. Yours alone. My resolve on this has dissolved a few relationships and I suspect was also the catalyst for losing a job I loved. That was hard. My work ethos has always been to give a hundred per cent – if I need to work longer hours to accommodate a patient or complete extra work then I'm happy to do so.

I went back to work fulltime prior to my radiotherapy, which was not an issue for me but I think people thought it was too much too soon after my chemo. I knew what I was capable of and I wasn't going to jeopardise my health … but I was asked to leave the position I was doing. One option was to return to ward nursing, which was too much for me, so I took a redundancy. I didn't hear from my work colleagues again.

With my surgery, I had a bilateral mastectomy with immediate implant reconstruction. This was my choice. I had to have a mastectomy, but I elected to have a bilateral one because I had these dense polycystic breasts. They were past their use-by date, so why not get rid of them both?

My surgeon was supportive of my decision. That was so important to me because it was my body and I had to think about what the best thing was for me.

The surgery was okay. I ended up having a nipple-sacrificing mastectomy. Not having the nipple there changed my perspective of myself, but again, that was my choice.

Once I'd recovered from the surgery, I had chemotherapy. The chemo was taxing; it was really hard. I didn't want to go back and have the third or fourth rounds.

*I had to tell myself, 'Put your big girl pants on. Get over it.'*

I was only sick for a week in each round – quite sick, actually. I had to have Neulasta injections to stop the reduction of my white blood cell count. I didn't like those injections as they were quite painful.

I lost my hair, of course. Surprisingly, it wasn't overly confronting because I expected to lose it. More confronting, was losing my eyebrows. I could pencil them in, but a couple of times I went off to work and I'd forgotten to do it. For me, that was horrific. Once or twice, I even rang my husband and asked him to bring me in my eyebrow pencil.

"No-one else is going to notice," he'd say. He was right, of course. But I'd know.

Sometimes, I'd have to go out to the front reception, where some of the younger women were. They'd always have something I could borrow so I could duck out and pencil in my eyebrows. It was more for me than anyone else.

Reflecting back, apart from the eyebrows, I didn't mind having no hair. It was quite good. I often think that if I hadn't lost my hair, I wouldn't have the short hair I do now. It would still be long.

---

*Now, though, I know I rock a short haircut.*
*I also know I rock a blue wig.*

---

My son and his girlfriend bought me a blue wig when I lost my hair. I looked really good in that blue wig; I still have it.

My poor husband ... he went over to England for his Master's course. When he left, I had hair. While he was away, I got sick of losing clumps of hair everywhere so when my kids came over, I got them to shave my head. They had great fun. I ended up with a mullet and then a mohawk, much to their delight. Then they just shaved it all off. So, my husband came back to his bald wife.

Although I didn't mind the no hair thing, I rarely went out in public without a head covering. One exception was the time I went to an ABBA concert, a tribute band, and it started raining. It's quite nice to feel raindrops on your bald head so I took my head covering off. Just that one time.

Apart from the blue wig, I did have another wig, which was quite bouffe. A lovely wig, but it wasn't me at all. We had to go to a few formal balls and events, so I'd wear it for that night but otherwise, I didn't use it much.

Hair loss can be confronting for other people, too. Particularly when you've also lost your eyebrows and eyelashes. They do grow back, of course, but often thinner. I've had some people comment, "Oh, you've got beautiful eyelashes." I sometimes respond, saying that they are much thinner now but people don't understand. They don't know or don't remember what you looked like beforehand – but you do. Although, your own memory can often be somewhat distorted.

Throughout my chemo, I fully intended to work when I could. I couldn't manage it during the first rounds because they were intense and

I wasn't up to it, but when I moved on to the Taxol, it was much better. My manager, though, made me seek permission from my doctor and my husband before I was allowed to return to work. Some people might ask, "Why did you have to get permission from your husband?" They knew me at work though; I had a reputation as a workaholic. I wasn't, I just gave a hundred per cent to everything. My manager wanted to be sure I wasn't going to overdo it. As it turned out, I only worked three days a week for half a day each time and that was enough. It was good to be back, doing something.

> *With radiation, the unit was barely a hundred metres up the road from where I worked. I'd go into work, do a bit of paperwork, head off to radiology, get zapped then return to work.*

The radiation therapy was okay. I didn't have any side effects apart from being a bit tired. My skin was fine, hardly any burns.

At the end of it all, once the surgery, chemo and radiotherapy are done – the major treatments – it's like you've been cocooned and well looked after. Then, suddenly, the cocoon's gone. In the acute phase, post-diagnosis, there is surgery and adjuvant treatment involving multiple appointments with different members of your medical team. Once the acute phase is over, normally after radiotherapy, you enter a chronic phase and then the appointments with the medical team are less frequent. Some people find the transition hard. For me it was a step closer to normality.

I still see my oncologist and surgeon once every twelve months, though. And I was fortunate to get onto a drug trial, so I still have a medical team, but not to the extent I had before.

The benefit of being on a drug trial is knowing you are part of a study that may improve outcomes for others. You also get extra medical input and follow-up from the trial team. I was involved with a drug trial and the follow-up for that is ten years. Another benefit of the trial was there was nil cost for the trial drug, which, at that time, was not on the PBS.

I'd worked with people who had cancer and I thought I'd be fine. I thought I knew what I was in for. Everyone is different, of course, but I wasn't too worried.

The side effects were frustrating, particularly the brain fog. I brought this up with my doctor but there's nothing much you can do about it – except keep your brain active with crosswords or Sudoku.

It wasn't just a case of saying stupid things sometimes because of the brain fog. I was at a soccer match, watching one of my kids play. I'm standing there and thinking, 'My bra feels so different.' I had no idea so I went to the bathroom to check. I had my bra on completely the wrong way. A combination of no real sensation in that area because of the surgery and that rotten fog.

There are also the physical effects, like hot flushes and joint pain. And then there's the financial expenses that nobody really talks about. The cost of the drugs and tests and doctors is to be expected, in some ways. But what about new clothes because you've put on weight or lost weight and your regular clothes don't fit anymore? Plus all the scarves and headwear and other bits and pieces along the way.

> *But, what can you do about it? Really, you just have to try and muddle your way through the best you can.*

Emotionally, I think it all got to me. I became quite down because there was a lot of stuff going on at work. I lost my position and that was hard. I felt like people may have thought I wasn't as capable now, perhaps because of what I'd been through. I'm not saying it was the sole reason, but it was certainly a contributing factor.

Returning to work was my choice. Physically, I knew I could do it. Mentally, I knew I could do it. It should have been my choice but it ended up that it wasn't. On the flip side, I've gone on to do other things. I'm in an area now that I may not otherwise have entered if all of that hadn't happened. I'm in a job I love. I absolutely love the work.

In hindsight, I now know that emotionally, I was in a dark place. That's when I started dragon boating. I knew I needed some sort of support and was tossing up between Bosom Buddies or dragon boating with Dragons Abreast. I'm so glad I chose paddling.

I joined in 2017 and the next thing I knew, the following year, I was off to Florence in Italy to paddle in a huge international regatta.

The trip to Florence was good, particularly so soon after my treatment experience. Certainly, there was a greater focus on breast cancer there and it made me realise how many people are affected by it. The *Flowers on the Water* ceremony is highly emotional at any time but in Florence, with thousands of people, wow!

My team, Dragons Abreast Canberra, are fantastic. It's a nice, supportive organisation. They don't focus so much on the whole breast cancer aspect; if you want to talk about it, you can, but it's more about the exercise and the camaraderie. I think that's the difference between Dragons Abreast and other support networks.

---

*Reflecting on that year and the years following, brings up a whole load of emotions. Everyone is different and everyone's experiences and emotions will be different. That's very clear in my dragon boating team.*

---

For me, I describe it as 'beautiful trauma'. I stole that from a Pink concert. I have the beanie with the words on it too.

To me, that's what it is.

It's traumatic because of the diagnosis, what you've got to go through and all the changes you face. The trauma is to be expected. It's also traumatic in that some doors will close. Some relationships will end.

At the same time, though, it's beautiful in the way that it opens up other experiences and other relationships. You come to see things differently; not through rose-coloured glasses, but things take on a different meaning. That's beautiful. For example, you see a sunset and realise they are so much better than they were pre-cancer. You stop sweating over the big things – and the little things – because what's the point?

Having cancer puts things back into perspective.

I tell people that, yes, cancer absolutely does change you. It changes you physically, emotionally, psychologically, socially and financially. But unless you let it, cancer doesn't need to define who you are. You will still be the same person.

And that's what I remind myself every day:

---

*Cancer will not define who I am unless I allow it to do so.*

---

# Bench 3 – Right

"Ready to go again, DA?" Jenny says.

A few of us nod. We're ready.

Twenty strokes to get the boat up and moving from a standstill is always an effort. A standard dragon boat weighs more than 250 kilograms – plus twenty-two paddlers, sweep oar, drum and other bits and pieces. But once the boat is up and moving, once everyone is paddling in time, it's almost hypnotic.

It's also easy to drift away into the thoughts in your head.

"Aah, sorry," April says to Anne as their paddles clash. "Lost my rhythm."

It's not hard to do.

"Up to seventy per cent," Jenny calls.

We all lean forward a margin more; with reach comes power. Done properly, dragon boating is a whole-body sport.

"Up to eighty per cent."

Twenty paddle blades bury themselves deep in the water, taking our hands with them, before pulling back parallel to the boat, lifting out at the hip and snapping back to the front, ready to bury again.

"Back to seventy per cent," Jenny calls. "Keep the leg drive on. Sit up."

Coordinating the leg drive and sitting up with the arm movements is not easy at first, but over time it becomes muscle memory. Not all of us in the boat can reach as far as we'd like, or sit up as tall – each paddler has her limits and niggles, depending on previous surgeries or ongoing issues. The expectation is only that each member aims to 'do your best'.

Connect. Move. Live.

"And easy," Lyndall calls at the end of the ladder. "Let it run."

April turns to Kathy. "I pinch myself every time I'm out here to make sure I'm not dreaming," she says. "I love this sport."

Kellie Nissen

**Name:** April Weiss
**Initial diagnosis:** 2017, HER2-negative, PR+, ductal cancer
**Age at diagnosis:** 57
**Job at diagnosis:** Associate Director Application Services (ANU)
**Job now:** retired
**Joined DAC:** 2021
**Favourite boat position:** anywhere
**Memorable DAC moments:** receiving the Rookie of the Year Award with Joanne in 2022
**Best travel destination:** our house in Mexico

## April's Story: A Process to Go Through

> *We have breast cancer in the family, so there was always an awareness that I could get it.*

I have always had regular tests for breast cancer.

I have ropey breasts, which makes self-checks a bit tricky. How on earth does anyone find anything among all that ropiness? It changes all the time. I'd be concerned, or unsure, and would take my concerns to my regular breast checks and screenings in Melbourne when I was living there.

"It's okay," they'd say. "It's just another cyst."

In 2015, I moved to Canberra and, in May of 2017, I went to the doctor for my normal check-up. She did a breast check and all was fine.

I wasn't being overly vigilant about doing my own monthly checks but, for some reason, when I was overseas later in 2017, I was doing a breast check and felt an interesting shape, like a starfish. I thought, 'Oh well, my ropes have turned into starfish now'.

After my trip, I sent holiday snaps to family and friends around the place. I have family in Guatemala, and a close friend over there who has what you might call 'interesting abilities'.

When my friend looked at my photo, he got in touch. "There's something very wrong," he said. "You must go to the doctor and find out what it is."

I'd only just had a breast check, but I'd had skin cancer a number of decades ago so I thought that might be what it was.

> *Maybe it's this. Maybe it's that.*
> *Make an appointment with the specialists.*
> *No, it's fine. I'd been through all of this before. Many times.*

It was November by this stage, and time for my mammogram. I hadn't had a mammogram in Canberra before so I went to BreastScreen ACT. They did the mammogram and left me there to wait while they went to get the films looked at.

The next thing I knew, the radiologist arrived, with that face they wear when they find something. "You've got something of interest there," he said. "We'd like to do some more checks."

They did various tests, including the delightful one – the biopsy. I was so well looked after. Everyone was highly attentive, trying to work out what it was.

Finally, they worked it out – cancer.

"Take these results to your GP," they said. "He'll arrange for you to see a surgeon."

By this time, it was early December and we were heading towards the middle of December when I saw my GP.

---

*Of course, everyone was starting to shut down because Christmas was coming.*

---

"I need to see a breast surgeon," I said to my doctor. "Can I see anyone before Christmas?" I didn't want to wait over the Christmas break.

She peered at her computer screen. "There's one surgeon who has opened up one more day," she said as she picked up the phone. "I'll see if I can get you in."

I couldn't believe it. Not only did she manage to get me in, but the surgeon was able to fit me in for surgery on 22 December.

When I went in, they told me they thought they'd be doing a lumpectomy but it would depend on what they found. So, I wasn't really sure what I'd find until I woke up.

As soon as I was released, I had a day of rest and then my husband Peter and I hopped in the car and drove down to Melbourne to see the family. I was still recovering but I thought, 'Oh well, it'll take my mind off it.' It would also distract me from thinking too much about the chemo, which I was due to start after we came back in the middle of January and had seen the oncologist.

I had a lovely time in Melbourne but as soon as we got back to Canberra, it was all systems go.

My oncologist was a very distinguished fellow. Very experienced, well respected – he'd apparently written over six-hundred papers. That was impressive. My first appointment was so good. He was incredibly patient and spent a long time answering all our questions and giving us lots of information.

I felt confident in the process but, as is bound to happen, people I knew were always saying things like, "Have you considered this?", "What about that?" or "Do you want to do this alternative thing?"

I do like a lot of alternative things, so I did a quick round of reading and came across Ian Gawler's books.

Ian Gawler lost his leg to bone cancer and was then given six weeks to live. There was nothing they could do, so he went on his own journey and ended up in the Philippines and tried this and that. He's still alive today, many decades later, which he puts down to a huge change in diet along with various other natural approaches.

---

*Dr Gawler's view, however, is that if there is a known conventional approach that has good recovery rates, take it. Don't think about anything else, just take it. Go on that path.*

---

I thought, 'Yes, I'll do the chemo.'

I had to get rid of my hair, though. So, before my first chemo, Peter and I went for a haircut. I'd always had super curly, super long hair. Before chemo, my hair was all the way down my back; it was wild and crazy and a reddish-auburn colour. Anyway, we went in and I said, "Shave it off. Maybe a number two or number three." The poor hairdresser: she was nearly crying.

Off it came. And then Peter did the same. I thought we both looked quite good.

On the drive to the hospital, the day of my first chemo, I remember saying to Peter, "Can you turn around and take me to the airport? I want to go to Patagonia." I was only half joking.

"You know I can't do that," he said. "I'm going to take you to the hospital."

Naturally, they couldn't find a vein. That was traumatic, maybe more so for the nurses than me. I did my best to go into super patient mode and make them feel at ease. I felt sorry for the poor nurse who couldn't find a vein in my arm; the other chemo nurses gave her a hard time over it. They're very close in there. Great senses of humour. I guess they need those.

That was the start of my three-weekly journey.

I probably should have watched what I ate and drank more. I was going to be sick anyway, but I think I'd have felt a bit better if I'd curtailed what I was eating. I was yet to discover that sugar did not agree with me at all when I was undergoing chemo. There was a woman who'd come around with these gorgeous chocolate chip cookies. The first time, I was like 'yum, yum' but afterwards … no.

Nothing really prepares you for how you're going to feel. I remember feeling simply awful but unable to be sick because of the drugs they gave me to suppress it.

I'd brought home a big wall calendar from the university where I worked. All my key dates were marked on the calendar and every evening, I'd mark off another day with an X – heading towards my end date.

I didn't work throughout my chemo. I felt like a bit of a fraud, particularly by the third week of each round when I didn't feel too bad at all. However, my oncologist had advised me not to work. "For decades, you've been paying so you can have some time off," he said, "and now's the time to have some time off so you can rest and take care of yourself."

When I hesitated, he added, "There's nothing worse than having to get up in the morning and brace yourself to go to work when you're having chemo. Just take the time out." He looked me straight in the eye. "I want you to have six months off during chemo and then we'll work out a plan around the radiation, if you want to go back."

I'm glad I listened.

Every third week, Peter and I would try to go away for a few days.

> *Kiama became my go-to place. I felt it had 'healing vibes'. I don't know whether it did or didn't, but I felt good there.*

I really loved the two rock pools. I wanted to go swimming in the ocean but felt I was like a wounded beastie and that if I went in the water, the sharks would hunt me down and eat me. I was convinced of it, but I felt happy in the little rock pools. Swimming in the beautiful salt water always energised me. We'd go for long walks and it was so beautiful. That became our routine – week three, off we'd go to Kiama.

Poor Peter became my 'nurse'. Not only was he doing his own PhD research but he had to care for me and my cravings. I'd get this urge for orange juice, water and ice. It had to be freshly squeezed orange juice, too. He'd race out and buy a huge bag of oranges to satisfy my craving, not only for the flavour – because I could actually taste it – but also the feel of it. I'd lost my taste for almost everything else.

The other thing my he had to do was get my drugs. I'd been told by the oncologist to take Endone.

"But I don't even take Panadol," I said.

"It's a different sort of pain," he explained. "You'll get sharp joint and bone pains from time to time. Just have them handy."

He gave me a script for Endone; for something like sixty pills, and I thought, 'Oh, I need to get them all, now.'

We raced to the chemist and I sent Peter in because I'd just had my first lot of chemo and didn't want to go anywhere I didn't have to afterwards.

In he goes and says to the pharmacist, "I need sixty Endone."

Well, didn't that start a chain reaction that went all the way up through the Department of Health! They sold him the sixty – of which I think I had maybe ten to fifteen throughout the whole process. However, you know you're sick when something like an Endone barely touches the sides and only takes the edge off the pain.

It was a process, you know. I lost all my hair. I lost my eyelashes. I kept riding my bike throughout and doing a few outdoor things and all the sand and dust would be getting in my eyes. And then, my body seemed to take over and work out a way to keep everything out of my eyes.

I didn't get a wig. I tried one and it drove my head crazy. They're so tight.

> *Around the house, I'd refer to myself as 'lizard lady'.*

If it were warm enough, I wouldn't cover my head but, in winter, of course, I'd have to sleep wearing a warm hat. It would need to be soft because I was so sensitive to everything. I went to that fabulous woman at HeadsUp Kippax who sells those cute little turbans and hats and scarves. We had a lovely time, trying on this and that.

I also went to the make-up sessions run by Look Good, Feel Better. Some of the women there were quite young. It was sad but everyone was so sweet. Trying to put make-up on when you've got no eyebrows is interesting.

Peter was so sweet and supportive through all my surgeries and treatment. During chemo, I said to him, "Look, I might want a dog for support or something."

I knew he'd probably be thinking, 'I'm not caring for her and a dog.' He didn't say that obviously, but I really wasn't expecting a dog.

Then one day while I was doing chemo he came in with a stuffed dog that I took to the rest of the chemo sessions for support. When undergoing radiation, Peter surprised me with a radiation rabbit. So unexpected and it really cheered me up.

I was also well supported by my work colleagues. They'd check on me regularly, ask how I was and if I needed anything. I'd try to go in to see my boss once a month or so, just to get out of the house. I'd go in, have a chat, see how things were going.

There was so much paperwork, though. Not from work but other cancer-related things. Insurance. Super payouts. Every day, I'd try and do a bit of paperwork because there were so much to do. There was lots of information to read. I tried to keep a diary of appointments and other related information as well.

It was the Easter long weekend and I was about halfway through my chemo when this really strange thing happened. I was lying in bed, although I was still awake. It was about midnight. I heard a loud knocking on the door.

Bang, bang, bang. Bang, bang, bang.

I shook Peter. "There's someone at the door," I said.

"I didn't hear anything," he said. "Are you sure?"

I was sure, so I got up and looked out the window. Our front gates were closed. There was nobody there. It freaked me out and I couldn't stop thinking about it. I got on my phone and checked to see what it meant.

Death. Basically. It was death knocking.

Now, a lot of people will think I'm crazy or was just dreaming, but I think it was a sign or a warning because when I got up in the morning, I felt a bit off. I checked my temperature and it was quite high. I checked again later, and again later, and it was going up and up. It was heading towards the danger zone.

"We have to go to Emergency," I told Peter. The rising temperature was one of the danger signs I'd been told to watch out for.

At the hospital, there seemed to be a hundred people in the waiting room. It was full. We walked up to the counter and I showed them my card. "I'm a cancer patient," I said, "and I have this temperature."

The lady at the desk told me to take a seat. I'd no sooner sat down than I was called in. Ahead of the hundred people who were there before me. I felt like a VIP.

---

*They whisked me into the positive pressure room and start checking me out.*

---

They couldn't get in touch with my oncologist so the doctor on duty came in and said, "We think it's probably neutropenia."

Because of the knocking the previous night, I couldn't shake the feeling that something bad was going to happen. "If I'm allowed to go home," I said, "please let me go home."

They gave me some injections and kept me there for hours. All the time, I kept saying that I didn't want to stay overnight. Finally, they let me go home. I wasn't far from the hospital and I think that helped, along with the fact it was Easter.

The Tuesday after the Easter weekend, I was sitting at home, still feeling pretty average and the hospital rang. "Can you come in?"

"Sure," I said, surprised. "Can I have a shower first?"

"Yes. Have a shower then come straight in."

There were no explanations and I suppose I didn't ask. Anyway, I had a shower. Pretty quick because, you know, no hair. After I got out, my oncologist rang. "Where are you?" he said. "We need you in the hospital. Now."

This was getting weird. I asked him if there was any particular reason.

"Just come in," he said.

I suppose, if your oncologist tells you to come in to the hospital, now, you do what he says.

As it turns out, when I was there on Good Friday, they were meant to give me a whole course of treatment, to take with me or have me return and give me an injection every day until my white blood cell count was back to normal.

Clearly, they hadn't. It was fortunate that my body kicked in after the first round of injections they did give me and it was enough to boost my white blood cells and keep me going over the weekend.

---

*It could have easily gone the other way, though.*

---

A lot of the time, during treatment, I couldn't talk to people. I didn't mind sending a text but I didn't want to talk to people. I'd talk to my children and Peter, of course, but I couldn't deal with random, social conversation. Sometimes, friends would call and insist on talking to me and I'd have to say, "I am so sorry. I can't talk but I'm happy to text." It was something people had to come to terms with.

Occasionally, people from the cancer support groups would want to come and visit. I did let a few people come over. They gave me a 'buddy', which was lovely. My buddy would come over and chat to me about this and that. A few times, she spoke about dragon boating. I thought, 'Maybe, some day.'

> *Finally, I got through my last chemo and then they started me on my thirty-five rounds of radiation. So off I went again, being very well looked after.*

One day, while I was waiting for my turn, a nurse came up to me and asked how I was finding the radiation.

"It's fine," I said. "So easy."

"You've had chemo, haven't you?" she said.

When I asked her how she could tell, she said, "All the women who've had chemo find radiation a walk in the park."

The worst part, actually, was trying to find a car park! I always booked in for a late afternoon appointment. That way, I was coming in when everyone else was leaving. By that stage, I'd decided to go back to work part-time with a limited role, so the late appointments suited me.

The people who work in the radiation unit are fabulous. When I'd gone in for the initial talk-through and to get my 'tattoos', they told me that because it was my left side, I'd have to hold breath. "But don't worry," they said, "if you can't hold your breath the whole time, the equipment will pause, you can take a breath and we'll keep going. But, you might want to practise holding your breath a bit."

We questioned this. Apparently it helps move your skin away from your heart. You don't want that getting zapped as well. So, that's what we did. Together, Peter and I practised holding our breath, just for fun.

> *When I went in for my first radiation treatment, I was determined not to let the machine get the better of me. I was going to hold my breath, no matter what.*

It was quite a long time, laying there, holding my breath. I was counting it down – it was about a minute. Then other bursts were shorter or slightly longer. But I did it.

Afterwards, the nurse said, "Wow, you held your breath all that time. Do you swim?"

I said, "No. I just practised. A lot."

There were a few strategies I used, too. Before each set, I'd ask if I needed to take a long breath or a short breath. If I knew that, I could gear myself up by breathing in the right amount. When I did that, I could hold my breath for a really long time.

The other thing I did, and people may think I'm crazy, was a visualisation. I'd do this particularly if they told me it would be a full minute. I would visualise this big seal that I called Sealy. I come from a part of Canada where there are a lot of seals.

Sealy's job was to sit with me while I was holding my breath. He'd stare at me and encourage me. If I needed air, I'd visualise Sealy blowing air bubbles as if we were underwater, and he'd give me air.

> *I certainly never told the people in the radiology unit what I doing. It was my visualisation. And it worked for me.*

Then, suddenly, I was having my final session. It was all a bit of a rush at the end. I just wanted to get out of there because it was late and I wanted to go home. I brought my radiation rabbit in to my last session because I wanted photos of it on the machine and other places. I don't think I took photos of the support staff there but I wish I had.

In fact, I wasn't even planning on 'ringing the bell', which is a tradition they have for when people finish their radiation treatment.

There was nobody around except for a male nurse – he was a giant of a man, really lovely but I hadn't had a lot to do with him. He said, "Is this your last time?"

When I said it was, he said, "Oh, we have to ring the bell. It doesn't matter that there's no-one here, you must ring the bell."

I rang the bell – I'm glad I did.

As we went to leave, he said, "I want you to promise me something."

I nodded.

> *"Sometimes people get slack about visiting their doctor, two or three years in, and then we see them back here."* He looked at me. *"So, promise me you will continue with your visits and your checks. Forever."*

I'd started all this treatment – the chemo and then the radiation – in January and it was nearly September. My hair had started growing back – it was all of about three millimetres – and I was sick of wearing the turban.

"The turban's coming off," I announced at work. "I hope nobody minds but I'm done with all of that. Here I am." Of course, they were all good about it.

It wasn't until December that I felt like myself again. This was highlighted to me by a colleague who, like me, had gone through a lot of operations and so on; we could always be frank with each other. He came up to me one day after a meeting and said, "And now, you're back."

Of course, the treatment doesn't end when you finish radiation; there's ongoing hormone treatment and tests. I was put on a drug called Arimidex. All the drugs have their own side effects, and one of the risks with Arimidex is joint pain and weakening. What I've realised is that the further you are from the 'end' of your active treatment, the more you forget about being careful.

One day, in 2019, I had a meeting with the new Chief Operating Officer and was racing across campus as quick as I could, worried I was going to be late. One minute, I was going to make it, the next minute there was what I can only describe as an explosion in my knee.

I called out to the people I was with, "Go, go, go. I'll be fine. It'll pass." And off they went. Meanwhile, I was standing there, doubled over. When I managed to stand up straight, I realised that, no, this wasn't going to go away. Luckily, there were some tradesmen nearby. I called them over. "I don't know what's happened but can you take me back to my office, please?"

They took me back and helped me upstairs. I sat in my office, waiting for this thing to 'pass' and it didn't. I couldn't get up. I couldn't do anything. Eventually, my colleague, the one who told me I 'was back' wandered past, then doubled back. "What's wrong?" he asked.

"I've hurt myself. I think I have to go to the hospital." I was thinking I'd have to call Peter and get him to pick me up. "But I'm not sure how I'm going to get back downstairs."

"Right," he said, "I'll wheel you down in your office chair." And that's exactly what he did – wheeled me to the lift, took me downstairs and wheeled me out to Peter.

It was a torn meniscus. They told me it was probably to do with the drugs I was on. I'd done so much damage that it needed an operation and at least two months in bed.

---

*But that's a whole different story – except to say when I woke up in the hospital there was Healy the stuffed hamster.*

---

Over the years, I've tried supplements and other things to help with the side effects of the drugs. I've looked into different types of exercise to help with bone density and joint issues – dragon boating was, of course, one of those I'd looked at on and off over the years. I'd never pushed myself to go along though.

Then, one evening, Peter and I were invited to the farewell dinner for the Timorese Ambassador. Peter was well known in that community because of his PhD and earlier human rights work. When we arrived, we were shown to our seats. The room was filling up and the two seats opposite ours were clearly being saved. People would come along and say, "Are these seats taken?" and someone would say, "Yes, they're reserved."

It turned out they were being held for the Ambassador of another country and his wife. The Ambassador knew of Peter's book, so there was lots of interesting conversation. His wife was lovely.

Then, the wife of the Timorese Ambassador came up to us and quietly said, "You both have a shared journey."

That started a whole new conversation as we discovered we had a lot in common. At one point, she asked, "Have you ever thought of trying dragon boating?"

I said, "Somebody did come to me in hospital when I was recovering from surgery and suggested it. I've always thought about doing it one day …" To be honest, I was nervous about going along – something new, people I didn't know and so on. As well as that, I had been in a dragon boat once; it was in Sydney a zillion years ago. We were paddling in a corporate crew for a construction company. The dragon boat tipped over and we all fell into the harbour. My foot got caught and I was under water for a bit, but I was fine. I did think, though, that would be my one and only paddle.

But then she said, "Look, there's an open day. Come along; I'll be your buddy in the boat."

She was very convincing and I agreed to go.

It was lovely. It was so nice to be out on the water and doing a mentally-focused sport. I was absolutely shattered when I got home, though, after that first session.

I went to more sessions and remember thinking I'd never ever make it through a whole session without having to stop paddling. But I love it, and the team is full of beautiful, supportive women who are very safety conscious.

The other thing I really love is the team aspect. I've always been more into individual sports rather than team sports; I never thought I'd like that, but I really do.

*It's funny, too, when people find out you do dragon boating, they're either really excited and interested – or they have no idea what you're talking about. I've never had that before with other sports I've done.*

When I think back on everything I went through with the whole cancer thing, I realise it was all a process. Something to get through then keep on moving forward.

On the other hand, there are some delightful learnings to be had – some surprising outcomes. Who would've thought I'd be on a dragon boat team, for example? Not me.

So many people look at cancer and think it means you're sick. Sure, you are, but it's not like it used to be. People used to say, "Oh, are you in remission?" Nobody talks like that anymore. Cancer always has the potential to be in all our bodies. Our bodies are processing cells all the time, some of which have the potential to become cancerous. In mine, it's gone. For now, it's all good. It's just part of the process of living.

# Bench 4 – Left

The wake slaps the front of the boat and swooshes along the sides – the sound of freedom as paddles are lifted from the water to 'let it run'. The boat glides effortlessly for several tens of metres, eventually slowing to a gently bobbing stop.

"Have a drink," Lyndall calls, partly to remind us to drink and partly to let us know it's okay and we have time.

Marion leans forward and taps Joan on the shoulder. "Do you have any plays coming up, Joan?" she asks.

"Not at the moment," Joan says.

"That's a shame. I did so enjoy seeing you in *Great Expectations*," Marion replies.

There's a chorus of agreement from the rest of us. Joan regularly performs in plays with the Canberra Repertory Society and other local theatre companies. Our social committee always organise an evening out – dinner and theatre – whenever Joan is performing.

We sit and take in the sunrise – slightly mottled through the cloud cover but lovely anyway.

"Sunrise!" Anita calls. "Can we take off our PFDs now?"

Life jackets – a necessary evil – are not the most comfortable to paddle in and many of us like to remove them at the first opportunity. Some keep them on though, for warmth or because they haven't done the swim and safety assessment. Treading water, huddles, practice rescues … then a hundred metres up and down the pool, all done in full dragon boating gear. It's worth it for the permission to paddle without a PFD when the sweep says it's okay – summer months only, though. Even strong swimmers would need a PFD if they were dunked in frigid Lake Burley Griffin mid-winter.

Within minutes, there's a pile of pink vests at Elly and Clare's feet.

"It's like a lovely pink mountain," says Joan. "I do love our pink."

Pink. The colour of breast cancer awareness.

"Go, Pink Ladies!" a walker calls from the lakeshore.

We've heard that call many a time. Pink PFDs have been part of the team's uniform forever. The pink makes us instantly recognisable on the lake – by other paddlers and spectators alike. Some feel it's a bit of a label but most of us see it as a source of pride.

Of strength.

And of belonging.

Stronger together – the DAA motto.

**Name:** Joan White

**Initial diagnosis:** 2013, triple negative

**Age at diagnosis:** 67

**Job at diagnosis:** retired

**Job now:** retired

**Joined DAC:** 2015 as a paddler, now a non-paddling supporter and committee secretary

**Favourite boat position:** any paddling position

**Memorable DAC moment:** paddling up the Yarra River in Melbourne, with my son and granddaughter cheering me from the bridge

**Claim to fame:** I won the Kashgar Cup – even though I'm no longer paddling

Kellie Nissen

# Joan's Story: Been There. Done That.

> *This is such a lovely life, I thought as I lay in bed, looking out the window at the sea and the palm trees of Horseshoe Bay on Magnetic Island. How lucky am I?*

We were on holiday and everything was fine. A few days on Magnetic Island then off to Airlie Beach to see my daughter and finally back down to Brisbane to visit my son.

The day before, I'd bought a new nightie, which was silky and soft and just lovely to touch.

That's what I was doing when I found the lump. I felt the other side and there was no lump. Just the one. That wasn't there before.

In my head, I told myself it could be anything. It could be cancer, I said to myself, but it probably isn't. I'm sure it isn't.

I got my husband Cliff to have a feel, too. "There's a lump," he said.

"Well," I said, "I'm not going to mess up our holiday. We'll go to Airlie Beach and we'll go to Brisbane. I'll go to the doctor when we get back." It was settled and I determined to put it out of my mind.

That was June 2013.

In August that year, I was due to go to England to see my sister. Her husband was ill and had not long to live, so I needed to be there with my sister.

It was definitely a cloud on the horizon and I hoped the lump wasn't anything that was going to stop me from travelling.

During my holiday, I did think about it from time to time – it's hard not to – and I'd wonder what it was. Two of my friends had been diagnosed with cancer. They'd both had a bad time with chemo but they'd come through and were both fine. So, I'd remind myself of that and thought:

> *Well, I'll be fine, too, no matter what.*

After my holiday, I went to the doctor and he sent me straight away for an ultrasound and a biopsy.

It's fantastic how quickly everything gets done.

I went back to him the next day with the results. "Yes. It's cancer," he said. He put me in touch with the surgeon. "See what she says."

We left the doctor's office and walked outside. I turned to Cliff. "I'm sorry. I'm so sorry." Because, that's how I felt – so sorry for him that he had a wife who had cancer.

"That's okay, we'll get through it," he said. "We'll be alright."

Then, of course, I had to tell my three children – they were all grown up. I didn't want to, but I knew I had to tell them. I had to do it over the phone, because they were all interstate. I'm not sure if that's easier or harder than telling someone in person.

My daughter was all teary. "Oh Mum, oh Mum," she said over and over.

My elder son was quiet. He's always quiet. I had to check in with his wife later to make sure he was okay.

And my younger son – whom we'd just been visiting in Brisbane – was all protective and indignant. "Why didn't you tell us before? How could you come and visit us and not say anything?"

Everyone reacts differently to that sort of news. We all deal with things in different ways. At the start, to be honest, I didn't want to tell anyone. I didn't want anyone to know. It was something I was almost ashamed of.

---

*I never actually said that word, you know. Cancer. I always said, 'I had a lump and it turned out to be malignant.' I never said I had cancer because I never felt I did.*

---

When people did find out, they made a big thing of it. Everyone was like, "Oh no. Oh, you poor thing. I'm so sorry." It almost made me wish I hadn't told them; it wasn't such a big thing for me.

The surgeon was a lovely lady – and straight to the point. "There are options. You can have a mastectomy or a lumpectomy."

It was a no-brainer for me. There was no way I was going to have a lumpectomy. "A mastectomy. Get rid of it. Cut it all off. Let's finish it."

And Cliff felt the same. He was there with me and we both agreed: why on earth would we mess about?

Other people feel differently, I know, but I felt strongly about it.

I suppose, if I had been younger and wanted to wear bikinis and that sort of thing, I probably would have thought differently but I was nearly seventy and didn't want to mess about. We made the appointment for the mastectomy.

"Will I still be able to make the trip to England?" I asked.

"You shouldn't travel within two weeks after the operation," she said.

I did the calculation – the operation had been booked for exactly two weeks before we were due to leave. "I'm going then." And she was okay with that.

After the surgery, while I was in hospital, a breast care nurse came to visit me. She was lovely – they all are. She sat and chatted then said, "Have you cried?" I remember thinking it was such a strange question. No, I hadn't cried. And then I thought that obviously people do cry because otherwise, she wouldn't have asked me. People deal with things in different ways. There's no right or wrong.

So, we made it to England as planned. I'd had a drain in after the operation, obviously, and it got removed the day before we left. The flight was a bit uncomfortable but we'd been able to book business class, which was nice.

My thinking at the time was that it was all done and dusted now. I thought, I've had the mastectomy so that's it. I figured I probably wouldn't need any further treatment – not everybody does, so that would be me, too.

*I totally convinced myself there would be nothing more; that was it as far as I was concerned.*

My brother-in-law passed away while we were there. I was glad we'd made the trip. Glad to be able to read at his funeral and support my sister.

When we returned to Australia, I had an appointment with the oncologist. I wasn't worried. By this time, I'd convinced myself there would be no treatment necessary. He sat there and looked at all the reports, and at the statistics and my papers. "We'll do the chemo."

"What did you say?" I said, shocked.

He repeated it, rather surprised, and showed me all the statistics again.

I looked over at Cliff and we agreed. "Yes, we'll have the chemo."

Four sessions that took me right up to December. Cliff was absolutely wonderful throughout the whole process. I had terrible sickness, loss of appetite, hair loss – the usual things – and he was there for me every step of the way.

The poor man would make me these lovely meals. "What do you fancy?" he'd say. I'd tell him and he'd get it all ready and then I didn't fancy it at all because I'd feel sick and had no sense of taste. Chemo does that to you.

Another of the side effects of chemotherapy is neuropathy – damage to the nerves. For me, this meant tingling feet all the time – walking on carpet felt like I was walking on nails instead. Shoes really hurt my feet, but there was one pair of thongs that were comfortable so I wore those everywhere.

Everyone who's been through this would have a list of side effects and other issues that crop up because of the treatment. For me it was managing my pre-existing atrial fibrillation because chemo drugs are pretty hard on your heart and I was already at a greater risk of having a stroke. I had to have cardioversion – where they use a series of short electric shocks to put your heartbeat back to a regular rhythm. Then they discovered a blood clot on my lung; there were more tablets for that. Thinking back, that clot may well have been caused by flying too soon after my surgery but, then again, had it not been for the chemo treatment, that clot may not have been discovered until it was too late.

The loss of my hair was interesting and is probably where my reaction is different from most other people because it didn't bother me. It helped that I had already retired, so I didn't have to go to work. I'd comb my hair and it would come out in clumps. I ended up cutting it very short and then my husband shaved my head – I found it all a bit of a laugh.

I got three different wigs. One was given to me and I bought another couple. Different wigs for different days. At home I was bald, but every time I went out, I wore a wig. I never wore a turban; it wasn't me at all.

*I didn't want to go out looking like a person who had cancer.*

My daughter overheard my four-year-old granddaughter talking to a friend: "My granny has to take medicine that makes her hair fall out," she said. "So she has to wear a ... a mop." You have to laugh sometimes. Kids are wonderful for that.

After thinking it was all over after the surgery – that I was fine – the initial shock of needing chemotherapy didn't last too long. I got on with it. I accepted it. A lot of it was about acceptance, really, and thankfulness that I was in Canberra among all these specialists. Everything I needed was here; so much support. I was very grateful.

Negative feelings were something I refused to succumb to. I just said to myself, well, this is how it's going to be. I'm having surgery. I'm having chemo. Let's get it over with.

And then, the chemo was over. It was done. I didn't have to have radiotherapy or hormone treatment – not with the sort of cancer I'd had – but, of course, it's not all finished once the chemo treatments stop. There's the six-monthly visits to the surgeon and the oncologist for the next five or so years. There were never any problems for me; everything was always okay. It became a routine, just something I had to do.

There's also the yearly mammograms. I have to be persuaded to have those. But Cliff says, "You've got to do it." And the doctor says, "You've got to do it." So I go and do it, but I'm so convinced it's all gone and there won't be any more. I'm the opposite to many other people; I don't believe in this saying that your life will never be the same again. My life is the same. It's what it is – for me.

There is so much support out there.

There is a group called Bosom Buddies. What a lovely name. I was invited to join but I didn't feel that I wanted to belong to a group where breast cancer was the main focus – although, it is a great support for some people.

However, I did join Dragons Abreast. It was funny, really, because I've never been a sporty person. I hadn't done any sports since I left school. Some years ago, I worked for the YWCA so I knew about their Encore exercise program. I went along to one of those and at one of the meetings, a lady from Dragons Abreast was there, talking about dragon boating. I found myself thinking it would be fun to try.

I went to a 'Come and Try' session and the ladies were so welcoming and lovely. It's a nice group and it was a new experience for me and exciting. It's hard work though – I was trying to do the right thing and was finding I was doing the wrong thing. It's all very coordinated. You have to be in time.

But I did it – I stayed. I paddled with Dragons Abreast for six years.

We went to Florence in 2018, along with 4,000 other breast cancer survivors from around the world. We went to regattas in Sydney and Melbourne. The best experience was paddling up the Yarra River in Melbourne. I miss that now that I'm not paddling any more – but I'm still involved. There are other ways to stay in touch. It's a great group.

---

*I always say there are three good things about when I had cancer.*

---

The first was that I suddenly realised exactly how wonderful Cliff is – I always knew that, of course, but this really brought it home to me. He was my nurse. He was my carer. He couldn't do enough for me. It was lovely. I also know I was lucky compared with other people – we were both retired, I didn't have children at home to look after, it was just us.

The second positive thing that came out of having breast cancer was the dragon boating. If it hadn't been for the cancer, I would never have become part of that community.

And the third thing was losing my hair. Not actually losing my hair – although I was fine with that, as I've said – but when it grew back, I loved it. For months I had this beautiful curly hair. I've never had a curl in my life, so I loved it.

So, positive things do come from awful things. But I'm done now. I'm not going there again. For me, it's a case of 'Been there. Done that.'

# Bench 4 – Right

Lyndall works the sweep oar, turning *GoAnna II* so she's facing the opposite side of the lake. "We're cutting across before the rowers come back," she says. "Are—"

The rest of her words are drowned out by the reverberating chimes of the Carillon – springing to life without warning. There must be some special occasion for it to be playing so early.

The sweep often takes us out and around the Carillon. It's sheltered and makes a good spot for novice sweeps to have their first go, or to practise manoeuvres such as drawing water or turning the boat in figure of eights.

From the drummer's seat, Jenny mimes the stroke rate to us, counting us in with large gestures and steady drum beats. Somehow, we all start in time.

"Now in time with the Carillon," Jenny calls when the boat is no longer directly underneath the iconic structure. Jenny dances with her arms and torso from the drummer seat and Lyndall joins in sinuously waving her arm that's not holding the sweep oar. Joan does a bit of a shoulder sway, and a few of us tap our feet – forgetting about using our leg drive.

Amanda shakes her head. "Can't be all serious, I suppose." She smiles.

The sisters love to dance but the resulting wobble and tilt of the boat, accompanied by a rippling cry of 'oooh', suggests that maybe dancing on the boat is not the best idea.

"Heads in the boat." Lyndall calls us all – including herself – into line.

"Oh, what a shame," Jenny says. "Alright, let's get ourselves over the other side then."

"Timing!" The call comes from Lyndall. "Pick the pace up a notch."

Once we've settled in to a steady and strong rhythm, Jenny stops drumming for a moment. Nobody misses a beat although we're all wondering why she's stopped. She doesn't leave us wondering for long.

"I nearly forgot," she says. "Congratulations are in order." She looks straight at Amanda. "You have news, I believe?"

"Oh gawd," Amanda says. She's not one for fuss and fanfare. "I made it into ACT Fire – the ACT representative team for nationals."

A cheer goes up. Pride for one of our own.

The thought makes us dig in a little deeper, with more power and drive and we get across the lake in no time at all.

Kellie Nissen

**Name:** Amanda Ferris

**Initial diagnosis:** 2016, Grade 2 invasive ductal carcinoma, ER/PR positive, HER2 negative

**Age at diagnosis:** 44

**Job at diagnosis:** preschool teacher

**Job now:** preschool teacher

**Joined DAC:** 2017

**Favourite boat position:** any paddling position

**Memorable DAC moment:** sitting in the boat in the middle of Lake Burley Griffin at 6:30 am on a Tuesday morning in the middle of winter – it's beautiful

**Favourite number:** 22

**Bucket list:** travelling the world

**Amazing moment:** being selected for ACT Fire – the ACT representative dragon boating team to compete in the Australian Championship regatta in 2024

# Amanda's Story: Just Make Them Even

> *I didn't say anything to anybody when I found that lump.*
> *It wasn't huge. I wasn't overly concerned.*

I can't remember exactly when I found the lump. I know I was at Mum's place on the south coast. It was the September school holidays in 2016. I was in bed and rolled over – and there it was. A lump I hadn't felt before.

In all honesty, I wasn't concerned. There's no history of breast cancer in my family so I'm not classed as at risk. Why would I worry? Getting stressed about it was pointless. There was still another week of holidays left and I knew I'd be able to get a doctor's appointment when I got home so I put it to the back of my mind. I also knew I didn't want to say anything to Mum; I didn't want to worry her because my father had passed away from cancer and she didn't need that extra stress when it was probably nothing.

When I got back to Canberra, I went to my doctor. I was due for my yearly check-up – I never went to the doctor otherwise. I don't get sick. I thought I might as well mention the lump to her.

It wasn't something I could feel all the time and she had a hard time finding it herself.

"It's probably just a cyst," she said, when she'd finally found it. "But let's be on the safe side and get you in for a mammogram and ultrasound."

Luckily, I was still on holiday, so I booked the checks for a couple of days later. I wasn't overly worried. Nobody came with me – I didn't ask. I thought they'd tell me it was a cyst.

The mammogram was first. Nothing showed up and I was ushered into the ultrasound room. That's when things started to happen. The minute the sonographer found the lump, I knew this was going to be more serious than I'd thought. The next thing I knew, the radiologist had been called in and I was having a biopsy.

"I know you're not allowed to tell me for certain," I said to him, "but should I prepare myself for breast cancer?"

> *He didn't beat around the bush.*
> *"If I was you," he said, "yes, I would."*

After the scan and biopsy, I stood in the hospital car park and rang my husband Michael. "I think I just got diagnosed with breast cancer." It was all a bit unbelievable; nothing had sunk in.

That was Friday and I was due back at school on Monday but had to wait until Tuesday to see my doctor for the actual biopsy results. Our children, Sam, Laura and James, were still young – between five and fourteen. We decided not to say anything to them until I'd seen the doctor on Tuesday. Those few days – the waiting – were terrible. Absolutely horrible.

Michael came with me to the doctor on Tuesday. The minute we walked in and saw the doctor's serious face, I knew it wasn't great news. My recollection of what was said is hazy; it was overwhelming. Surprising. Totally out of the blue. I was forty-four.

"You'll need to see a surgeon first," my doctor explained, "and then an oncologist – but the surgeon will recommend someone for you."

I nodded.

"Do you need me to recommend someone for you?" she asked. "Or do you know someone already?"

"We don't know of anyone," Michael said, looking at me.

"But we can work it out ourselves," I said. I like to be organised. I need to know what's happening and the best way to do that is to take control of it myself. "I know someone who can help us out," I added.

Whether or not anything sunk in with Michael, I can't say for sure. Neither of us knew what to think or expect. We had no idea what sort of impact this might make on our lives as a family.

Family.

Now we had to tell the kids.

As soon as we were all home, Michael and I sat down and told them. There was nothing much to say as we didn't have much idea about the type of cancer or the treatment I'd need. "We just need to hope for the best," I told them.

Telling Mum was going to be harder, and I chose not to say anything to her straight away – not until I knew more. Dad's cancer – and my sister's – meant she would take the news badly, so I decided to wait until after I'd seen the surgeon and knew what we were dealing with.

---

*It's just that word. Cancer. It has the ability to set people off.*

---

It was like being on autopilot and going through a checklist. Do this. Now this. And now this. The next item on my checklist was to find a surgeon.

The mother of a child I'd taught years ago was the head of Emergency at the Canberra Hospital. I'd got on really well with her, and she'd always said, "If you ever need anything, get in touch."

I sent her an email: *Here's my situation …* I began and told her what had happened and what I needed. *I'm happy to travel. To Sydney or wherever if needed. If you were in this situation, who would you go with?*

She said she'd ask around and find out for me. *I'll get back to you as soon as I can.*

Less than a week later, she rang me. "I have a name," she said.

I wrote down his details and then rang him straight away.

"We can fit you in next week," the receptionist said.

Quick.

I'd been working at Girls' Grammar for quite a long time. Funnily enough, I'd decided – prior to all of this – that I was going to give my notice and go to the public system. I guess I'd had enough of the private 'world'. I had it all planned out – go to school as normal, make an appointment with my principal and then give my notice on the Monday, or Friday at the latest.

I found out I had breast cancer on the Tuesday of that week.

It seems my principal had an inkling I was going to resign. It was like she was actively avoiding me. Once I knew my diagnosis, however, I looked harder. I started lurking in the places she could usually be found.

"I need to have a meeting with you," I said as soon as I had her cornered.

Her eyes widened. She thought she knew what I was going to say but she was wrong because everything had changed. "Okay," she said. "Make an appointment through the front office."

I went straight there and did it.

She cancelled.

I made another appointment.

She wasn't there.

I didn't bother with another appointment after that. I went straight to her office when I knew she'd be there and blurted it out. "I know I don't have an appointment, but I need to tell you this right now." I paused. She stayed silent. "I need my sick leave – I'm letting you know I have breast cancer."

Her face fell and she went pale. She opened her mouth to say something, then closed it again.

Hearing a staff member is going to resign is very different to hearing the staff member tell you she has cancer. That word again. It's hard to hear.

What's harder, though, is telling people.

---

*Everyone seems to jump to the worst-case scenario.*
*I suppose, at the time, I'd done the same thing.*

---

My entire world was consumed by the whirlwind of cancer – one thing after another. And now, I can't remember any of it.

Keeping it all together was something I felt to be important for my family – and for me. But it's hard. You don't know how bad it is – or how well the treatment will work. You're bombarded with information, from everyone. Doctors. Specialists. Family. Friends. Sometimes even people you don't know. Everyone has some advice, or a story, to share. Making a choice for yourself is difficult.

Finally, I found myself in the surgeon's rooms.

In the days before, I'd pretty much decided that if he suggested my only option was to lose the breast, he'd have to take both of them. No way did I want to be lopsided. My chest size was quite big, so losing one would be instantly obvious. I didn't want to live like that so I'd convinced myself that taking both would be the better option. No boobs had to be better than a big one and nothing.

I made sure I told the surgeon this before I could change my mind. "If you take it," I said, "I want you to take the other one too."

He stared at me for a moment. "Let's just back up a little," he said.

I steeled myself to dig my heels in.

"You do have options."

They'd have to be good ones.

"We can remove the cancer on the right side." Where the cancer was. "Then, if you're open to it, I can reduce the left to meet the size."

Smaller breasts versus no breasts? It was a pretty good option.

I agreed to go ahead with that plan.

To be honest, I think if he'd taken both of them, I may not have coped very well after the fact. I don't know. It's hard to know. It all happens so fast. One minute you're planning school lessons for the next day and the next you're being asked to make decisions – right now! There's not any time to process anything but you're expected to make decisions that could affect the rest of your life.

---

*I'm forever grateful, however, for those words –*
*"Just back up a little."*

---

My surgeon explained the next steps as clearly as he could. "It'll be a lumpectomy," he said. He'd take out the cancer, and the margins needed. Then he'd reduce the other side to match. "But you don't get to pick the size," he added. "You go with what I can do."

Honestly, I didn't care. They could be small or big – but they wouldn't be nothing. "Just make them even," I said.

Exactly two weeks after I received my diagnosis, I was operated on – 27 October 2016. There was no point in waiting; whatever I needed to do, I wanted to get it done. I only took a week off work because, for some reason, that was how I coped. I needed normalcy, a regular routine.

Everyone said, "You're crazy." Or words to that effect.

"Nope," I said, every time, "this is what I'm doing." Luckily, my recovery from the surgery was relatively smooth.

A few weeks after the surgery, I was back in with the surgeon so he could check how things were going. He was pretty pleased. "Do you have an oncologist?" he asked. When I said I didn't, he recommended one of the oncologists whose rooms were in the same building as his, just upstairs. "Go up now," he said. "She can see you now."

Off I went.

Next thing I knew, I'd been booked in for chemo. I was due to start the Monday after school finished for the year – just before Christmas.

Throughout all the treatment, I tended to keep my feelings to myself. I didn't talk about things to anyone else. I wanted to keep my kids' lives as normal as possible. Michael was wonderful – and we both tried to keep things like they used to be before the diagnosis.

What I realised though, was that I needed my mum.

Luckily, she was able to be there for me. Mum moved in with us for about three months. She kept things going; she'd do the grocery shopping and the cooking – she was just there, whatever we needed. As much as I needed her, I also think she probably needed to be there as well. I think she needed to know I was okay, and to feel like she was doing something to help me.

There were others too. I had lots of people come and drop meals off and check in on me. It was nice; good of people to do that. But often it felt like I was trying to convince everyone that I was okay; like they needed reassuring – "I'm fine. Yes, I've got breast cancer, but I'm going to be okay." It may have been me trying to convince myself I was going to be okay, but I also couldn't help feeling I was being written off somewhat because of my diagnosis. 'Poor Amanda.'

On the other hand, one of my good friends was just amazing. Before I started chemo, she took me over to HeadsUp – where they sell wigs, hats, scarves and other things. Hair loss is confronting, as is shopping for headwear before chemo, but she made it fun.

"Let's go," she said. "We can try everything on together." And off we went. She tried on everything I tried on. It was nice, doing this with someone – and laughing about it. Rather than being a case of 'oh no, I'm going to lose my hair, so I need to find something to hide that', it became a fun afternoon out with a good friend.

## Bench 4 – Right

*I don't know how she knew I needed that.*
*I didn't even know I needed that.*

She bought me a little case with nail polish and creams, plus a blanket and a wheat heat pack. I don't know where she got it from, but once I started chemo everything in that pack was perfect. Just what I needed. She had an innate ability to come up with little things that meant so much.

Being around her was refreshing too. Never did I feel had to convince her that I was going to be okay. Nothing was about her – and being around her was a completely different feeling. She knew I was going to be okay, but I needed a little help at the time.

Another person who inspired me was one of the girls at the CrossFit gym I'd been going to before I was diagnosed. She'd also been diagnosed with breast cancer – perhaps around five months before me. I'd seen her go through her treatment and the whole time she was still going to the gym. She had no hair and sometimes looked like death-warmed-up, but she'd show up and do whatever she could do. I remember hearing her say, "They pump all these poisons through me so the best thing I can do is move them around and pump them right back out." In other words, her idea was exercising and drinking heaps of water would help sweat it out.

So, once I'd started chemo, I was determined to follow her lead and keep going to the gym.

Before that, though, I had to get through my first chemo session because I had no idea how my body was going to react. Everyone is so different; there's no set pattern.

The side effects of chemo almost creep up on you. After my first chemo, I felt okay – a little bit odd but okay. Sam had her end-of-year awards ceremony scheduled for the week of my first chemo session and I didn't want to miss it. I was feeling okay at first but remember sitting there and it all hitting me about ten minutes before the event was due to end. I could literally feel something working its way through my body like some sort of beast, almost leaching the life out of me.

> *It was the longest ten minutes of my life.*

I barely made it home and it was all I could do to fall into bed. I stayed there for three days. I was done. My head ached – not a headache, it really hurt. At some point, I remembered someone telling me: "If you get pain in your head, shave your hair. It's the weight of your hair on the skin."

After three days of putting up with the pain, I called Michael. "I want you to shave my head," I said. "Shave all my hair off." It was going to fall out anyway, but I couldn't put up with the pain until it did. He was so good about it. We went outside and he shaved all my hair off. The pain went away.

Chemo runs in a three-week cycle. The first week, you feel like rubbish – obviously I wasn't up to doing anything then but as soon as I started feeling better, I'd head off to the gym.

I'd talked to the people there beforehand. "Look," I said, "I'm going to come in. I'll wear a hat but if that doesn't work for me, I'm going to take it off."

The gym staff were all fine with it. They'd had the other girl in doing the same thing, so nobody even blinked. Lucky, because I was amazed how hot I got – and I was doing very little. The hat didn't last long at all. No-one reacted in the slightest. They treated me the way they'd always done.

I made sure to wipe each piece of equipment down really well after I'd used it. With all the chemo drugs, even your sweat can be slightly contaminated, and I certainly didn't want to share anything around. I was super careful.

For me, it was all about having a normal routine. I honestly didn't do much at all, but it was the act of getting up, going out and turning up. It was an outing. It got me out of the house and out of my head, and I felt like I was doing something. Anything was better than nothing, and it helped with my attitude and mental state.

All that said, I doubt I would've done it if the other girl hadn't done it before me.

In all honesty, I don't understand why they don't have exercise plans as part of active treatment. They have recovery sessions, once treatment is done, but I really think there needs to be something for people who are in active treatment.

*Exercise and routine helped me so much.*

So much of how you react, mentally, has to do with mindset. Exercise helps with that.

One of the things recommended with the type of chemo I had was to paint my fingernails and toenails black. They also put my hands in an ice bath while the infusions were happening. Both of these were apparently to stop me losing my nails, which was very common with my type of chemo. The black polish on the nails was there to block the UV rays from my nails, which would have reacted to the drugs and weakened my nails further.

"If you lose your nails," the chemo nurse told me, "they can take up to five years to grow back."

I didn't fancy that happening, so I wore the black nail polish – quite the fashion statement. It was also a bit of a pain because I had to remove the polish and reapply it at least once a week because even a chip could affect the nails.

When it came to painting my nails, I was always careful with my fingernails but a bit slap-dash with my toenails. I did end up losing the nail off one of my toes – and it's never been the same since. It's brittle; cracks easily and falls off all the time. I'm constantly waiting for it to grow back again.

With the ice bath, this was to slow the circulation in my hands as an extra precaution – again, for the nails. It was uncomfortable. They'd fill the bottom of a black bag with ice, and I had to put my hands in it. Not pleasant.

In the middle of my trio of treatment – towards the end of my chemo – my best friend passed away. It was awful. She'd had an autoimmune disease that affected her lungs. Eventually, she needed a double lung transplant, which had major complications. She was in and out of hospital during fourth term and throughout my chemo, and sadly passed away at the beginning of January 2017. Her memorial service coincided with the last week of my final chemo. Not the best timing but I was determined to go. I had to push through for her.

I was as sick as a dog during her memorial. Felt awful. Drained. Pasty. Just horrible.

But I went.

I pushed through it.

For her.

Four rounds of chemo took me through the school holidays and then, after a couple of weeks' break, I went straight into six rounds of radiation — that's five days a week for six weeks. My radiation oncologist was lovely; I was lucky.

Radiation wasn't as bad as chemo obviously, but it was tiring. And the burns! They'd given me all sorts of creams and gels to put on, and I was doing that regularly. I thought I had it all under control then — bam — literally overnight, I had burns.

The radiation oncology centre has a bell for patients to ring to celebrate the end of their treatment. You can hear it being rung almost every time you're there.

"Make sure you ring the bell," someone said at some point, "because you'll regret it if you don't."

I didn't ring it. At the time, it seemed a silly thing to do. James came with me and Mum to my last appointment, and I think he might have rung it.

---

*Ringing that bell ... I think I should have.*
*I do regret not doing it now.*

---

My chemo had mostly happened during the school summer holidays but the radiation wasn't so I took Term 1 off school; daily radiation sessions wouldn't work for a preschool teacher. Especially in first term.

Surgery. Chemo. Radiation.

Boom. Boom. Boom.

Done.

And back to school I went.

With no hair.

The students were all told that I'd had cancer. Some of their parents were a bit weird about it, though. As for me, I was absolutely knackered. Looking back, it wasn't the best decision – for me, for my colleagues or for my students.

I didn't allow myself any time to adjust to anything that was happening. Blinkers on, I was so set on getting things done.

Too late, I realised I shouldn't have done it. Too late, I realised I'd gone back too early.

---

*On the other hand, I'd likely do the same thing again, because that's who I am. It's my personality.*

---

I didn't want to be in my head. Staying at home – to recover – also meant more time to think. More time to be plagued by wondering and doubting.

Not allowing myself any time to catch up with what had happened, process things along the way and heal – mentally as well as physically – ultimately led to me crashing and burning. And part of that was this anger I felt once I'd gone back to work.

I'd chosen to go back to work – that, in itself, wasn't the source of my anger – but when I was there, I'd become frustrated and angry at everyone and everything. I wasn't too bad around my family, but it was a different story with the outside world. It was like the chemo had killed off the filter in my brain that regulated what I said. I found myself saying things – bitchy things – to people, trying to get a reaction from them. And in my head, I'd be saying, 'You can't say that. Don't be like that,' but there was no control. The words kept coming out of my mouth. I was particularly horrible to my assistant at school. I've apologised since then, but I know it was way past that stage for her, which I completely understand. I shouldn't have treated her the way I did.

I was very angry for a long time.

Eventually, I had to go and see my doctor. I'd reached breaking point and knew I had to do something. Since my cancer diagnosis, I'd had a very good relationship with her.

"After everything you've been through, you have every right to be angry," she said after I'd told her what had been happening. "But you don't have the right to hurt other people."

It was interesting that she was the one who said that to me. She could obviously read me very well. I'd never been like that with her, but she could tell.

This was my turning point.

She sent me to a psychologist, who I saw twice a week for around six weeks. To be honest, the psychologist never said much. She listened. She sat there, asked one little question and off I'd go. She let me talk. Allowed me to be heard. And at the end of every session, I always felt fantastic.

Through these sessions, I came to realise that one of the reasons I was so angry was because I didn't like how I'd changed. It annoyed me. I was pissed off that I'd become 'this' person and I didn't want to be 'this' person. I wanted to go back to the person I was – pre-cancer – but I couldn't.

My psychologist gave me a heap of strategies. Walking became important for me. I'd always done a lot of walking before my diagnosis, but I found I needed to walk a lot more. Music was another strategy I found useful, and I still find that if I'm home by myself and not feeling the greatest, it really helps to pump the music up and sing at the top of my voice – not necessarily the correct words, but who cares?

Seeing the psychologist didn't 'fix' me; I wasn't 'over it'. There are still days I'm not great. But the difference is that I now have a raft of strategies I can pull out to help me get through things. It's the main reason I've continued exercising. I know some people think I'm crazy, but I believe eighty per cent of the reason I exercise is for my mental health. The other twenty per cent is probably for the social side of it. I like having a chat; it makes things more enjoyable. I don't have any particular desire to be ultra strong or muscular – it's not a body thing for me. If I work out, I feel a lot better. That's all.

> *I'll probably continue to use all the strategies the psychologist gave me for the rest of my life, to be honest.*

I'm coming up to seven years since diagnosis now, but about two years ago, it suddenly hit me. I was with my doctor when it dawned on me that I was never going to be the same again – not in a physical sense, but mentally. I don't think in the same way I used to, and I know my brain doesn't work the same as before. One hundred per cent, it was the chemo. It does something to your brain. My thinking processes are different; I have trouble remembering numbers and names. I hate the fact that when I'm talking, some words escape me – I know that I know the words, but I can't get them out. It's particularly annoying when I'm talking to parents at school.

I'm also much less patient. Less tolerant. I definitely have more of an attitude that life is too short. I can't put up with 'bullshit' as much as I could before this whole thing. I'm more 'black and white' in my thinking. If I want to do something, I do it. And I don't care if people think I should or not.

I suppose this is the remnants of all that anger I had.

> *It's probably also that realisation: 'Oh, shit. This has happened. To me.'*

The other thing that's changed is that, a lot of the time, I just 'go with it'. If something's going to happen, and I don't have control over it, I don't care anymore. I don't worry about it. If I don't want to be involved, then I don't do it. I think more about myself now.

I joined Dragons Abreast Canberra around October 2017, the same time as another couple of ladies. I'd seen a poster up somewhere for one of their Come and Try sessions and thought: Why not? I took a photo of the poster, thinking that dragon boating was something I'd like to try. My brother had done dragon boating in the past and loved it.

At the time, I still wasn't back to feeling a hundred per cent normal. I was on Tamoxifen, which was causing some issues with aching bones and general joint pain. Getting out of bed was painful. So, not a hundred per cent but I wanted to do something.

I loved it. Right from that first session. And I knew I was definitely going back.

It was tricky, not knowing anybody – it's always hard in anything that involves a group – but the ladies on the team were friendly. 'Newbies', as we were called, were given a buddy whose job was to keep in touch with us and answer any questions we had. Sometimes they sit with you to paddle but the coach we had at the time used to allocate seats, so there was never any concern with trying to find someone to sit with in the boat.

The year after I joined, a large number of the ladies in the team were heading to Florence for a huge international regatta. The coach gave me the information and said I could go but that I'd have to organise my accommodation as a lot of the organisation had been done the previous year. I thought about it but decided I couldn't go to Italy by myself.

The time I joined was the start of the local regatta season. Lots of racing over different distances. I didn't go to regattas for quite some time; I was just enjoying the training and the routine.

Something that did surprise me a bit was how little people talked about stuff. It's great all the conversations don't focus on breast cancer – because sometimes I craved being known as a person rather than a 'breast cancer survivor' – but there were times I would've liked people to talk a little more about the medications they were on and what they were having trouble with – and how they got around things.

It can be hard when you feel you're on your own and are being left to make decisions when you don't really know what all the choices are. For example, Tamoxifen didn't work for me. I had to be taken off it and put on blood thinners because I ended up with a ten-centimetre blood clot under my arm.

At the time, Tamoxifen was the only oestrogen-blocker medication available for women who are premenopausal. To have the same effect, I was told I needed an injection every month, which would put me into menopause medically.

> *Nobody ever told me that another*
> *option was to have my ovaries removed.*

If I'd known there were other options, and I'd had that procedure, not only would I not have had to take the medication, but I also wouldn't have had to get the injections.

In the end, I had my ovaries removed but that was only because I found out about it – through my doctor – and insisted.

I don't blame anyone for this but can't help wondering why all the options aren't given to us to decide for ourselves. It's our body, after all. At the end of the day, the procedure is now day surgery.

Day surgery.

I had an injection in my stomach every twenty-eight days for years – and I could've just had day surgery.

Options. It's important to know them – be given them and have them explained – so you can go into things with your eyes wide open, and knowing you have a say as well.

Even though it sometimes took a while for me to find out certain information, I'm glad I always pursued it. Doing this meant that I felt like I was in control and, as hard as it's been at times, I am now stronger for it.

Kellie Nissen

# Bench 5 – Left

Lyndall calls for twenty more strokes and we all comply, not stopping until we hear her voice again. "Easy."

Over to the left of the boat, a pair of swans are feeding. One keeping watch while the other tilts, its head disappearing and its rear pointing skyward. We sit for a while, silent. Just enjoying the morning quiet.

"It's like being in another world, isn't it?" Marion says.

We all agree. There's something very special about being able to view our city from the middle of the lake, first thing in the morning before everything awakes.

"I think we need one of Marion's poems before we start off again," says Joan.

Each of us in the team has something to give, and one of Marion's gifts is her poetry recitations. With the water still, and the sun casting its glow over the sky, now is the perfect time.

A chorus of agreement ripples through the boat.

"Yes."

"That would be lovely."

"Please, Marion."

"Of course," she says. "And how fitting that I'm sitting in Anna's seat this morning." Pulling herself tall and straight on the left side of Bench 5 – the seat our founder, Anna Wellings-Booth, always paddled from – Marion tilts her chin, raising her face to the pink-orange sky. "William Wordsworth would be perfect for today," she says, and begins her recitation of 'On Westminster Bridge'.

Everyone is silent; everything around us is at peace. There is only Marion's strong clear voice. Beautiful words, spoken with passion, entwine their way around our bodies until that delicious moment of complete peace descends, between the end of the poem and the realisation there is no more to be said.

It's like coming out of a trance.
We are uplifted. We are ready to continue.
"Thank you, Marion," says Joan.
"It's my pleasure," says Marion. "I do hope you enjoyed it."

Kellie Nissen

**Name:** Marion Leiba
**Initial diagnosis:** 2000, invasive lobular carcinoma, ER+
**Age at diagnosis:** 54
**Job at diagnosis:** landslide scientist
**Job now:** retired
**Joined DAC:** 2000
**Favourite boat position:** paddling from benches 3 to 8
**Memorable DAC moment:** placing in a race at Darling Harbour, Sydney
**In my spare time:** I love walking around Lake Tuggeranong, seeing how many different species of bird I can identify and stopping to drink a mocha

# Marion's Story: No Room for Complacency

*She started doing the breast check and then stopped. "You've got a lump," she said. And that's the first I knew about it.*

Here's the crazy thing about breast cancer for me – I had no idea anything was amiss.

I went to see the GP for a pap smear. The doctor I ended up seeing wasn't my regular GP; she was a new young doctor in her first year out, where they do the first twelve months under supervision. Anyway, she was doing the smear and said, "Would you like me to examine your breasts as well?"

I thought that was a good idea; I hadn't had that done for a couple of years.

It was a good thing she asked.

"A lump?" I said. "Well, I have a mammogram coming up in about a week. Can it wait until then?"

She nodded.

I didn't think too much about it after that. I was only 54.

When it came time to do the mammogram, my daughter Nadine said, "Would you like me to come with you?" I wasn't concerned – it was just a mammogram – so I said no.

*Perhaps that was not wise.*

After I'd had the mammogram, the sonographer said, "They'd like to do a biopsy."

This was unusual; I'd never had that request.

If you've had a biopsy, you'll know they're not pleasant. By the time I left, I was pretty shaken and wasn't sure I should be getting in the car to drive myself home.

I thought I'd wait a bit to try and settle down. I went across the street and got myself an ice cream. It didn't make much difference and I had no option but to get myself home.

My golly, let's just say the force was with me while I was driving. I drove straight through a red light; fortunately, no-one was coming in the other direction. I'm not sure how I made it home.

The following week, I was booked to go to Cairns. In my role as a landslide scientist, I was giving a lecture to some building people there, and do some landslide work. I was to be away for the whole week.

I put the whole mammogram and biopsy thing out of my mind and went to Cairns. Not long after I arrived, I got a message from my husband Courtney to call my doctor. This couldn't be good. The conference was about to start and we were all so busy, but I had to know what was going on.

"We have your results," my doctor said. "When do you get back? We'll make an appointment and talk about it then."

There was no way I wanted to wait. "No," I said. "Tell me now."

My doctor didn't want to tell me over the phone but I kept insisting. "You've got breast cancer."

Wow. I think deep down I must have known — but it still came as a shock.

I was on my own up in Cairns, away from my family, about to present a paper at a conference and was not booked to go home for another six days. Yes, I was scared. I thought I was dying.

An unchangeable week with a lecture, meetings and field work that I couldn't pull out of; it was going to be tough. I knew I had breast cancer but I had no idea how bad it was. I didn't have anyone to talk to about it – it's not like I could sit down next to other colleagues there and say, "By the way, I've just found out I have breast cancer."

I spoke to my family, of course. I also spoke to the people I worked with. But I was still on my own. It was like having my own personal thundercloud above my head, with a background movie playing in my head all the time – what if, what if?

When I finally got back to my room after my first presentation, I opened the door to find a beautiful, bright bunch of flowers sent by my workmates in Canberra. It was very thoughtful and cheered me up a bit.

The next day, I had a meeting with the head of the Emergency Services and the Deputy Mayor. I have no idea what was said, or what I said. I imagined them thinking, 'What the heck is this woman doing here?' I'd met them both before, a while back, but I definitely wasn't myself this time.

Somehow, I managed to make it through the rest of the week. The day before I left, I went up to the Copperlode Dam. There's a big, windy road to get there and it suffers from lots of landslides. It's a terrible road to drive on but I was determined to make it to the end, and I did. There was a café at the end of the road. I went in and started talking to the woman who ran the place.

---

*I suddenly found myself finally talking about it all. She listened. She was lovely. Then she gave me a free coffee and said, "It's going to be alright." People are so kind.*

---

On the Monday after I got home, I had an appointment with the surgeon. He was just lovely and booked me in straight away for a lumpectomy.

I still couldn't believe it. Even while I was having all the tests, the bone scans, the ultrasounds – I was in a state of disbelief. Cancer happened to other people.

The morning after the surgery, the surgeon came to see me in my hospital room. I could tell by his reaction that he wasn't super happy with how it had gone. "We'll know more when we get the pathology back," he said. "Come and see me then."

I had another visitor during my time in hospital as well – a lady from Bosom Buddies. She'd had breast cancer herself and came to talk to me. She brought me some things from Bosom Buddies as well. I said to her that I thought it was lovely, all the things that people were doing and the support that was out there.

> *"Oh, we can do lots of things," she said.*
> *"We even have a dragon boating team." I thought,*
> *'That's something I'm going to do when I get out here.'*

I went to see the surgeon later that week when I got out of hospital. I took Nadine with me this time.

He pulled out his notes and the images and started pointing at different spots. "Well, you've got a grade two there and a grade three there. There's a bit of cancer there and some precancerous cells there …"

> *I decided to save him the trouble. "I have to*
> *have a mastectomy, don't I?" He looked at me.*
> *"How about next Monday?" I was booked in exactly*
> *two weeks after I'd had the lumpectomy.*

I went home and told Courtney. "Will you still love me if I lose a breast?"

I was suddenly reminded of the sketch on *The Comedy Company* where the young woman said to her husband, "Would you still love me if I had no arms? Would you still love me if I had no legs? Would you still love me if I were just a stump?"

Courtney said, "Of course, I'll still love you."

I went into hospital the following week. I was being stoic – yes, this breast has to come off. This is going to save my life. I have to lose this breast. And I was fine – until the orderly pushing my trolley had to stop at the nurses' desk before he took me into the operating theatre. I dissolved into tears.

Finally, we trundled along to the holding room outside the theatre. One of the nurses there asked me what I was having done. "A mastectomy," I said.

She shushed me. "You don't have to talk so loud."

I didn't understand. I hadn't spoken loudly but then I realised that she didn't want me to say that word out loud. As if I should be keeping it a big secret; keep my privacy. I thought that was a weird attitude. Why should it be something to be embarrassed about?

I was in hospital over Easter. I even had some 'bikies' come in with some Easter eggs on Easter Sunday. That was nice.

On the Sunday, in my hospital room, I was listening to *Australia All Over* on the radio. Then I thought, 'I'm going to phone in and talk to Ian McNamara.' He was the host of the show and I used to talk to him a lot about earthquakes. This time, though, I wanted to urge other people not to be as complacent as I was.

So, I rang him and explained my situation. He put me on air. "I was complacent," I said, "I just didn't check. Please remember and don't be like me – check your breasts more often."

Once I got out of hospital again, I went to see the oncologist. Both he and the surgeon were happy with how everything had gone. "They got it all," the oncologist told me. "Your prognosis is excellent. You'll live a long and happy life after you have completed treatment."

I was feeling really nervous. I was to have six months of chemotherapy, then five weeks of radiotherapy. "Then you should be right," he said.

I was dreading the chemotherapy. It's not something one looks forward to at all.

At this point, Nadine was working in one of the department stores and was able to arrange a day off every two weeks. So, that was the day I was booked in for each chemo treatment. She'd drive me into chemo, sit with me while I had it and then drive me home. I'd take that afternoon off work as well.

---

*I'd decided to try and work through my chemo, which turned out to be a big mistake.*

---

My first chemo session was terrifying.

We went in and they got me all set up and explained what was going to happen. They also explained that after chemo it was important to flush the toilet twice and things like that. Then a lady approached me – and I nearly fainted in fright – she was wearing a big purple outfit, with big purple gloves and a purple bucket. I found it so scary.

After that session, I became more used to it. I knew what to expect. I used to have a joke with the nurses because that was the best way I had of handling it.

I was partway through my chemo when I noticed a flyer for a Come and Try session with Dragons Abreast. I'd been waiting for this ever since I'd had that lumpectomy and, even though I was still doing chemo, I went along for my first paddle. I loved it, but afterwards I knew I'd need to get fitter before I did it again and thought I'd try swimming for fitness.

I also ended up with a blood infection not long after that. I was very fortunate that I was at work when I started feeling unwell. I was so ill, all I could do was lie on the floor. My boss found me and helped me up. Then he rang Nadine to come and pick me up. Courtney came too and drove my car home. By coincidence, I had an appointment with the oncologist that afternoon, which Nadine took me to.

The oncologist took one look at me and said, "Go straight to hospital." Do not pass go. Do not collect $200. Before I knew it, I was on an IV drip being fed antibiotics. I was in hospital for about five days. My immunity was incredibly low – anything that was there to pick up, I would have picked up.

All throughout my chemo treatments, I felt nauseated. Having to work was difficult because I wasn't up to scratch; I made some poor judgements about various things and I was supposed to be supervising someone who was struggling a bit, but I was struggling too.

It wasn't always awful, though. On occasion, I'd feel like myself and remember one day feeling particularly pleased because I wasn't nauseated and had a good creative idea to solve something. It was comforting to know my brain did actually still work.

However, if I had the time again, I would have taken the time off, and that's what I tell people now. If you have the sort of job where you have to make decisions and use your brain, it can be really hard.

Somehow, though, I managed to get through the chemo and then it was on to the radiotherapy, which wasn't nearly as bad. I'd arranged to work in the morning, have radiotherapy in the afternoon and then go home straight afterwards. By the time I got to the fifth week of radiotherapy, I was so tired. I got into work on the first day of my fifth week and all I could do was put my head in my arms on my desk. I took the rest of that week off work; I just couldn't do it.

Once I'd finished the radiotherapy, I couldn't wait to get back into dragon boating. I took it a bit easier this time, and started out doing the drumming while I was recovering from the radiotherapy.

The team was a new team at that stage – they'd only formed the year before. The coach was a male and he'd stand up the back teaching us how to paddle, how to sit – that sort of thing.

Even though I often wasn't well enough to actually paddle, I'd still go and meet the team for coffee after their training. I needed to mix with other people who'd been through what I'd been through. I needed that support and the support was there; it was strong. I was terrified for quite some time that I was going to get it again; I'd feel phantom lumps or some sort of pain and get really worried, so having the other ladies around me was wonderful.

*All the treatment just finishes you off. I think it must have taken me about a year to get back to normal.*

I was diagnosed in my fifties so I was a lot younger than I am now – this all happened twenty years ago – but it took a toll on me and even though the active treatment had finished, I still wasn't myself.

At the time, my boss was based in Brisbane and would come down to Canberra once a week. One week, he walked over to me and said, "We'd like to have a talk to you. Come on, we'll take you out for lunch."

So, off I went with my boss and his wife. They bought me lunch and gave me a lovely gerbera. Then, after lunch, they said, "Here, watch this video." It was about depression. After we watched it, he said, "We think you're suffering from depression. It might be worth getting it checked out."

It hadn't even crossed my mind. I didn't think of myself as suffering, I was doing my best, trying to survive and get my work done.

I went to see a psychiatrist who prescribed me some antidepressants. I took them for a few months and then decided I didn't need them anymore. I would never have realised if my boss hadn't shown me that video.

Nadine and my son Kenrick were incredibly supportive through all of this. And Courtney, of course. But, in terms of other support – remember, this was more than twenty years ago now – they didn't have breast care nurses or the other support groups they have these days. I did have a homecare nurse come to check my drains and wound after the surgery. I was always so glad to see her. She'd been a palliative care nurse and was so supportive. When I saw the McGrath Foundation come out in support of funding breast care nurses, I remember thinking, 'What a good idea.' I wish they'd had that when I was going through it all.

It's been twenty years for me now.

*You can get complacent after a while, but it's important to remember that this thing can come back and whack you at any time.*

I still make sure, when I see my GP, that I ask for a referral for a mammogram and ultrasound every year. I'm strict about checking my armpits too because even though I had a full clearance, I still have two lymph nodes there.

Any joint pains or unusual twinges – I get them checked too. "I want to get this checked," I say to the doctor. "Remember, I had breast cancer." The type of cancer I had – invasive lobular carcinoma – is, I believe, one of the ones that can come back and affect you, years and years later.

I'm finished with being complacent.

# Bench 5 – Right

The sun's finally shown itself and is working overtime to inject some warmth into our bones.

Nadine casts a sideways glance at her mum, sitting beside her. Marion's in her late seventies; the oldest, still active paddler in the team. Things are getting harder each year. Harder to get in and out of the boat. Harder to get going on the cold mornings. But Marion gives her all during every session … because that's what being part of a team means. No complaints.

Marion pats Nadine on the knee. "You alright, love?"

Nadine smiles. "Of course, Mum," she says. "I'm more than alright."

"I do love being out on the boat, in the fresh air," Marion adds. "Don't you?"

"Absolutely," Nadine replies.

Over to the left of the boat, a carp jumps from the water and flips back in with a splash.

The lake is full of carp. Often there are people stringing in fishing lines from the shore, or sometimes from kayaks, but who knows what they do with the carp they catch. They're not good for eating.

"What else is in this lake?" Gillian asks.

"Who knows?" Nadine says. "We do see the occasional kangaroo."

She's right – there have been times when a kangaroo has strayed off course and ended up in the lake. They can swim – or stay afloat at least – but find themselves unable to get out over the stone wall.

"And there was also the time we managed to rescue a young one," Katherine says. "It was only small but it was a heavy bugger. Years ago, that was."

"We're not allowed to do that anymore," says Nadine. "Have to call a ranger, so let's hope we don't see any."

Kellie Nissen

**Name:** Nadine Leiba

**Joined DAC:** 2000 as a supporter member with her mum, Marion

**Favourite boat position:** engine room

**Memorable DAC moments:** that first regatta in Penrith, paddling for Chinese New Year in Sydney

**Favourite colour:** burgundy

**In my spare time:** I love listening to music and trying new food

# Nadine's Story: Your Own Emotional Roller-Coaster

> *Mum had a cyst in one of her breasts for ages.*
> *I remember saying to her, "Is this just another cyst?"*
> *She said it wasn't. This time it was cancer.*

The day Mum had 'the' mammogram, the one that found the cancer, I'd asked her if she wanted me to drive her to the appointment. In her usual fashion, she said no. As it turned out, they gave her a biopsy after the mammogram.

When she came home, she looked at me and said, "I wish I'd taken up your offer to drive me." She'd run through a red light on the way back. Her mind was on other things.

The day after the appointment, Mum had to go up to Cairns for a landslide field trip. That's where she was when she found out about the breast cancer. Alone, away from family, up north.

Her GP rang here initially, not knowing Mum was away. She didn't say anything to me obviously, but I had the feeling that it was cancer. You just know.

It was all such a long time ago – 2000 – it's hard to remember some of the details, although a lot of it still feels really recent. I'd given the GP Mum's mobile number to call her in Cairns and later Mum rang here. I can't remember the exact conversation and I suspect she mainly talked to Dad, but it wouldn't have been a fun one.

After the field trip, she came back to Canberra and went straight into specialist appointments and those tests. Dad went with her to all of these appointments. I was working two part-time jobs at the time – Kmart and Grace Bros – so I'd call her after each appointment to see how she went and ask what was happening.

The surgery was booked in quickly. She had a lumpectomy to begin with, then, around two weeks later, she was called back to have a mastectomy.

Watching your mum, or anyone you love, going through this — it's like being on your own emotional roller-coaster, but different to the one Mum was on. It was scary. For me, at first, it was like, is this really happening? Is it really cancer? I was pretty much thinking like that until she went in to have surgery.

I don't think I ever said anything to Mum but I was absolutely terrified about her surgery. On the day, I was there, wondering how long it was going to take. Was she out yet? What's happening in there? I was there when she woke up.

---

*No-one makes much sense straight after they wake up from surgery — you can't exactly have a conversation — but I needed to be there. To see her and know — okay, she's come out; she's still alive. There's some kind of reassurance in that.*

---

After Mum had recovered from the second surgery, she had roughly six months of chemo. Actually, it probably ended up being longer than that because she there were a few times where her cell count was way too low to have chemo.

Even though Mum often felt like rubbish, she'd go in to work each day. The problem was that people would walk in and tell her she looked so well. She was good at hiding it.

We had some scary episodes during the chemo period. One day in particular, I remember getting a call from one of Mum's work colleagues. "She's really sick," they said. "She's vomiting. We need someone to come and pick her up."

I went in and Dad came too, so he could drive her car home. Fortunately, she already had an appointment with her oncologist that day. So, after she'd had a rest, we went in to her appointment.

Her white cell count was very low.

"You have to go to the hospital immediately," the oncologist told her. "You'll need a course of IV antibiotics."

I went home and collected the things Mum would need and Dad drove her to the hospital. She was so sick. It all came on incredibly quickly.

We went together to all her chemo appointments. It was basically a whole morning. I'd sit with her, and we'd be home again around lunchtime.

I also took Mum to one of her radiotherapy appointments. She didn't really need anyone to drive her by then, but I was curious to see the whole thing. The staff were great. They let me in to the room to have a look at the machine and where Mum would be lying. Obviously, I had to go out while she had the radiation, though.

*The biggest thing about watching someone go through all of this is that you feel so helpless. There's nothing you can do to magically take away the cancer.*

Of course, the whole thing doesn't end with the last radiotherapy session. Mum was on tablets for a while. Tamoxifen at first, then something else. Plus, there's regular appointments and checkups. There's always that nervous wait with every check-up; hoping she's still clear.

With dragon boating, I'm pretty sure she went along to one session early on — I think she was still having chemo at the time. They told her to come back after the chemo — and she did. She was keen.

Still undergoing treatment — radiation — she started off with Dragons Abreast as a drummer. Then, once she was medically cleared, she got into the paddling. She was always telling me to come along so I did, a couple of months after Mum started.

All of a sudden, I found myself in the boat at my first ever regatta. We were in Penrith and the team was down a paddler — so I was it. It was the first time I'd ever paddled properly; I might have been to maybe one training session at that stage.

*I remember thinking, 'this is going to kill me'. But, at the same time, it was so much fun.*

The added bonus was this one sweep who was there. He was gorgeous. I think he may have been Filipino and he was sweeping bare-chested. We made him wear a pink boa.

As a supporter member of the club, I don't feel any different to the paddlers. The dragon boating community in general is very friendly, welcoming and family oriented. I feel like I'm part of the group.

It's been twenty-two years since Mum went through all of this but my supporter role is still there. My dad has cancer now, too – prostate. It's ongoing – but not in a bad way. It's just how it is.

Mum is so independent but sometimes, in that supporter role, I tell her how things are going to work on any particular day. I think having gone through this together definitely brought us closer. I think there's a definite friendship there – more than your average mother-daughter relationship. Plus, there's the dragon boating that brings us together.

Being in a support role can be tough. You want to do everything but you need to know when to back off. You want to help but the person doesn't want your help – fair enough. You need to let them do what they need to do. Although sometimes, when they've knocked back your help and then they're really tired afterwards, it is tempting to say, "You know, I did offer …" But you don't.

There are probably a few things, in hindsight, I'd have done differently. I was a bit too anxious. I tried to keep a lot of the worry to myself because I didn't want to put it back onto Mum; she had enough to deal with.

At times, it would have been good to have other supporters to talk to about what we were going through. Sort of like unleashing your burden onto someone else but not onto the person who actually has the cancer. Helping someone out through their cancer treatment is such a huge thing and, while there's lots of support for those people, there doesn't seem to be a lot for the supporters. I think it's the same for all supporter or carer roles, whether it's cancer, dementia, special needs or whatever. Even simple things like accessing leave to take Mum to her chemo appointments – you have to rely on the goodwill of your employer to a certain extent.

---
*Being a supporter is as much about being there emotionally for the person as it is about advocating for them.*
---

In Mum's case, she can more than speak for herself but sometimes, when she was in the middle of chemo particularly, I did find myself stepping in.

One time I remember was with our doctor. Mum had been trying to ring to get an appointment. They were super busy and when she finally got through, the receptionist told her there was nothing available. I rang back and said, "Look, my mum has cancer. She needs to see the doctor now." They found an appointment somehow. It's a small thing but it's part of your role – and it's important.

Looking back now, there are some days it feels like such a long time ago and others where it feels like yesterday. Some days, I find myself thinking about it; then I can go for weeks without giving it a thought.

On the whole though, it really is that never-ending roller-coaster.

# Bench 6 – Left

Just in front of Commonwealth Place, Lyndall calls for us to slow the boat, then stop it. We comply, paddles holding against the water, then plunging deep to a hold.

There's a bootcamp in action and a few of the participants wave as they run sprints up and down the adjacent hills.

"Are we stretching?" asks Marion.

"Sure are," Jenny says. "Let's do this."

Not every club stretches half way through a session – but perhaps they should. Nobody can quite remember if it's a Dragons Abreast thing, or something that was instigated by one of DA Canberra's founding members. More probably the latter. Either way, it's a beautiful thing to do.

Elly and Clare start counting as all twenty of us lift our paddles above our heads, holding them parallel to the water.

"I love this," says April, "but could do without the water running down my arm and into my armpit."

"Eight … nine … June."

Clare and Elly finish their count and it's over to Megan and Anne to continue counting while everyone moves on to the next stretch. "One, two …"

"Slow down," Denise calls. "June would not approve."

"Ohhh … is June a person?" asks Sugar. "I've never understood why we say 'June' instead of ten."

"June McMahon," Marion says. "She was a paddler right back when DAC first started. We even have a bench named after her at Lotus Bay. Anne organised that, didn't you, Anne?"

Anne raises her hand in acknowledgement.

"We all did what June told us to do," added Denise. "Like stretching. We used to get into trouble if we rushed that."

"And when she wasn't paddling with us any more, Patsy suggested we replace 'ten' with 'June' to remind ourselves to slow down and stretch properly." Marion finishes the story.

"She was a wonderful lady," says Denise, "but I'm still scared of her."

Kellie Nissen

**Name:** Denise Brown
**Initial diagnosis:** 2012, can't remember what type of breast cancer
**Age at diagnosis:** 59
**Job at diagnosis:** aged care worker
**Job now:** aged care worker
**Joined DAC:** 2013
**Favourite boat position:** near the front
**Memorable DAC moment:** going overseas with the ladies
**What I love:** clothes, plants, my sons (not necessarily in that order)

# Denise's Story: Live in the Now

*I was scared. Really scared. I've never smoked.*
*I breastfed. I'd never had any problems before …*

I was having a regular annual mammogram. It was fine. Nobody suggested that something might be wrong so I didn't give any thought to it at all.

A couple of weeks later, I had a call. They'd found an anomaly and wanted me to go back in for a biopsy.

The whole experience was uncomfortable – the biopsy itself, of course, but also the fact my son was there with me. It was overwhelming for both of us.

After I got the results, they sent me to a specialist – a surgeon. He said he would take what they call a 'chicken fillet' out – just a piece. A lumpectomy, in other words. "We'd like to get it tested," he said.

I went along with that, of course. I was told it wasn't a big drama but it was still frightening.

The whole thing was scary. You know all the old wives' tales – breastfeed to prevent breast cancer and all of that – well, they didn't come true for me. It was a shock.

A couple of days later, I got another phone call to say that they hadn't got a clear margin and I needed more surgery.

*They then told me my surgeon was going on leave for six weeks. Six weeks. It did my head in. For the whole six weeks, I think I just about went nuts with fear.*

One of the receptionists must have realised how scared I was. "I've got the phone number of a lady who's been down this path," she said. "Would you like her to contact you so you've got someone to talk to?"

"Yes, please," I said. I'm not really medically minded and I didn't want to go to a large group like Bosom Buddies. I was petrified and didn't know where to turn.

I got in touch with this lady and it was wonderful. She just talked to me. She'd ring me three or four times a week. If I was having a bad day, she talked me through it. She was a former Dragons Abreast paddler, which was really good. I honestly didn't know how I was going to get through everything and she was so helpful.

Even though she only lived a couple of suburbs away, I didn't actually meet her until after my surgery. I was very protective of myself. I wasn't comfortable with people coming to the house either. It might have started when I had my son Daniel – he has special needs, Downs Syndrome. A lady once brought her two-year-old over to play and I remember thinking, 'I don't want my son to be like that.'

It was the same with the breast cancer. I wanted to go through the process and not start comparing myself to others and thinking negative thoughts. When you're so scared, you can't control what you think. So, I only talked to her on the phone.

---

*My brain was busy enough as it was. Who would look after my family? Would I die from this? I didn't really understand what was going to happen – would they just cut it off and, with a bit of luck, it would be fine?*

---

Once my surgeon returned, I was booked in for my second surgery.

It wasn't the best experience. I was very self-conscious.

My appointment was in the middle of the day and I was so upset. My surgeon came to see me before the operation. "Why are you crying?" He couldn't understand. Another doctor was just looking at me.

The anaesthetic must have been slow working because I remember watching them stretching my arm out on a board and taping it down – not a pleasant thing to witness.

The next day, it didn't get much better.

I was supposed to be seeing a breast care nurse first but she couldn't make it in. Then, a young student nurse came in to help me have a shower. I was bruised, as you could imagine, with stitches everywhere and blood and stuff. All I wanted was someone to help me get cleaned up but this young nurse stood at the door and stared at me. Maybe she was overwhelmed, or not sure what to do, but she didn't offer to help me at all. That made me feel even worse.

Thankfully, somebody went and got one of the breast care nurses for me. That made things a bit better. The breast care nurses were wonderful. They were friendly and very helpful.

---

*I was fully prepared to have to lose my hair with chemo. While I was waiting, I wore a big hat all the time because I figured I'd have to get used to not having hair.*

---

I ended up not needing chemotherapy – or radiation treatment. Just the mastectomy. Even today, I can't believe that.

Other people can't believe it either.

Afterwards, I threw all my paperwork in a box in the garage. I didn't need to look at it. I didn't need it in the house. A couple of my friends, who've had breast cancer too, went and found the paperwork. They started going through it and I said, "I'll go and get the shredder and shred it right now." I didn't want it around and I didn't want to start wondering whether I should have had this, or had that.

You have to trust the medical profession.

My surgeon was thorough. He didn't speak much though, and didn't offer a lot of information. That made me more insecure. Now, I understand different things and maybe I should have asked different questions but, at the time, I didn't know what to ask. However, he was a good doctor. He was reassuring and he was one of the people who told me about dragon boating. He was friends with the husband of another lady who did dragon boating so he knew about it and about Dragons Abreast in Canberra.

> *I ended up having to take about eight months off work.*
> *The work I do is physical and it was a major operation,*
> *so I wasn't able to do anything like I used to for quite a while.*

It was a lonely time. Not being able to work in my job as an aged care worker, and with the rest of my family at work during the day, I was at home a lot by myself. It was a big decision, too – would I go back to work or not?

More than anything, I was still worried. Would the cancer come back? Would I be able to go back to work afterwards; should I go back? I was 58, but I loved my job and the money was handy.

Daniel was twenty-three and my older son, Adam, was twenty-five at the time. They both became most attentive. Adam said, "Mum, if you died … well, you're my only real family that I've got left." It was traumatic for all of us and they became protective of me. My partner Malcolm was the same. He hid a lot of his fear at the time but he was so supportive.

I used to love nice bras and other things like that. For a long time after the surgery, and even now, I don't like looking at the pretty bras.

> *"I'm a reject now," I'd sometimes say to my partner.*
> *He'd tell me I wasn't – that I was fine –*
> *but I know I've lost a lot of confidence in that way.*

Psychologically, the experience has affected me a lot – having the mastectomy. I still have days where I feel uncomfortable about it. I have low self-esteem anyway and I've never been a confident person, so this hasn't helped.

What has helped, though, was joining Dragons Abreast. I've made good friends in the team.

A few people had told me about the sport and about Dragons Abreast so, one day, in February the year after my surgery, I went down to the lake with my friend – just to watch. Some of the ladies saw me there, watching. "Come in the boat," they said.

"Oh no, I'm just watching," I said. "Then we're going to have lunch." It was my birthday.

"No, no," one of the ladies insisted. She was one of the founders of the club and was very persuasive.

Everyone was so lovely. They all said hello and made me feel welcome. So, I went out in the boat.

I was hooked.

I joined and started going to training, three times a week. Sports had never been my thing; I'd never played much, but I'd found something I could do – and enjoyed. I'm not a great swimmer, and I don't have a great love of the lake, but I don't think about that. I tell myself to just think about the dragon boating.

---

*Joining the team took that big cloud away;*
*the one that had been hanging over me for a long time.*

---

I'm still very self-conscious. I still have days when I feel insecure. And, as for the 'Why me?' – well, breast cancer was never in my family. So, for me, it was just one of those things. Nobody knew why. It just happened.

Occasionally, I find myself thinking, 'Surely I didn't actually have cancer?' Cancer is something that happens to other people. I often wish, too, that I'd known more at the time. For example, if I'd known more, I would have insisted on the mastectomy in the first instance so I'd only have the one surgery.

A few people have suggested that I 'should' have the other one cut off. I couldn't do that. I couldn't go back into hospital again. I say to them, "You don't know what it was like. It was such a terrible experience for me."

---

*Fear makes you do and say weird things.*
*It makes you act in ways that you wouldn't otherwise act.*

---

I didn't think I would get there. I didn't think I'd come through it all — I even went as far as planning my funeral. I made a friend come with me to find out what to do and how to make sure everything was planned properly. I was thinking, 'The boys wouldn't know what to do.'

It's funny, the connections you make with people, though. It's not like we all walk around with a sign above our heads, but sometimes you'll be talking to someone and they'll mention something about having had breast cancer.

"Oh, me too," I'll say.

Then they might say something like, "Which side was yours? Mine was left."

"Mine was as well," I'll say.

Then, all of a sudden you find you've got something in common with a person who was a stranger a few minutes earlier.

Getting cancer was a major pain. It was an upheaval in my life, another one. I think I'd had my fair share of that already. But I had it, and that's it.

Now, I believe it's important to take each day as it comes. Follow the doctor's orders and just get on with each day, because you simply don't know what's coming. And you won't know it's over until it's over.

# Bench 6 – Right

"Swapping from the front," Lyndall calls. "Paddles flat when you're not swapping."

Bench by bench, each pair balances their paddles across the boat, grabs hold of the gunnel and moves across to the other side. It's not an easy task, swapping sides on the bench while the boat is floating. Keeping paddles flat helps, but there's always a bit of rock 'n' roll and a few gasps as the boat tilts one way or the other. It's definitely a skill. The paddler on the right stands – just enough to be able to step across to the left. The paddler on the left has an easier task, just needing to slide along the seat to the right. Although, they bear the experience of having their bench buddy's rear pass by their face at close quarters.

"There's no privacy," Katherine says. "But we're all friends, right?"

"When we do the Ord," says Jenny, holding tight to the drum seat, "we'll have to swap on the move."

"What?" says Denise. "While we're paddling?"

Jenny nods. "None of us can paddle for a whole day without changing sides."

The boat tilts again and Denise grabs Katherine's knee.

"Well, hello there." Katherine purses her lips and winks at Denise. If anyone is able to take the stress out of a situation and lighten the mood, it's Katherine.

"You okay to swap?" Janet asks Deb. Not all of us can paddle on both sides. More often than not it's a short-term thing – usually an unrelated injury. Paddling just on one side is never a preference, although many of us are stronger on one side than the other.

The swapping continues down to the back of the boat and before long, Lyndall calls, "Bum mats and drink bottles." This is the signal that all benches have swapped and we can now do the necessary adjustments like repositioning our 'bum mats' that stop us sliding all over the seat and placing our drink bottles back at our feet.

"Warming up on this side," Lyndall calls. "Attention. Go."

Once again, twenty paddles drive into the water as one, pulling the boat up and forward, keeping time with the drum.

"It always feels weird on this side," Katherine says.

Others agree, but thirty seconds in, the body remembers what it should be doing.

*Bench 6 – Right*

**Name:** Katherine Davis Kralikas
**Diagnosed:** 2000
**Age at diagnosis:** 52
**Job when diagnosed:** teacher
**Job now:** carer, teacher
**Joined DAC:** 2001
**Favourite boat position:** Bench 2 or 3, but if I'm on the boat, I'm happy
**Memorable DAC moment:** that very first time I sat in a dragon boat
**What I love:** the beach, it's the freedom of being on or near the water that brings such joy

Kellie Nissen

# Katherine's Story: No Time for This – I'm Booked on a Dragon Boat

*From the start, I decided I was going to do this on my own. Everything's fine.*

It was only the second mammogram I'd ever had. I'd not long turned fifty.

I was supposed to have the mammogram in September, but I'm a teacher and that's one of the times of year when you're flat out. Like most teachers, I often put appointments off until the holidays. That's what I did with this one.

By the time the October holidays rolled around, I'd decided to take study leave for a year and do my Graduate Diploma in Special Education and Graduate Diploma in Religious Studies. I'd be working part-time too. Enrolling in my uni courses was my priority so the mammogram was put off again until the Christmas holidays. I made an appointment for early January 2000.

On the day of the mammogram, I didn't expect to be in there for too long. They did it and asked me to wait. Then they came back in and did it again for 'clearer images'.

I'd just gone back to my teaching job, and my university course was due to start when I got a phone call. "Can you come back in?" the caller said. "For a biopsy."

It all went south from there.

I wanted to get this done on my own, without anyone else there, so I deliberately booked the appointment for one of the days I usually worked and a day I knew Edmund would be in a meeting.

It was a great plan – until he came home early.

I couldn't believe it. I was about to leave and there he was, in the driveway. I'd just missed out on getting away.

"Where are you going?" he said.

"For a biopsy," I said. "I won't be long."

Well, he went into overdrive. "Come on, then," he said. "You can't drive yourself. I'm taking you …" Blah, blah, blah.

He dropped me off at the clinic and went to get a park. When I walked in, the nurse looked up at me. "Did you come on your own?" she said.

"Well, sort of," I answered.

"Where is he?" she said. A couple of them went running out to the street to find him.

I don't know if they were worried about him being in shock or something but all I could think was, 'I don't give a damn. This is about me.'

They found him and brought him inside. Then they called me in.

Getting undressed in the cubicle, I could see in the mirror that my right breast was much larger than the left. It's not unusual to have different sizes but the odd thing with me was that it was the wrong way round. Normally, my right one was smaller.

The nurses were absolutely amazing. I can't praise them enough. They knew exactly what was going on – I could see that much – but were unable to tell me anything. They're not doctors so it's not their job.

It was a tumour. In the right breast.

"You can't go home until you've phoned your GP," the nurse said to me.

All I wanted to do was go home. "It's okay," I said. "I'll go and see my GP later."

They wouldn't have a bar of it. They actually dialled her number for me and waited while I told her.

---

*My GP was my neighbour – we'd been friends for years – so that part wasn't too bad. When I got home, she came over and we discussed it all over a glass of red wine.*

---

Funnily enough – but not funny – about eighteen months after my diagnosis, my GP found out she had breast cancer. "It's all your fault," she said. Then she started sending me off to find out what this doctor was like or that one. When I got back, she'd drill me for feedback.

Anyway, after we'd had the wine, she gave me a referral to a specialist. A breast surgeon.

On the day of the surgeon's appointment, I was sitting in the waiting room, checking out the other patients. I've never seen so many sickly-looking people in the one space in all my life. Bandages, pale skin – you name it. It was depressing. The room was dark and crowded. Not pleasant.

When I was called into his office, it was much the same – crowded, though not with people. In my usual style, I was thinking about how I could best communicate with this man. I wanted to build a rapport. Looking around the room, I could see he'd graduated from Monash University at almost about the same time as my sister had, so I thought I had a talking point.

Silly me! As if I'd need a talking point when I'd just been diagnosed with breast cancer. The surgeon wasn't the slightest bit interested in making small talk.

"Right," he said, "I'll book you in for a mastectomy on Monday."

This was Thursday, or maybe Friday. There was no time to think about it or prepare. It was a massive thing to have to come to terms with and he was so matter-of-fact. There was no explanation other than 'you've got a tumour'. I had no idea what was going on or what to expect.

Back at home, I got straight on to my doctor. "I don't like that man," I said. "I'm not letting him do things to me. This is ridiculous."

"I didn't think you'd get on too well with him," she said. "I'll line you up with someone else." She did, and that was so much better.

---

*There were a few coincidences along the way. My new surgeon and I both had the same surname. The ward I was in after the surgery had the same name as the suburb I lived in. Silly things like that, but they make you laugh and think it must be meant to happen.*

---

My new surgeon was the most wonderful man who explained everything. We got along really well.

"No wonder it was so hard to detect," he said at one point. "It was really well hidden; really deep. You'd never have felt it."

I had the surgery about a week after I saw him.

Having the wire put in beforehand was a ghastly experience. The wire is there to guide the surgeon so they cut out the right bit. They tell you not to cough and you immediately want to cough. You're lying face down with your breast hanging through the hole and they're trying to get you to look up at the screen so you can see what's happening. I didn't care to know.

Once they finally had the wires inserted, they sent me to hospital for the surgery. My husband drove me and we waited together to be called in to the theatre.

The day after the operation, my surgeon came to see me. "I'm going to apologise now," he said. "I had to cut through some major nerves to get at that tumour, but I wasn't taking any chances. You're very lucky they found this with the mammogram."

I wasn't feeling too lucky.

About a month later, I had to go to Melbourne for a family wedding. I come from a large family – six children. My oldest brother had been killed in a car accident a couple of years earlier. My eldest sister had also been diagnosed with what they initially thought was ovarian cancer but it turned out to be cancer of the fallopian tubes. She'd been diagnosed about a year before me – and she died fifteen months later.

After the wedding, everyone was standing around at the reception. I'd not long had the mastectomy and was still self-conscious; wearing a gown with little baubles all over it to try and hide the missing breast.

My remaining siblings were huddled around each other, having a chat. I marched over and pushed my way into the huddle. "Okay," I announced. "I'm here and I'm alive. You can stop talking, now."

They all froze.

"You're all fine," I said. "It's only the odd numbers in the family that have to deal with this crap." My eldest brother was first-born, my eldest sister was number three and I was fifth born.

There was a stunned silence for a second then they all laughed. "Yeah," they said. "We'll all be fine. That's great." Then we all got on with the party.

> *That's the thing I found, continually, through my cancer journey — I was the one who had to open the conversation and lighten everyone else up. It was never the other way around.*

No-one ever asked me how it was going. It was like they were too scared of what I might say.

I was teaching in the Catholic system and we always had prayer on Tuesday mornings. Most of the teachers were religious to some extent. I walked into the staffroom one Tuesday, feeling like death-warmed-up — I was in the middle of chemo. Somebody said 'hello' or something and that was it. I let loose.

"Well, it's all your fault," I said.

They all looked at me in horror.

"You haven't been praying hard enough for me," I said. "I failed another blood test."

I was joking, of course — not about the blood test but about the praying — but you should have seen the expression on their faces.

"What?"

"Sorry."

"Oh no."

There were all sorts of mumblings and awkwardness. A few relieved smiles.

That same afternoon, we were having a little celebration for something. I'd forgotten about my comment in the staffroom from that morning until one of the teachers came over and said, "What did that mean about the blood test?"

It was one of the blokes, actually, and it was really good. I started talking about it all — the diagnosis, the treatment — and suddenly everybody was on board. They'd all been too scared to ask me anything before.

> *The misinformation around cancer —
> the scare factor — is unbelievable.*

My boss basically expected me to run away and hide and not come back after that year. "You've had cancer," he said. "There's no hope for you." He even gave my teaching position away — who does that? It was a nightmare. I had to bring the union in to get my job reinstated.

My colleagues initially ran a mile. So did my family. It was too confronting for people. My only guess is because I was 'the life of the party' person. I was the one who made things happen. I was the organiser. I was in control. So, for me to go down was a blow. People must have thought: 'If she can go down, then so can everybody.'

I'm a fairly independent person but it was still hard to take.

One of my teaching friends was fabulous. She'd retired at the end of the previous year — before I was diagnosed. When she found out, she said, "Right! And this is why I retired. To take you to chemotherapy."

Once I started the whole chemotherapy cycle, my friend would pick me up and take me over. Edmund took me once, but I think it was too much of a shock for him to see me with all these things happening to me; tubes and needles and things like that.

My sister also said she'd take me if I ever needed her to but that never happened. She was a teacher too. It's hard to get time off. She did buy me a hat, though. "For when you lose your hair," she said.

My surgeon and my oncologist were having a bet about my hair. One of them said I'd lose my hair and the other one said I wouldn't. My sister lost her hair after her second or third round of chemo treatment, so I was waiting for mine to fall out, too.

I sort of did half and half — so neither of them won.

What happened though was that I started getting all sorts of rashes over my body. I turned bright red. There was concern among the medical staff so they sent me off to hospital and stuck me in an isolation room like I had a highly contagious disease.

The doctor came in to see me and said they weren't sure what it was but they'd find out. He left the room to have a pow-wow with some of the other staff.

When you're sick, there's often one of your senses that is heightened. At that time, for me, it was my hearing and it was like I could hear right through walls. I heard everything they were saying.

"It looks like measles," one of them said.

"No, it's not that."

Then my oncologist came along and put them straight. "Don't worry, she's not contagious," he said. "It's just that every hair follicle on her body has opened up."

The nurses came back into my room, completely unaware I'd heard what they'd been saying. "Look," one of them said. "We think you're losing your hair. It can be quite distressing for people because once it starts coming out, you tend to lose it in clumps."

I nodded. I knew that already.

"So we suggest you wear a cap, particularly at night, so you don't roll over and get a mouthful of hair."

I wore that blessed cap for months. It never happened.

All my body hair, all my facial hair, including my eyebrows and eyelashes – that all went. But not the hair on my head. It thinned. It moulted, more than anything. I ended up having a short haircut to make it look a bit thicker but I didn't go bald. I had hair on my head the whole way through chemo.

---

*"You were both right," I said to my surgeon and oncologist later. "But neither of you get the money because neither of you were a hundred per cent right."*

---

Chemo was chemo. That was it. The nice part was that my appointments were always around midday. I'd be brought in some lunch and a glass of red wine. You've got to take what you can get.

Throughout chemo, I kept working. I'd taken sick leave for the surgeries but worked the rest of the time, with the exception of the six weeks I took off about midway through my chemo treatment. It was 2000 – the Sydney Olympics. We had a short term that year because everything revolved around the Olympics, so I took the whole term off.

Back in 1956, when the Melbourne Olympics was held, my parents bought us this fabulous present. There were six of us kids in the family and Mum and Dad decided it was worth spending a bit of money. It was a big secret until we all went into the lounge room on the day the Olympics started. They bought us a television set. We watched the Olympics.

I'll never forget that, so, with the Olympics being back in Australia, I thought, 'Why not!' I splurged and bought tickets to the swimming and went to watch the marathon. I felt like I'd walked a marathon the day we watched it. I was in between treatments and it was a sweltering hot day. I couldn't believe it when I finally made it back. I thought I wouldn't. I wasn't doing too well but I kept going because I'm that sort of person. If I say I'm going to do something, I do it.

I'm pretty determined. Sometimes to my detriment.

After the chemo, they wanted to give me radiation.

The thing with radiation is that I had a bit of a family history with it. My dad had all these spots and things but was otherwise a very fit guy. Maybe because of that, or because he was old, they didn't test anything. The next year, he had full blown cancer – he ended up with a brain tumour. They tried to give him radiation but he died within three months. He was eighty-one.

In my sister's case, they'd done so much radiation on her bowel, she ended up dying of septicaemia. Basically, they killed her trying to cure her.

---

*When I was offered radiation, what do you think my response was?*

---

It was all raw because my sister had only just died when I got asked the question.

"Not unless I absolutely have to," I said.

Apparently, I didn't. "But it wouldn't hurt," they added.

"No, thanks," I said, "I'll pass." That wasn't the end of it all, though. I was put on Tamoxifen, which is a whole new journey of side effects.

There are some things in life that you just have to get on with by yourself because nobody else can do it for you – breast cancer treatment, for example. However, there are some things many of us need support with, even if it's just moral support.

My children were grown up when I received the diagnosis. They'd been travelling the world, living overseas. They weren't around at the time and although they sort of knew what was going on, I don't think they were coping very well with the idea.

I found that very difficult.

BCNA run a range of events and I started going to a few. I remember doing one of the walks they'd organised around Regatta Point at the lake. For the whole walk, I'd been crying because everyone else seemed to have family there, supporting them, and I was on my own. I needed to do it, though, because I had to face up to this thing.

It was on that walk when I saw people on a dragon boat.

"It's the Pink Ladies," someone in the group said. Everyone was waving and the ladies in the boat were waving back.

I was shocked. All these women out in a dragon boat, flaunting the fact they'd had breast cancer. 'How ghastly,' I thought. 'Dreadful people. They should go and hide.'

A couple of months later, I'd taken myself off to a counselling course – the type where you all sit around in a circle and share. It was rather depressing, to be honest – not really my thing. However, while I was there, I saw a flyer for dragon boating. I was a swimmer and love water. I love outdoor stuff. I'd forgotten how horrified I was at the ladies flaunting their stuff earlier and thought, 'I might go and have a look at this.'

It was a Come and Try session, but for some reason I thought it was a meeting where we'd sit around and hear about what dragon boating was. Anyway, I went off to the Yacht Club on the right day and went inside. There was nobody there, of course. I went back outside and wandered around – totally missed seeing all the dragon boats on the shore.

> *I was just standing there, looking at the water and wondering if I had the wrong day or place and the next thing, I hear these people yahooing at me from a boat.*

Someone came over. "Have you come to have a go at dragon boating?" she said

Then, suddenly, I'm in the boat.

And I've never got out since— except for when my doctor tells me I'm not allowed to do it because of my heart. That's really tough, to be honest.

I'd been paddling for a while – and loving it – when I found out there was an international regatta coming up in New Zealand. It was the inaugural South Pacific Dragon Boat Regatta. Why not! I decided I'd go. I booked all my tickets and organised long service leave.

That's when I found out I had uterine cancer.

I was finished with all my active treatment by this stage, but was still on the Tamoxifen. Awful thing nearly killed me, the uterine cancer. I needed another operation for that, which looked like it would be after the regatta, so I knew I'd have to take sick leave straight after my long service leave.

I told my principal – because that was the right thing to do.

"Well," she said. "That's absolutely ridiculous. I'm cancelling your long service leave."

I was in shock for a moment, until she went on.

"You'll take all of it as sick leave."

I guess that was a bit naughty but I had the blessing of my boss.

My surgeon had other ideas. When I told him I was booked on a plane to go to New Zealand for dragon boating, he said, "Well, that's not happening."

"Yes, it is," I said.

"No dragon boating then." He tried to negotiate because he knew how stubborn I was.

Did I go dragon boating?

I sure did!

The regatta was fabulous. We ended up having too many for our boat, which meant some people wouldn't be able to participate in all the races. As it turned out, the organisers wanted some extra people for an international composite boat.

"I'll be in that," I said.

I met some wonderful people and we had an amazing coach. One of the other paddlers was a school teacher too, and she invited me to visit her school down near Wellington. Next thing I know, I'm paddling in a Wellington regatta as well.

When I returned, it was straight off for surgery.

---

*To me, it seemed to have gone okay – but apparently it didn't.*

---

There was some bleeding and a few other things going on and the surgeon wanted me to go back in.

The second time round, he figured he'd got it all. As a bonus, he didn't think I'd need any further treatment.

A few months later, I went to see my oncologist. It was the middle of winter. Nine degrees at the most and I was in a T-shirt and sweating like crazy.

My oncologist took one look at me. "This isn't working, is it?" he said. "I think we'll take you off Tamoxifen. It seems to have caused you more problems than anything else."

Problems.

He wasn't wrong about that.

At the time, when you're in the middle of treatment, you're so busy. You're just trying to keep ahead of things and trying to get through and survive the experience. It's one day after another and you don't realise it. But I think, physically – and emotionally – it hits you after the treatment is done.

Because, of course, it's not done.

Physically, things often keep coming back and testing you again and again.

Take my breast reconstruction as an example.

I'd always planned to go for the reconstruction. I was set to do it but didn't like the first doctor. I didn't care for the next one either. There were various reasons – I was at the stage, though, where I didn't want just anyone. Then – before I'd decided – I got the uterine cancer. 'Whoa,' I thought, 'best wait and see what else God's got in store for me.' So, I waited. I got through it and then finally had the breast reconstruction.

Fast forward ten years – lump in the new, reconstructed breast.

My doctor sent me straight back to the specialist. That was interesting; the plastic surgeon thought I was back in to show him what a wonderful job he'd done. Here's another beautiful example of my work … he grabbed his camera, ready to take a photo.

"Excuse me," I said, "that's not why I'm here."

He took a look. "There's a lump there," he said. "It shouldn't be there; it needs to come out."

That particular appointment took longer than it should have because when I'd finished, the waiting room was full of people. There I am, walking out with the surgeon by my side – he was a very big man and I'm there under his armpit – and he says, "Everybody, this is trouble."

They managed to get a clearance the first time, which was fabulous. The interesting thing about that lump was that when they dissected it, they discovered it was full blown cancer. They were saying it wasn't possible because the reconstruction used stomach tissue.

Obviously, it was trying to assimilate to my breasts really well. Ha!

Cancer is not only a debilitating and exhausting life experience, it's a complete about-face. It takes a long time to get back on top of things.

---

*What you knew is no longer what you know.*

---

In my case, it's been one ride after another. Not everyone gets this, of course – I must be special or something. I always try to keep positive. Stay determined. Have a joke and a laugh when I can.

There are many judgemental people out there, though. People who don't get it or who think they have the answer to everything. I've had people tell me that my lifestyle contributed to the cancer – "It's because you drink."

Honestly, on hearing that all I want to say to them is, "Would you like a drink?"

I've had people tell me I got cancer because I do too much. "You do too many things and don't get enough sleep." I've been told that on a few occasions. I just look at them and hope it makes them feel better – judging me for doing the things that they don't do.

It's a bit naughty, but sometimes when people say these ridiculous things, I find myself thinking, 'Well, you won't get cancer because you wouldn't be able to handle it.'

Maybe I'm wrong. I knew some amazingly tough people who didn't make it. It never quite leaves me and I go through stages where I think, 'Why me?' Not in the sense of 'Why did I get cancer?' – I don't ever think like that – but 'Why am I still here?' I start wondering what has given me the right to still be here when others, who were just as worthy of life, aren't here anymore.

---

*The only thing I can put it down to is that there must be something more I have to do. There has to be a reason for my existence.*

---

I was in hospital recently and they'd been doing all these tests, trying to work out what I had this time. One afternoon, a doctor pulled up a chair beside my bed. I had no idea who he was because I had a massive fever and I wasn't with it at all. However, I distinctly remember him saying, "It just keeps coming for you, doesn't it?"

"Well, you're a cheery soul," I said.

He looked at me and said, "You've got pneumonia."

That wouldn't do. I had no time for pneumonia. "I've got to be out of here by the end of the week," I said. "I'm booked on a dragon boat in Port Macquarie."

"I don't think you'll be dragon boating," he said. "But maybe you'll get there in time to cheer your mates on."

The next day, I was worse. The doctor came back in and I said, "Don't forget, I have to be on that boat on the weekend."

He lost it. He got really cross with me. "I told you it's not going to happen," he said.

Although I may have been partly serious, there are some people you can't have a joke with.

You have to joke about things – I do, anyway. What's the point, otherwise?

*Sometimes you have to turn the 'Why me?' around and make something positive out of it. Anything – as long as it's positive.*

The best advice I can give people is to be aware that this could be a long journey. Of course, it depends on the treatment, the type of cancer and so on, but it all takes time – longer for some of us, but it's best not to wallow in that thought. In fact, I'm about to have some tests because I've found a couple of lumpy bits that shouldn't be lumpy. I'm hoping it's something else – anything else. I've been in hospital so many times … so yes, a long, long journey.

I also want to emphasise the importance of hanging on to anyone who's interested – anyone who truly wants to give you support. Take all that support; welcome it with open arms. Don't tell yourself you're fine to do it all on your own – at some stage, you won't be and you'll need some backup.

On that, the support, one of the very best decisions of my entire life was to go down to the lake that day and hop on that dragon boat. I've met the most incredible people – amazing people I wouldn't have met if I hadn't had breast cancer. People from all over Australia and all over the world. I can't imagine life without Dragons Abreast and I really value the support and friendship I've had. Right from the start, I knew you could get on that boat and say anything. You'd sit down and people would say, "How are you?" It didn't matter what you said, people got it – they still do. Then, once you've said it on the boat, you can get off and leave it there. Get on with your day.

Sometimes, I feel like I'm on a train that keeps going round and round the same track – like one of those novelty trains. The scenery is sometimes a bit different but you know it's the same old train. It's the same route and you're thinking, 'I've been here before, let me off.'

I have things I want to get on with. Things other than waiting in doctors' surgeries and the like. Of course, if you think like that all the time, it can get very negative. And where does that get you? By all means get mad, throw a few vases, yell and scream 'I'm sick of this stupid cancer' – but then move on.

There's more to life.

# Bench 7 – Left

Jenny keeps drumming but leans forward slightly. "Keep going," she calls, over the drum beat. "So, who's going to Penrith on the weekend?"

"Me," Janet says. "Woo hoo!"

This is followed by a chorus of 'me' from the majority of us. It's the twenty-fifth anniversary of Dragons Abreast Australia. Racing, dinner and a big cake – a great way to celebrate a great sport.

Events like these are frequent and well attended by breast cancer survivor teams from all over Australia and New Zealand. The Pink Paddle Power regatta in Melbourne. Nipples on Ripples in Hobart. And the big one, the International Breast Cancer Paddler Commission (IBCPC) world events – Canada, Australia, US, Italy, New Zealand, France.

Once every four years, the IBCPC participatory dragon boat regattas draw breast cancer survivor teams from all over the world. You have to be at one of these events to believe the atmosphere of understanding and celebration, as well as the sombre overtones, knowing what breast cancer can do, and does, to people.

"Stop the boat. Stop it hard," yells Lyndall. The boat grinds to a splashy halt.

"Back to the weekend," says Jenny, after waiting out a couple of minutes of reminiscing about the New Zealand regatta – our most recent IBCPC. "Right now, we need to get some race starts and race practice in. Are we ready for this?"

There are a couple of groans but they're in jest. Racing is one of the reasons many of us are here. The adrenaline rush and the sense of achievement are empowering.

"Seven. Seven. Seven. Then thirty at race pace, long and strong," says Jenny. "A few times through, with a stop after each thirty."

Lyndall calls the team to hold the boat. "Hold hard," she says. "In-water start. Are you ready. Attention. Go!"

Kellie Nissen

**Name:** Janet Olsen
**Initial diagnosis:** 2017, ductal carcinoma in situ
**Age at diagnosis:** 54
**Job at diagnosis:** executive assistant
**Job now:** retired
**Joined DAC:** 2017
**Favourite boat position:** sitting down (i.e. not sweeping)
**Memorable DAC moment:** surviving my first regatta one month after my first paddle
**Bucket list – tick:** jumping out of a perfectly good plane at 16,000 feet

# Janet's Story: A Bit of a Detour

*There's no history of breast cancer in our family but those yearly mammograms — they still cause anxiety. You sit there and wonder what's happened; what's changed since the last one? You can't help it.*

I had my first breast check in 2013, after I turned fifty. There seem to be many medical things you suddenly have to do when you turn fifty.

Someone had said to me, not long before, "I can't believe you're fifty and you haven't had a mammogram yet."

I said, "But why? I don't have a history of breast cancer in my family."

I have always had lumpy breasts so that first check was all about capturing a record. A biopsy was performed on some tissue thought to be cancerous. The results came back negative, so that was fine.

My 2015 breast screen came and went with no issues.

Then 2017 rolled around.

I had been feeling a bit tender on the side of my right breast for a while but I nearly didn't mention it at the time of the breast screen. Fortunately, I did.

"I'll check everything out, then," the radiographer said. "We'll do both sides and compare it to the results from your last appointment."

They did another biopsy, too.

Laying on the table, I said, "We're heading off on a cruise next week, for a week."

"We'll make an appointment for when you get back, to go through the results," the nurse said. "Go and enjoy your cruise. Don't worry about anything."

*Well, that's easier said than done.*

Of course, we had fun. We were away with another two couples and we had a good time. I didn't think too much about the results. Why ruin a good holiday? Besides, the nurse had said not to worry.

The appointment was scheduled for Monday morning, 10 o'clock, right before work. I didn't think much of it, dressed for work and off I went to the clinic. My husband Mark came with me.

When we walked into the room, we saw the doctor but there was also a nurse sitting beside her.

"This can't be good," Mark said.

We sat down and the doctor looked at us and said, "I hadn't seen your results before now. So, honestly, I'm not sure what I'm going to tell you."

---

*Before she even mentioned it, we knew.*
*And nothing prepares you.*

---

I was diagnosed with DCIS.

I remember being thankful Mark was there because I shut down. It happens – as soon as you hear the diagnosis. Your brain says, "Oh. Okay." So, I'm not sure, but I think we talked through a couple of things and next thing I knew, the doctor was on the phone to my GP, making an appointment for me to see him as soon as possible.

So, we went from our 10 o'clock appointment to see my GP that afternoon. He started going through the options and talking about different things. And then he said, "I'll give you a referral to a breast surgeon."

He mentioned a couple of names. "This is who I think you could see."

It wasn't like I'd ever sat and researched breast care nurses or doctors because why would you? "I'll go with her," I said when he mentioned the next surgeon's name.

There was so much information to process and I found it overwhelming. It's hard to remember the details.

Anyway, after the GP appointment, we were heading home and Mark asked, "Do you want to go for coffee?"

I looked at him and said, "I'm exhausted. I just want to go home and rest." It's funny to think I was initially planning on going back to work after the appointment.

Once we were home, I lay on the lounge, trying to absorb everything: What's going on? What just happened? Who do I tell? How will I tell my family? All sorts of questions. There was so much emotion and I had to prepare exactly what I was going to say to our kids and my parents.

Once I'd told the family, and started talking about my diagnosis to others, it became a little easier. I had to let people at work know what was happening as I'd need time off for surgery and treatment.

Even though I'd been talking about having surgery, it didn't really sink in until I got a phone call to tell me my surgery date — 3 May 2017 – exactly a month after I'd received my diagnosis. I remember thinking, 'Okay, I've got a date. This is happening. I'll just go with it now.'

I was inundated with information from the day I received my diagnosis. It felt like a real overload so I decided not to read too much straight away. There's a great little kit produced by BCNA which contains all sorts of information and a journal. I found excuses not to read some of it. I told myself I was happy to wait. I wanted to see where I was at, post-surgery, and what the treatment was going to be before I read about every possible scenario.

I flicked through some information but I didn't take in much. It was overwhelming and I kept thinking: 'Oh, my God, I don't know if I need to read all this. Do I need to take in this information if it's not going to apply to me?'

But everyone's different. Some people need to know all the facts; I'm not one of those people.

For me, this is where the breast care nurses were particularly wonderful. They'd say something and, maybe because I hadn't read the information, I'd say, "Okay. And what's that?" And they'd explain it in a way that was easy to understand and only had the information I actually needed.

I kept working right up until the day before my scheduled lumpectomy. Keeping busy.

On the day of surgery, I was supposed to be operated on in the morning but I didn't get in until two-thirty that afternoon because things happen in hospitals and priorities change.

Kellie Nissen

> *I spent the whole morning sitting there in the waiting room, wearing my lovely stockings and dressing gown.*

Mark and our daughter accompanied me for the day. At one stage, they went off to get coffee but I couldn't have anything, of course. "Don't you dare bring coffee back in here," I said.

When surgery time finally arrived, I walked myself into the operating theatre and put myself up on the trolley. I was wheeled into the prep room for the anaesthetic.

The anaesthetist was a beautiful lady. "You're smiling," she said in her German accent. "You're very positive."

I hadn't realised I was smiling.

"This is very good," she said. "Everybody comes in here and they're glum."

I remember asking a couple of the nurses if I could also have a couple of skin tags removed while I was under! Fortunately, I recovered well from the surgery and was allowed to go home the next day.

Prior to my surgery, my surgeon had said she was fairly confident they'd get all the cancer. But you never know, right? And even if she did get it all, I was told that radiation was going to be part of the package. I was okay with that – it is what it is. I was mentally prepared by this stage – surgery, referral to an oncologist, then radiation. I'd done the numbers and figured I'd be finished with treatment around September 2017.

After a lumpectomy, you usually need to wait a few weeks for the results. They have to check they have everything; that you have clear margins. When we went back to see the doctor for the results, I wasn't sure what to expect but she looked at me and said, "I've got it all. There's nothing there. Clear margins."

I felt so lucky. The lump itself had been quite small. Plus, it was in the milk duct so it had been contained. All credit to BreastScreen ACT for even picking it up.

"Everything's good," the doctor said. "However, I'm not sure what to do with you, now."

That was a surprise.

"I've been telling you that radiation is the next step but I don't think you need it. In fact, I don't even think you're going to need medication."

All I could say was, "Oh. Wow! Okay."

"However," she said, "I want to take your results to our group of oncologists and pathologists. I want to make sure that what I'm telling you is right; that I'm not giving you a bum steer."

"Look," I said, "I'll do what I'm told."

We left the office hopeful but not too hopeful – just in case. The following week, we were called back in. She'd had her meeting with her group and they'd discussed my results, offering their recommendation.

---

*"Don't waste her time. She's fine. It will probably take her longer to find a carpark than it will to get the treatment."*

---

That was it!

Mark and I walked out of her surgery. We walked down the corridor, past rooms and offices, then found ourselves in the atrium at the front entrance.

I had to stop.

I turned to Mark. "Oh my God. That's it."

It was all so overwhelming – the relief and the realisation of just how lucky I was. I still get emotional about it now because it's still raw, five-and-a-half years later.

It had been such an emotional roller-coaster. All the 'what ifs' and all the information about possible treatment.

I returned to work ten days after my surgery. I received a call from the surgeon's receptionist. I'll never forget her words:

---

*"We've withdrawn your referral to the oncologist."*

---

I didn't have to do anything else. That was it. I put down the phone. I had to go for a walk out of the office into some fresh air to clear my head. All I could think was, 'What was that all about?'

It was like I'd been on this emotional roller-coaster ride for two or three months, then suddenly been kicked off.

It wasn't how I thought it would end.

So sudden.

I didn't even need medication.

I still have my annual mammogram and ultrasound – that's non-negotiable. Every May.

When I reached my 'five years', my GP said, "You can keep going for these annual checkups for ten years if you want. It's totally up to you. There's no hard and fast rule about how long you want to continue."

"I'll do ten years," I said. It's part of my annual routine now. Off I go, every May – mammogram and ultrasound.

My first twelve-month check-up was pretty hard. They thought they'd found another lump.

I think the lump was at the top of the breast. I sort of knew even though the sonographer didn't say anything – she was looking around on the screen, then she went out and came back a few minutes later. "I'm going to bring someone else in to have a look at the screen," she said.

I lay there thinking, 'Oh, really!' But there's nothing you can do.

The radiologist finally came in. "Nice to meet you," he said. "We need to do a biopsy. We can do it now or you can come back later."

"I'm here," I said. "Let's do it now." I didn't want to muck around.

They'd already brought the trolley in, so they were going to do it anyway. It wasn't really a choice. Then it's the waiting – again – waiting for the results. So, I'm just lying there and thinking, 'Oh man. What now?'

The lump was benign. The biopsy was recorded; they can look back the next time and know it was okay. It had been checked.

Still, each time I go for my annual check-up, I just hope everything will be okay.

I remember when I was first diagnosed, one of my work colleagues said, "I can't do anything for you."

I said, "Yes, you can. Go and get your breasts checked."

My colleague was ten years older than me. "I haven't had a breast check in about fifteen years," she said. So, she went and had herself screened. She got the all-clear.

"Well, there you go," I said. "You've made me happy." She thought she couldn't do anything for me, but she did. And that's part of it – you just don't know. You don't know what's going on inside your body.

I'm lucky, I know that. I'm a good news story.

I know that if it wasn't for BreastScreen ACT being so thorough, noticing something so small and acting on it … well, who knows?

---

*And each appointment is the same.*
*I was lucky that time but what about this time?*
*What if they do find something else?*
*I don't know how I'd react if they came back and didn't say,*
*"You're good to go. See you next year."*

---

Receiving a breast cancer diagnosis was a wake-up call. At the start of 2017, if someone had said to me, "You're going to be diagnosed with cancer, then you're going to get the all-clear and by the end of the year, you'll be retired," I would have laughed at them.

I honestly think if I hadn't had that diagnosis, I'd still be working now. When I did get the all-clear, around June 2017, Mark and I went to the coast. We were sitting there and I thought: 'What am I doing still working?'

It doesn't matter who you are or where you're working – it doesn't count for anything. There's more to life than sitting behind a desk. I loved my job; I loved it till the day I left, but I thought: 'Well, someone else can have it now.'

We wanted to travel. We wanted to do things we'd always dreamed about. Autumn is the best time of the year in Canberra and I'd always wanted to take leave in autumn. I was always saying, "I'm going to take March off one year." Then 2018 rolled around and it's March and I didn't have to apply for leave!

---
*All the stuff I was going to do 'one day' —
now, I can do it. It's a whole different mindset.*
---

One of those things I'd always wanted to do was dragon boating. I'd often see the boats out on the water and think it would be good to have a go one day. It never occurred to me there were 'Come and Try' days. Anyway, I was at Manuka in June 2017 and there were two Dragons Abreast ladies promoting the next 'Come and Try' day, which was to be in September. I took a flyer and stuck it on my fridge. I registered for the Come and Try.

I was hooked!

Everyone was so welcoming. The coach at the time forgot my name and called out, "Come on, chicken legs." I was wearing an Australian cricket hat that had the KFC logo on it. Hence, chicken legs. It was all in good fun.

Dragon boating, or 'paddling' requires strength and technique. I remember thinking I would never make it through a session without having to pull my paddle in.

At the time, 'newbies' had three free sessions, so I did three and then joined DAC. It wasn't until my fourth or fifth time out that I managed to get through a whole session without having to stop and rest.

I did my first regatta soon after joining, and not long after that someone mentioned the team trip to Florence in July 2018 for the big international breast cancer survivors' regatta. "Are you coming?"

As it turned out, Mark and I were in the initial stages of planning a trip to Norway about the same time so we thought, why not go to Italy as well?

So, there I was, with our team, paddling on the Arno River in Florence.

Being with Dragons Abreast Canberra is wonderful. We don't always sit around and talk about cancer — in fact, we rarely do.

However, when the topic comes up, I often stay out of it. My experience was 'straightforward' and I was so lucky in that I didn't have to have medications and ongoing treatments. If some of the ladies happen to be talking about what meds they're taking and the different treatments they are undergoing, it sort of goes over my head because that wasn't my experience. I don't get it. I don't say anything. I just listen because it's not my place to say, "Oh, well, I didn't have that, you know."

It's not a competition!

Everyone has their own experience that's unique to them and should be acknowledged for what it is. Although, sometimes it's hard not to feel guilty when I think about how lucky I was and then hear about what some other women are going through.

Sometimes it's almost like I forget but then I catch a glimpse of my lumpectomy scar in the mirror and think: 'Oh, that's right.' It's a reminder. There are little triggers, too, that bring it all back and suddenly you're in tears and you don't know why.

That scar is a reminder of one thing life threw at me. The roadblock it put up. The detour that I dealt with and got around.

I always try to put a positive spin on things. Life is what you make of it.

Appreciate it. Live it.

# Bench 7 – Right

Seven strokes to get the boat up and moving.
"HUP!"
Seven more strokes, building pace.
"HUP!"
Seven strokes – race pace and power.
"Long and strong. Long and strong. Drive. Reach. Drive."
Continue for twenty.
"Easy."
Jenny checks the speed coach. "Nice," she says. "Catch your breath. And we'll go again."
There are a number of variations on the race start; it varies widely from team to team. It's all about finding one that suits the crew, allowing them to lift the boat and get it moving as efficiently as possible. There have been a few changes to the DAC race start over the years. Different coaches. Different ideas.
"That seven-seven-seven start was a great suggestion, Kathy," Deb says.
From Bench 3, Kathy raises her hand in salute. "You're welcome," she says.
"Let's go again," Jenny calls.

*Bench 7 – Right*

**Name:** Deborah Lopert
**Initial diagnosis:** 2014, ER/PR+
**Age at diagnosis:** 58
**Job at diagnosis:** government lawyer
**Job now:** retired
**Joined DAC:** 2018
**Favourite boat position:** front half – but not the stroke
**Memorable DAC moments:** receiving the Rookie Award with Che in 2019, the first time I competed in a 2 km race
**Little-known fact:** I ran a vegetarian restaurant in Queanbeyan with some friends

Kellie Nissen

## Deb's Story: This Too Will Pass

*I've often wondered about it. I had regular mammograms and then I started taking HRT. Two years later, I had the cancer. I'm not saying that was it; nobody has said it, but I don't know. I really don't know.*

I had no inkling anything was wrong, no family history and no other reason to be concerned.

Every two years, I'd go for my routine mammogram. It was never something I worried about; I never had any sense there was a problem. There was absolutely no reason that this one, in 2014, should be any different.

Two weeks later, they rang me.

"Can you come in again?"

"Ah, there must be a mistake," I said. Years before, I'd been called back – it turned out to just be a lymph node. "It's probably the lymph node again."

"No," they said. "Please come back in."

They were pretty adamant about it so back I went. There was a lot of poking around but nobody could feel anything. Not even the breast care nurse. No lump. Nothing. So, they did another ultrasound.

On that particular day, they had a visiting breast surgeon in. Terrible bedside manner. She walked up, looked at the screen, sort of huffed and said, "I don't like the look of that." I got a glimpse of the image too, and thought I could see something there – a shadow of some sort. Then they did the biopsy and sent me home.

"We'll call you when the results are back," they said.

*I'd more or less worked it out by then, though.*

I was lucky. The day my results came through, I managed to get in to see my GP that afternoon – and she arranged for me to see the surgeon the next morning. I was amazed by the speed of it.

The surgeon took me through my options and what was going to happen. I don't remember much of that consultation; I suspect I was in shock.

At one point, I recall being offered the choice of a mastectomy or a lumpectomy. A choice? I suppose there were pros and cons to this but I thought being asked to choose was a bit silly, especially as I didn't remember her giving me any kind of tips.

In the years since then, many people have told me they had a mastectomy so they didn't have to have radiation. In hindsight, if my surgeon had told me I wouldn't have to have radiation if I chose the mastectomy, I would have gone for the mastectomy.

It was all a bit surreal and confronting. My daughter Natalia was at uni at the time and she was freaked out. I don't blame her. It's scary. Lots of people were freaked out, as it turns out but, right from the start, I realised there was no point in thinking, 'Why me?' That's just hopeless. Instead, I remember thinking, 'Well, this is a bloody nuisance. Let's get it over with.'

---

*I started to think of the situation as similar to having a house with a really bad tenant. I'd be kicking the tenant out with the surgery, and then I'd have to clean everything up – that was the chemo and radiation. I knew it wouldn't be the same house afterwards, but it would still be a good house.*

---

It was quick – being diagnosed, seeing the surgeon, having to make a choice and then two weeks later, I'm scheduled for surgery. At the time, I was happy with the quick turnaround because I thought it would be good to get it all over with.

Friday of the October long weekend is not a good time to be in hospital. There's not a lot of staff; not much support. Everyone's in a hurry to be somewhere else.

At one stage, someone hurried into my room and put a bag next to my bed. "This is from the Breast Cancer Network," she said. Or something like that. She didn't stop and chat, so I had no idea what was in the bag or what anything was for.

When I looked through the bag, there was a little horseshoe-shaped pillow. I had no idea what that was for. Nobody said to me, "You might want to rest your arm on it." There were a lot of pamphlets and other bits and pieces too, but I didn't take much notice after the pillow.

After the surgery, my surgeon came to see me and I'm sure she said she'd only taken three lymph nodes. I was quite happy with that.

They sent me home at the end of the weekend with a drain. After a day or two, I checked the drain bag and thought, 'Oh, how fabulous!' There was nothing coming through the drain so I figured the surgery must have been healing really well.

That wasn't right.

When I eventually had the drain taken out, they discovered it was blocked. The wound leaked for twenty minutes. To top it off, I ended up with a big seroma – a build-up of fluid under my skin – that took ages to go.

Even now, when I have my ultrasounds, someone always comments, "Oh, there's a bit of a fluid collection there."

It's nothing like it was, though. For a long time, it was huge – a massive bulge under my arm. I used to go and get it drained regularly but, of course, it would fill up again.

---

*"Nature abhors a vacuum," someone said to me once.*
*They were certainly right.*

---

Two weeks after the operation, I went back to the surgeon for the post-operative review. Something came up about the number of lymph nodes she'd removed. "Oh no," she said, "I took fifteen." Then she added, "I'm not happy with the margins so I've scheduled you in again for next Tuesday."

This was the first time it dawned on me that I was a little cog in a machine. Nobody cares about you as a person. You're a problem to be solved. Nobody was ever unpleasant or anything but, as the person with the breast cancer, you have no say. You're an anonymous thing to be dealt with. That's what it felt like to me, anyway.

This time – the second operation – it was just day surgery, which was lucky, because two or three days later, I was giving a reading at a friend's wedding. I was so taken up with the surgery that I didn't have time to get nervous. I was the least nervous I've ever been doing public speaking. It was quite a funny poem that I had to read, too.

After the ceremony, there was a reception for everyone and then a whole bunch of us were going to dinner. Between the reception and dinner, I went home to put a great big ice-pack under my arm, it was so sore and swollen. There was no way I was missing the dinner though.

So, that was my introduction to the wonderful world of breast cancer – of course, there was more to come.

When I went to see the oncologist, she started talking about the tumour. "I'm surprised nobody could feel it," she said. "It was a big tumour, around twenty millimetres – and it was a funny shape. It had tendril-like growths."

I had no idea what that meant but it didn't sound good.

"It's borderline whether you need chemo, " she continued, "but if I were you, I'd have it."

That was all I needed to hear. She was, after all, the expert. "I'll do the chemo," I said.

She told me I could start next week or wait for up to twelve weeks.

"No," I said. "Let's get this over with."

She booked me in to have my first chemo the following week.

---

*The first thing I thought about was my hair.*
*'It's going to fall out,' I thought, 'so I'll have it cut short.'*
*And off I went to the hairdresser.*

---

I was on a contract at work at that point, but they were really good about it all. My oncologist had written me a medical certificate, which said something along the lines of: 'She's having this treatment. It may make her feel unwell at times. If she feels unwell, she shouldn't work. If she feels okay, she can work.' It was perfect, and my employers were happy with that.

Every three weeks, on a Wednesday, I'd head off to have my chemo. By the time Thursday and Friday of the following week came around, I'd be feeling pretty awful so I'd take those two days off. Then I'd go back to work for a week-and-a-half, until the next chemo session.

Given that I was on a contract, they were within their rights to terminate it but they didn't. There were only two of us in my section and they got someone else to cover for me on the days I wasn't there. Plus, they showed me how to make the most of my leave so I wasn't too much out of pocket. I felt incredibly supported. There are some horror stories around about the way people are treated, but I wasn't one of them.

In terms of physical effects, my first three rounds of chemo weren't too bad. My hair fell out, but I'd expected that. However, they decided, for whatever reason, not to give me a portacath. I noticed an issue with my veins straight away.

After the first cycle, I said to my oncologist, "Look at this." I showed her my arm.

She shook her head. "We're coming up to Christmas. We can't get a theatre now. Can you persevere?" What choice did I have?

My veins are totally stuffed on that arm now.

My second lot of chemo was the week before Christmas. And then I had my first injection of Neulasta – the white blood cell booster – on Christmas Day. I went in to the clinic and they'd set up a table for their Christmas lunch. I was sitting there, watching them get ready and waiting for my injection.

Normally, my husband Francois and I go to a friend's place for Christmas lunch, but not that year – not with my white blood cell count so low. Instead, I sat at home with my dog watching the *Luther* DVDs a friend of mine had lent me.

My friend makes this fabulous trifle. I love it. I eat trifle once a year and then don't think about it again for the next twelve months. "Bring me back some trifle," I said to Francois when he left.

> *That was my Christmas Day –*
> *the dog, Luther and uneaten trifle.*

I didn't change too much about the way I lived my life. Basically, I did everything I needed or wanted to do, although sometimes I'd be tired. I tried to retain a sense of normal – I'd walk the dog, exercise and socialise – but my immunity was low and I was finding I had to cut back on what I was doing.

The thing is, when you're an extrovert like I am, it's hard to be told not to go out and see people. In hindsight, I suppose it was good practice for the pandemic because people would come rushing up when they saw me and I'd step back – "Have you got a cold? Have you got gastro? No? Let's have a hug then."

Friends would come and visit regularly when I was at home. I had hand sanitiser for them to use at the door before they came in and so on. Now, there are certain hand sanitisers I can't use because the smell reminds me of having chemo; it takes me right back.

Being so susceptible to infections, it seemed like I was always at the doctor. I cut my finger on the cutting edge of the cling wrap box; a tiny nick but my finger blew right up. I kicked my toe against something and it came right up, too. I couldn't get in to see my normal GP that time so I saw another one and he thought I had gangrene. He sent me for blood tests straight away. A day later, this doctor rings me, which I thought was a bit odd. "I've got your blood test results. You've got no immune system," he said. "You can't go out for two weeks or see anyone."

I had two friends visiting me when I got that call – they're both introverts – and I walked out to them and said, "The doctor says I can't see anyone for two weeks. I've got to stay home." They both looked at me and I knew what they were thinking – wow, that would be the best thing anyone ever told us.

It worked out fine in the end because my doctor hadn't realised that the following day I was due for my next Neulasta injection.

In February 2015, we threw this huge birthday party. It was Natalia's twenty-first, Francois' sixtieth, and my mother was turning eighty-seven

– all within two days. We thought we'd have a combined celebration – a 168th birthday party. We'd invited a lot of people – friends from Sydney and all over the place. A lot of people I hadn't seen for a while.

That day, three people cried when they saw me. I was in the middle of chemo and had no hair and I suspect it must have been a shock, but still, you don't want people to cry when they see you. I wanted to say, 'I'm getting on with it guys. It's fine.'

*People's reactions often took me by surprise. When it's you going through it, you're looking out at the world and, basically, the world looks the same – but you don't look the same to other people.*

I suppose the thing was, with the hair loss, I hated the idea of wearing a wig. I didn't even consider getting one. A lot of people had given me cute caps to wear, but I've got a small head so most of those came down well below my eyes. I was left with buying hats in the kids' section unless I wanted to go around bald. I did try a scarf one day. "That just screams cancer," Francois said. He was right.

Eventually, someone gave me a little black-and-white cap; a small flat one that you might see in Morocco or somewhere similar. I wore that; it seemed fine. As far as I was concerned, that was me. Take it or leave it.

People generally wanted to help – like with the hats. I had a friend come down from Queensland to give me a pampering night with lots of nail polish and foot cream and a lovely dinner. People would come and visit or send me little gifts.

A few people wanted to question me about everything. There was no malice or anything like that, but it could be a bit intense. And people would always be trying to give me advice. It's like when you've had a baby and suddenly everyone's an expert.

I'd just smile and say, "Thanks."

Although, some of the advice was a bit wonky. One of my neighbours decided I needed to have a tub of — I don't know what it was – vital greens or something. Yuck.

There was plenty of advice about food and what to eat but I'd pretty much decided I'd eat anything I wanted, in moderation. So, if my body said it wanted Vegemite and banana, that's what I'd give it. Even if it was weird, my body was going to get it.

I was worried about losing my fitness. I had been going to a personal trainer twice a week before the diagnosis and he was an absolute 'suck it up, princess' kind of trainer. There was no slacking off because of the chemo. Too bad.

---

*After a bit of research, I found a trainer who'd had breast cancer herself. She was wonderful. I just adored her. We became close friends. She died of breast cancer in 2018. It was her third time and she'd had enough – refused to have chemo and went down the natural therapy path instead.*

---

The first three cycles of chemo were pretty average; I didn't feel too bad. However, the last three cycles were Docetaxel; they just about did me in. I had a terrible reaction to it, plus, it gave me horrendous fluid retention. I could barely walk and remember begging my GP for diuretics.

"Okay," she said, "take half a one of these."

My sister's a doctor and when I told her what I'd been prescribed, she said, "That's practically homeopathic!" She was right, they didn't do much.

All anybody was interested in was whether I was breathless. I wasn't breathless but I could barely get my trousers on because my legs were so full of fluid.

I tried again, with my oncologist. "Look, I can't walk," I said. "My legs are really slow and heavy. And they're painful."

Finally, my oncologist agreed to give me something. "Take two tablets in the morning and come and see me again next week."

I was six kilos lighter when I went back the following week. "See, see?" I said. I felt a lot better. She agreed that I could keep taking the tablets for a while and it sort of settled down.

The Docetaxel also gave me a terrible rash. I had to take antihistamines a few days before so I ended up with a really badly coated tongue.

"You've got a fungal infection," I was told.

"It's the chemo," I insisted. "I'm not taking anything else."

I got through it, though, and then they wanted to start the radiation treatment. Thank goodness I had a few days off in between the end of chemo and starting radiation – it may have even been a week. Either way, it was so good not to have anything. Not to have to go anywhere.

I was worried about the radiation. Not only because of the radiation itself but because of the parking situation. Anyone who's tried to get a park at Canberra Hospital will understand what I'm talking about. I was trying to juggle work and didn't want to take any extra time than necessary, because radiation is every day.

All throughout my treatment, up to this point, people were always saying, "What can we do?" It was nice and now, I had something for them to do.

"Take me to my radiation appointments," I said. I ended up putting together a roster of people who'd take me to radiation and pick me up afterwards. It was five weeks, four or five days a week, and it was fabulous. It made my life so much easier.

I was lucky with the radiation treatment. I hated it, but I didn't get that extreme fatigue or much skin burning. By that stage, I was ready for it to be over. I'd be on the table ready and looking at the screen above my head where I could see my details and the end date. I was always thinking, 'Oh, come on, come on.'

---

*They used to practically have to hold me on the table because the minute they'd say I was finished for that session, I'd be trying to get off.*

---

I was so happy when I finished. I bought chocolates for the technicians. I bought chocolates for the people at the reception desk. When I finished chemo, I baked a big cake for the staff. I kept saying to people, "Don't take this the wrong way, but I hope I never see you again."

My active treatment finished up during 2015, but it doesn't end there. You still have to see the surgeon. Still have to see the oncologist. Take medication.

The thing I've come to realise is that you've absolutely got to be your own advocate.

I'd been put on hormone blockers – initially for five years. It's not fun. Your hair gets thin. Everything dries up. It's quite shitful. At the end of my five years, I was looking forward to coming off them but my oncologist said, "There's new research that seems to suggest you boost your chances of not having a recurrence if you take the blockers for up to ten years."

All I could think was, 'God, no!' So, I looked at the research. I got advice from my sister and a good friend, both of whom work in the health area and have epidemiology expertise. They agreed with me that the advantage of going an extra five years was small. Sure, it was an advantage, but not much.

I ended up negotiating a drug holiday with my oncologist. If I kept going with the hormone blockers, I could have three months off every year. However, after six years, I told her I wasn't going to take them anymore because I had developed osteoporosis. "I'll come and see you every year," I said, "and I'll keep up the regular mammograms and ultrasounds but I'm not taking the drugs anymore."

And that was it. I was done.

---

*It makes a permanent mark on you, though.*

---

When I had the breast cancer and was going through all the treatment, I wanted nothing to do with any breast cancer charities or associations or groups. I didn't feel the need to have an affiliation just because I had breast cancer. It was important to me not to be engaged in that way or labelled.

Then, at a friend's birthday, I met a lady who started talking about dragon boating. I'd always been interested in dragon boating – even before the cancer – but for some reason, I thought you had to do it kneeling.

"It must be terribly uncomfortable," I said, "kneeling the whole time."

After a moment of confusion, she said, "No, no, you don't do it like that. Come to a 'Come and Try' session."

"Okay," I said. "Why not?"

At the 'Come and Try', I met another lady who I'd known years earlier. We'd been good friends but had sort of drifted apart. It was so good to see her again.

That's the interesting thing about it all. When you get breast cancer, so many people say, "Oh, I've had it," or "my sister had it," or "my mother had it," and you realise, shit, it's everywhere. It's like a silent community. People don't reveal themselves until you're a part of the community.

I remember being on a plane and when we'd landed, I got up and saw another woman who, like me, had her sleeve and gauntlet on. We looked at each other – we didn't know each other at all – and did this funny little high five at each other. Like a secret society.

Lots of things happen that you just need to laugh about.

I was in the US at one point, not long after my treatment had ended but before my hair had grown back properly – it had started growing back but was still really short. I handed over my passport at immigration and the officer looked at it, then looked at me. "Why did y'all cut your hair?"

"Oh, I didn't," I said. "I had cancer. It all fell out. It's coming back, though."

His face dropped. He was speechless. I ended up getting a free pass through security though.

There's a few times when you can pull out the 'cancer card'. Mum sort of did it. She bought me a Thermomix. I'm sure she did this because she thought I wasn't going to be around for very long and when I pulled through she was so happy to have me back. She organised to buy it through my cousin in Melbourne, who was a Thermomix consultant. Apparently, they're strict about the areas they're allowed to sell in, but Mum convinced her to get special permission to sell me one because I was the 'cancer-ridden cousin' or something like that.

Part of the deal with Thermomix is the consultant is supposed to come to your house and show you how to make all sorts of things.

We did it on FaceTime and went through the motions of making something – I have no idea now what it was –thinking 'Oh God, this is the last thing I want in my life right now.' I've still got the Thermomix, though. It's handy for soup.

I never dwell on what things might have been like if I'd done something differently or known something more.

*Life's full of sliding door moments.*

You have to roll with the punches. Make the most of whatever situation you find yourself in. Have a laugh.

I organise brunch once a month with some friends. There's seven of us. We all used to work together and we've been friends for what feels like a hundred years. One day, someone said something about the stats for breast cancer – something like one in seven or eight women get it.

"Well, I've taken one for the team," I said.

# Bench 8 – Left

If adrenaline had an aura, it would be pink. Not just any pink but the strong pink of the lotus flower, resembling enlightenment and resilience.

The sense of satisfaction and determination in the boat keeps the momentum high.

"I love this," Anita says when the boat comes to a stop at the end of the second set. "The racing. Regattas."

"It's hard work though," Sugar says.

"Yeah," Anita replies. "But it's why we're here. And you love it. You know you do."

Sugar nods.

"That was better," Jenny says, her eye on the speed coach – her newest 'toy' for keeping tabs on our speed, stroke rate and power. "But room for improvement. Let's head for the race course. We'll do a full 200 metres this time."

We use the paddle to the race course as an opportunity to catch our breath and loosen our limbs. Not quite a warm-down paddle, but we're in no great hurry to get there either.

"Focus on technique," Jenny calls. "Be your own coach. Pick one thing to work on."

Leg drive. Getting an extra centimetre forward with your blade. Pulling strong. Sitting up. There are a number of areas to focus on.

"The buoys have moved," Lyndall says.

She's right. The starting buoys marking the lanes are not exactly in alignment. Makes actual racing tricky, but training not so much.

Lyndall angles the boat, positioning it in the centre of the lane as best she can with the increasing breeze and the current. She uses the paddlers at the back to move the boat forward a smidge. "Hold. Hold hard," she says. "Hold for drift."

Twenty blades turn in the water so they are now parallel with the side of the boat — hopefully keeping the boat from drifting into the next lane.

"Two hundred metres. Full race," Jenny says. "Gillian, you might want to sit this out. Just enjoy the ride. Your boat, sweep."

Kellie Nissen

**Name:** Anita
**Initial diagnosis:** 2014, HER2+
**Age at diagnosis:** 48
**Job at diagnosis:** senior library technician
**Job now:** aged care
**Joined DAC:** 2015
**Favourite boat position:** close to the front – for a good view
**Best thing about DAC:** the friendships
**Little-known fact:** I love crocodiles

# Anita's Story: But I Don't Have Cancer, Do I?

> *"Look, I'd like to do a biopsy – but I'm eighty per cent sure it's nothing." That was an eighty per cent chance of it not being cancer, which means a twenty per cent chance that it was? Where do they pull these figures from?*

I didn't have a lump.

I'd started having regular mammograms at the age of forty because my maternal aunt died of breast cancer. It didn't put me in the family history category, but I wanted to do it just in case, so my doctor wrote me a letter to allow me to start having them earlier than the recommended norm of fifty.

My first mammogram came back normal.

I had another one around two-and-a-half years later – also fine.

I didn't have another one until I was forty-eight.

I was working at the Australian Catholic University library at the time. All the staff there were women, and one day we were all talking about mammograms, pap smears and the like. I said, "Mine's overdue."

"Go and book one," my boss said. "Just go and book it."

So, I did.

That was the appointment where they wanted to do a biopsy as well – even though they were eighty per cent sure it was nothing.

"We can do it now," the radiologist said, "but you won't be able to play sport for a week."

I deferred the biopsy for three weeks because I was in the women's senior netball team, and I was pretty sure we were going to get into the semi-finals. I wanted to be able to play. The doctor agreed, saying they'd pencil me in for three weeks' time in case I needed it.

> *As it turns out, they did call me in for that biopsy.*

I thought it was going to be a waste of their time because of the eighty per cent comment but when I got there, the doctor must have been able to read my mind because he said, "This isn't a waste of time. We think you need to have it."

It was hideous. I passed out and they had to give me adrenaline.

They sent me home afterwards, saying that they'd let me know the results, which might take up to a week.

While I was waiting, and at every stage of the process thereafter, I had this recurring nightmare. This witch-like figure would appear between my bedroom doorway and the hall and she'd just be dangling there. I can still see her now. It sends shivers up my spine. When she was there, my husband was even scared; sometimes we had to sleep with the lights on.

The morning I went to get the biopsy results, I asked my husband if he wanted to come with me. Normally, I wouldn't have – not to collect results that were probably going to be okay. We sat in the waiting room for ages, watching people walking out with manilla folders packed with information. The nurse came out at one point and said hello but didn't take us in. I thought that was a bit strange – she even looked a bit sheepish. Sort of awkward and uncomfortable.

I turned to my husband. "This doesn't look good, does it?"

It wasn't.

They were waiting for the big guns.

By the time we finally got called in, I was expecting bad news. Although, listening to the doctor, I wasn't sure what was going on. The doctor never said the word cancer. She talked about different things, but nothing that registered with me as cancer. I'd had a lump when I was in my twenties. It was benign and they checked on it every so often and eventually took it out – I assumed this was the same thing.

Then I heard the doctor say the word "invasive".

"What?" I said. "But I don't have cancer, do I?"

"No," she said. "You do."

It was confusing. My husband said later that he realised what was being said but the message didn't sink in with me. I was too shocked.

> *Looking back, I think the first sign that something was wrong was that nightmare. The next sign was when we were sitting in that waiting room — watching people walk in and out. In and out.*

All of this happened in the space of a couple of months in 2014. Mammogram in August, biopsy in September, lumpectomy in October. I had just turned forty-nine.

The surgeon I was referred to didn't have the greatest bedside manner. Everyone's different. He explained the whole lumpectomy procedure to me, including the hook-wire process.

The image that came to mind the minute he said 'hook-wire' was of a dirty, rusting fishing hook. It freaked me out! I was okay with the idea of the operation but the hook-wire idea sounded hideous.

It was.

Basically, they use a local anaesthetic to numb your breast, then use an ultrasound or something similar to insert the wire – which acts as a marker for the surgeon, like a map so he can find the lump.

The procedure took a while and I was standing up most of the time, barefoot and my feet were freezing. I'd asked if my husband could come in with me and ended up sending him to get me some socks.

I also had an MRI with the dye injection into my vein, which provides a clear picture of where the cancer is. I had heard that was a painful procedure.

There were four people in the waiting room about to have the same procedure when I walked out afterwards.. One of the ladies said, "How was it?"

"Actually, not too bad," I said. "Not as bad as I thought."

When I saw her again later – we were in a ward together with the others who were getting lumpectomies or mastectomies – she said, "You lied to me. It was horrible."

After I woke up from the lumpectomy operation, I was lying in the ward waiting for the surgeon to come and see me. He didn't – it was one of his team. A female doctor.

"Looks like you're allergic to nursing tape," she said.

I had a red rash all over my stomach from the tape that held the hook-wires in place.

Then she said, "Look, it was a difficult operation so we'll have to wait and see."

"What do you mean by that?"

---

*Who says that to a person who's just come out from under an anaesthetic?*

---

She didn't give me an answer. "We'll have to wait and see what the results come back with." Then she left.

Two weeks later, I got the call from the surgeon. I knew what was coming because I'd been having that same nightmare again.

"We didn't get clear enough margins," he said. "We're going to have to do a mastectomy."

"Can't you just take out a little more?" I asked.

He told me it wouldn't be aesthetically pleasing. All I could think was — yeah, neither is no breast, mate!

As it was, he'd already removed thirty per cent of my breast and my nipple was facing outwards and although the breast itself was quite perky, it looked hideous. When he said the breast would have to go, I thought, actually I could live with the hideous breast.

Ever since this whole thing started, I'd been researching every step of the way. This time, I'd been looking up reconstructions.

"I'd like to have an immediate reconstruction," I said when we went back to see the surgeon.

He shook his head. "No. It's better to wait for a year."

I couldn't believe it. In America and England, they do reconstructions straight away. From what I'd read, it was standard procedure. Why not here?

I stood my ground. "No, I really want it." I knew my surgeon had plastic surgeons on his team. I knew he could organise it.

Still, he wouldn't commit.

The mastectomy was pencilled in for about six weeks later.

About two weeks before the mastectomy, I was heading to Sydney to see the Rolling Stones in concert. I was really looking forward to it. I still hadn't heard anything about whether or not they were going to do the reconstruction at the same time. I'd pretty much resigned myself to the fact that I'd be living for a year without a breast. Then I got the phone call.

"You'll be having a joint operation," my surgeon's receptionist said. "You'll have the mastectomy and the plastic surgeon will put in an implant."

I was really, really happy! The surgery was booked for 23 December. They told me I would be in hospital for six days.

---

*My breast felt like a melon.*

---

Being in hospital over Christmas, I was pretty sure I'd been forgotten about. I was stuck in the general ward with amputees, stroke patients, people who'd been in accidents – it was a mixed ward, too. The doctors would come in and do the rounds but they skipped over me because I was a 'Plastics patient'. Apparently, 'Plastics' didn't come in every day so it was ages before I saw anyone who was there specifically for me.

The nurses were great, of course. They did all the checks and made sure I was as comfortable as I could be but they didn't have the answers I needed. I felt isolated, forgotten and felt alone.

My new breast was higher up than the other one and I assumed it was swelling. The plastic surgeon said, "No, it's just the implant."

I was thinking, well that's not going to look great, one high and one low. It was like a melon – and that is exactly how the plastic surgeon described it in my consult!

Apart from the size of my breast, another thing that worried me was blood clots. I have something called Factor IV Leiden – it's a gene mutation that can lead to blood clots and DVT. I was paranoid about it. I wouldn't sleep in the bed and spent all my time in the recliner that was next to my bed.

It was such a horrible week. I was too scared to sleep and felt like I wasn't getting the professional medical attention I needed. I had been told about my multidisciplinary medical team – who were they exactly?

When it was time to be discharged, I waited all day for someone to come by and sign the discharge papers. Nobody seemed to know who had to sign them. Was it the surgeon's team – or Plastics? In the end, they said, "Just go home. We'll post the papers out to you." So that's what I did. I received those papers a month later.

Christmas period: try to avoid operations!

On New Year's Eve, the community nurse came around to remove the drains.

The next morning, when I woke up, the wound didn't look right. It was all oozy. My husband was a nurse and he said, "I think we should go to Emergency."

---

*Honestly, I was expecting them to tell me I was fine and send me home, but they didn't. They admitted me – but just to the day stay ward.*

---

I was there for three days.

Public holidays!

Eventually, I was released with intravenous antibiotics. Somebody would come by every day to check it – or we'd go in. It was a busy time of year with staff away.

For the next three weeks I went into the community health centre for my dressing to be changed. As Alan was a nurse, they let him change it every second day so I didn't have to attend the clinic daily. Once a week I would see the Plastics team. Plastics ended up saying that I would need a debridement to make it better.

"You'll go in for day surgery," they said. "We'll open up the wound, flush it out and sew it back up. You'll be fine."

You have to trust the professionals, right?

When I woke up in the recovery room, I had a bad feeling. There was a lovely nurse sitting with me, monitoring me. I said to her, "They've taken out my implant, haven't they?"

She went and got someone from the Plastics team and they said they had no choice, it was never going to heal.

---

*It felt like a slap in the face. I cried for the next five days.*

---

After that I was emotionally low. All the breast care nurses were on Christmas leave but eventually I contacted Bosom Buddies and told them what had happened. They did a ring-around and found someone who supported me over the phone. She did that for quite a while; we even met up a couple of times. Bosom Buddies – they're lifesavers.

At some point in that month prior to the implant being removed I did have a visit with a breast care nurse.

"Did the doctor give you a special bra to keep the implant in place?" she asked.

"No," I said. "Should I have one?" I knew nothing. I'd been given verbal instructions with the post-op dos and don'ts – keep your arm by your side, don't reach for anything overhead and so on – but nothing about a bra. Did that contribute to the implant failing?

After the debridement debacle – as I like to refer to it – I had a post-op appointment with Plastics. Who should walk in but the plastic surgeon who I'd had for the implant surgery.

My husband said, "Are you going to talk to him?"

"I'm not leaving here until I get to talk to him and get some answers as to why it happened."

So, I was called in to see him. His whole team was there.

He was so apologetic. "I'm so sorry, I don't know how this happened to you. It's not your fault. It's not my fault. It's not the breast surgeon's fault."

I stayed silent. What do you say to that? Of course, it wasn't my fault.

He went on. "We can still do a reconstruction. Not the silicon implant though. That won't work for you."

I ended up seeing the plastic surgeon again, about three months later to discuss a reconstruction using my belly fat. The doctor had blood all over his shoes; he'd just come out of a ten-hour operation performing that procedure. As I left his rooms, I decided – nope, not getting that done. A high-risk op, and emotionally I didn't think I could handle it. I ended up having another day procedure with my original breast surgeon to tidy up the excess skin Plastics left behind, then I had it tattooed.

A gorgeous pink lotus surrounded by pink frangipani flowers. When I look in the mirror, I don't see that I'm missing a breast, I see my beautiful tattoo.

Throughout the surgery debacle, I often wondered about other treatment – whether or not I'd need chemotherapy. Luckily, the cancer hadn't been found in my lymph nodes but I still wanted to know – so I asked.

"We may as well get you set up with an oncologist now," my doctor said in response. "We'll do the referral, then the receptionist will give you a call to organise an appointment. You may need to wait a little while."

I waited. No phone calls.

A week, or more, went by and I still hadn't heard anything. Nobody rang me. There were no missed calls or voice messages. I rang the cancer clinic at the hospital but didn't get anywhere. It was like they hadn't heard of me. I had no idea what was going on. Would I need chemo? Radiation? Surgery?

Eventually, I went into the clinic in person. Even then, it took me breaking down in tears before I finally got to see the oncologist.

Way too late, as it turned out.

Sitting in his rooms, my oncologist's registrar was talking to us, but the words were like background noise – a hum. He said something about a six-week window and how that was gone. I don't know. I didn't get it. They'd been crunching numbers to see if I still needed chemo or not.

Then the registrar turned to me. "With the numbers, I think chemotherapy will be the recommendation."

I heard those words loud and clear. Apparently, chemo would only improve my chance of not having a recurrence by some miniscule per cent. I can't remember exactly what it was but it seemed barely worth it.

Bench 8 – Left

He stared at me for a moment. Like I'd said something, although I was sure I hadn't. "I'll just confirm," he said. "Give me a moment."

I turned to my husband once the registrar left the room. "I'm not doing it. That's ridiculous. I'm not going through chemo for that tiny improvement to my risk factor."

We sat in silence until the door opened again. This time, it was the oncologist. He sat down and smiled. "I don't think you'll need chemo."

Woo hoo!

"Great," I said. I wasn't going to have it anyway but that wasn't the point. I wasn't entirely off the hook though.

"You'll need monthly Zoladex injections and oral meds," the oncologist said.

For some reason, I was under the impression the injections were only for one year, but they went on for four years. They were okay, done at the Canberra Region Cancer Centre, but I thought it was a waste of nursing and medical resources and felt I didn't need them.

I wouldn't wish cancer on anyone. It was a hideous and consuming experience.

---

*Never once, though, did I think I was going to die.*

---

The thought of dying didn't really cross my mind. I was scared, but that was more about the operations and not knowing what was coming next.

Even though I didn't feel heard or seen by some of the medical professionals, my family and friends were there for me and helped me get through. My family was my rock.

And – dragon boating.

It's funny. I'd never even heard of dragon boating before I was going through the little goodie bag they give you in the hospital before surgery. The bag is full of all sorts of information and other things, and there was a brochure about Dragons Abreast Canberra. I remember looking at it and thinking there'd be nothing worse than hanging around with a bunch of people who'd also had breast cancer.

Then, after my implant failed, I had second thoughts. Being with other people who 'got it' might actually be good. So, as soon as I was able, I went along.

I loved it. I'm still doing it.

All that treatment – the operations, the stress, my emotions – it takes a toll on your mind and body.

Everyone reacts differently.

Everyone has a different experience.

Ultimately, you need to look after yourself.

I've moved on from breast cancer. My life doesn't revolve around that illness now. My life is about me.

# Bench 8 – Right

The team knows that, at any time, we can pull our paddle in if necessary. Even in a race. We're reminded constantly, by both coaches, that safety and preventing injury trump everything.

It's one thing to know this, and something else entirely to enact it – especially in the middle of a race, training or otherwise.

The call of the sweep, the thump of the drum and the bellow of the drummer are all there to drown out the voice in your head that says it's too far, too hard or too fast. The voice that says you can't.

"Nearly there," Jenny yells.

Lyndall calls for a lift and everyone digs in deeper. More power.

"Bring it home," they both yell. "Go. Go. Go. Go."

Jenny raises her hand. The dragon head has passed the finish line.

"Easy," Lyndall calls. "Let her run."

A cheer goes up from the back of the boat. Gillian. "Woo hoo. What a ride!"

Red faces. Deep breaths. Pounding hearts. Splashing water. We congratulate each other on a job well done. Support. Companionship. Teamwork.

Sugar turns to Anita. "I did it!"

"And?" Anita says.

"It was awesome!"

**Name:** Sugar Masangcay
**Initial diagnosis:** 2019, HER2+
**Age at diagnosis:** 38
**Job at diagnosis:** stay-at-home mum
**Job now:** administrative officer
**Joined DAC:** 2020
**Favourite boat position:** pacer – but usually put at the back
**Most memorable DAC moment:** competing in my first 2 km race without stopping. I was overwhelmed with joy – and annoyance that it took breast cancer to make me do this. My eyes welled up as we paddled back to shore
**Little-known fact:** I'm from the Philippines but I'm of Japanese and Spanish descent

## Sugar's Story: An Awakening

> *We kind of ignored it at first, I guess.*
> *Just tried to forget about it …*
> *until the lump didn't go away like everyone expected.*

It was April 2019.

My second son, Kaleb, was about eight months old. I was breastfeeding him when I felt the lump.

We'd had such a lovely day the day before. A good friend had gotten married; we'd had a beautiful night and were sleeping in, lounging around in bed. I felt happy and loved. It was perfect.

My husband Kai was next to me and I got him to feel the lump too. I'd had mastitis – I was used to it. It's not pleasant, but for us it was 'normal'; we agreed it must be a mastitis lump. Deep inside, I knew there was something wrong but I tried to shrug it off.

That week it was the Easter weekend and we'd planned to go away. Kai suggested I go to see the doctor first but I said, "It's just mastitis again. I'll see the doctor when we get back."

We had a nice weekend away with our boys, and when we got back I went to see my doctor.

"It's probably just milk," the doctor said, "but go and get an ultrasound to be sure."

I had the ultrasound and, even there, they were reassuring. "It's probably nothing. You're breastfeeding; it could go away." They also said they didn't want to do a biopsy at that moment because it would put me at risk of more problems.

The lump didn't go away.

Another ultrasound was booked and then they were saying the lump was growing. Fast. But still, they assured me it was nothing to be worried about.

By this point, Kaleb was about to turn one and Keiran, my older boy, was turning three. It had been nearly four months since I first found the lump. My doctor suggested I start weaning Kaleb off breastfeeding and then they'd test again.

I was sent for a biopsy on 24 July. Three days later, I saw I'd had three missed calls – all in the afternoon. I called back. It was the clinic. They asked me to come in to see the doctor and booked me an appointment for Saturday.

The poor doctor we saw was not my doctor – the one who'd requested the biopsy – so he didn't know me, didn't know my background and had to give me the information factually.

---

*The word 'carcinoma' was all I really heard.*
*English is not my first language*
*but I knew this wasn't a good word.*

---

I felt bad for this doctor. I wasn't his patient but he had to give me the news. He did his best to refer me to specialists; he organised the referral in a timely manner.

Because it was a Saturday, my family was with me. Kai had dropped me off to go into the clinic and then went with the boys, to look for parking. My family came into the consultation room later. When they walked in, I was already crying so Keiran and Kaleb started crying too. Kai had a lot of questions but he stayed quiet. He walked us outside and we sat on a bench next to a playground so the boys could play while I processed everything.

Keiran and Kaleb had no idea what was going on, they were too little. It was such a gloomy afternoon. I'll never forget that day – 27 July 2019.

Sitting in the park, the first thing that came to mind, was that I'd already scheduled a trip to the Philippines for the end of the year. I'd already booked it. I needed to go, no matter what. The tickets were non-refundable.

The problem was that I hadn't sorted our insurance. A voice in my mind said, 'Maybe I'll get the insurance now and pretend I didn't know I had a terminal illness. Then I can move the dates if I have to, or cancel it and claim the money back.' That's where my mind was at.

Of course, I didn't do that.

Then, out of the blue, I was watching my boys playing and that same voice said, 'No. I can't die. I just can't.' Keiran and Kaleb were my driving force. I didn't have the option of giving up or looking for alternative types of treatment. 'Just go with the science,' my inner voice said. 'Surrender to the people who've studied this.'

Once I'd had that thought, other questions came flooding into my mind.

---

*The main question I was asking, though, was not 'Why me?' it was 'Why now?'*

---

I had one child who could barely walk and a three-year-old who very much needed his mummy. I had no idea how I was going to do this. I was barely sleeping enough as it was, let alone having to deal with all the treatments and their side effects.

It was a strong reminder of the need to look after myself. To do the treatment and listen to my body.

So that was Saturday, and then on Sunday, I first tried to call my mother-in-law because she's a GP. They were at church, so I spoke to my friend who's a nurse.

"I have this invasive carcinoma," I said. And blah, blah, blah – I was trying to make it a bit of a joke; lighten it up because my friend is Filipino as well and that's what we do.

"Are you okay?" she said.

"I've got this," I replied.

"You'll be alright," she said. "You'll be alright."

My friend was on her way to Sydney at the time so we were doing a video call and all I could see was her lipstick. I noticed it because she didn't normally wear lipstick.

"Oh," I said, "this is a good day for you. You're going out; having a day off?" She was a mum with young kids, too.

For me, this conversation was important because it lessened the burden of all the emotion I was feeling inside – before I could tell my own family.

That was going to be the hard part because I knew they would be worried and that I would then be overwhelmed with worry for them. I felt like I wouldn't be able to handle any more worries.

First, I spoke to Kai's family because they're in Australia.

When I spoke to my mother-in-law, she said, "Okay, I'll come to your appointments." She also explained things that she could do or help with, because she was in the medical profession.

So, that was my Sunday – trying to tell people.

I did send a message to my family in the Philippines – but not my mum.

"This is what's happening," I said to my sister. "Don't tell anyone yet."

The next day, Monday, the boys were having a nap and Kai and I lay on the floor and cried.

We cried the whole afternoon.

Then, we spoke to Kai's nana.

"It's not a death penalty," Nana said.

"I know, I know," I said. "It's just not timely. But we'll get there."

---

*When do you choose to get sick? It's never timely, is it?*
*I had to keep reminding myself – I can't die. I can't die.*

---

I also saw my doctor on the Monday. He referred me to a different surgeon to the one on my original referral and I was booked in to see him on the Thursday.

In the meantime, I had playgroup with the kids. Kai was going to take the week off, but I told him I was fine and he should go to work. "I'm not dying just yet," I said. I wanted things to be normal for a while before they started getting crazy.

When we got to the playgroup, I saw all the mums who'd become my friends. I stood at the door and blurted out, "I don't know how to say this, but I've found out that I've got cancer."

They were all shocked, of course. Everyone was saying, "I'm so sorry," and things like that.

I told them I was okay and, after a while, we carried on like we normally would at playgroup. I felt like I'd released something that I was hiding; something that was bothering me. It helped me, knowing that other people knew.

The waiting game was agonising – waiting to see the surgeon and not knowing anything.

I had heard of this surgeon because my friend had seen him earlier that year, when she'd had cancer. She didn't stay with him, though, because she didn't like his bedside manner. "He's an excellent surgeon," she said to me, "but I needed someone who was willing to talk more."

I didn't mind. I needed someone who was factual. I was open to the harshness because I just wanted to know and I needed to trust as well.

It's sort of lucky that I did feel that way because when I did finally see him on the Thursday, the three words I remember him saying were 'big', 'bad' and 'aggressive'. He didn't say them in the same sentence but those are the words I remember. All I wanted to know was my probability of surviving, but he couldn't tell me that.

What I understood, however, was that because it was big, my surgeon needed the cancer to shrink before he could operate. So, he referred me to the oncologist and managed to get me an appointment for the next day. I guess that was because of the 'bad' and 'aggressive' nature of my cancer.

Kai wanted to know more. I was satisfied – okay, he can't operate and needs the cancer to shrink. That was enough for me but Kai had questions. He wanted to know probabilities and chances and to understand the medical words.

---

*Even as my surgeon was standing and showing us to the door already, my husband didn't have all the information he wanted and was still talking. In my mind, though, I was already on my way to my next appointment.*

---

My mother-in-law flew in from Melbourne the day of my oncology appointment, just to sit with us in the consultation room.

There was a lot of information. The only thing I knew about chemo was that you lose your hair. I didn't know anything else so when the oncologist started talking about this 'cold cap' that I could wear that would help me keep my hair, I was surprised. "I'm fine with losing my hair," I said.

I didn't say much else. Kai and my mother-in-law asked all the questions. Kai was worried about other things, more important than hair. And my mother-in-law was asking about the technicalities of the procedure and stuff like that.

I sat there and waited for what was coming next.

If I'm honest, I was probably thinking about what I was going to do for dinner that night. About all the laundry that needed to be done. What we could do with the boys this weekend – everyday things.

I was also wondering where I was going to squeeze in the time for treatment.

One of the biggest concerns was cost. Thankfully, the oncologist was reassuring about it all. A lot of breast cancer treatment is covered on the PBS and Medicare. I also remember telling my husband something like, "Don't worry about the money. I don't want to feel sick and poor at the same time."

It was true. I wanted to focus on getting better, not worrying about the money.

I kept telling myself, 'I'll get there. I'll get there. I'll come out of it.'

The two or three weeks after seeing the oncologist were a blur of appointments and everyday tasks. Drop off the kids, get a biopsy, go and do the grocery shopping, get a blood test …

In among the routine, I found time to get my hair cut to prepare for it falling out. I also decided to buy the new furniture we'd been needing for a while. So, off we went to Ikea. I wanted a lounge that had a chaise so I could lie in the living room with my kids.

When we found what we wanted, the lady asked, "When do you want this delivered?"

I said, "I'm going to be having treatment soon so can you schedule something around that?" Even then, I was still focused on organising the household. It was how I coped.

Then, all of a sudden, it was chemo time.

We were well into winter by this stage. I always get sick during the flu season so, naturally, the day I was due to start chemo, I had all these flu symptoms – sore throat, aching and so on. But I still had to go through chemo. It wasn't the best timing.

My father-in-law came to help us during the first chemo round.

Apparently, what usually happens is that people have their chemo and are good for a few days until it starts to take effect. That's what I was expecting, but I got those awful effects two hours later.

Luckily, I'd done a bulk cook and had already prepared meals for the family. My father-in-law was a great help but he doesn't know how to cook and I needed to make sure my boys were fed.

Another thing I'd prepared was a walkie-talkie. I had one in the bedroom and the other in the kitchen. It was so handy because I needed to use it straight away as I had no energy at all. I'd be in the bedroom and pick up the walkie-talkie and say, "I need some water."

---

*The walkie-talkie was kind of fun for the kids.*
*I was trying to make it all into a game for*
*them but still keep things as normal as possible.*

---

We had a lot of help from our neighbours, the mums in my playgroup and the Filipino community. Receiving that Filipino comfort food was wonderful. We didn't have enough space in our freezer or fridge so I ended up scheduling people on a roster. I was still doing the organising, even from my bed.

After my first chemo, everything settled into a sort-of-normal routine. Tuesday was my chemo day and Wednesday was playgroup. I'd take the boys to playgroup but would get really tired, so when I got home, my father-in-law took the kids.

The thing was, I didn't realise I'd been risking getting even more sick by trying to do everything I usually did. I'd be okay for one day, but for the following four days I was not myself at all. I was sick and weak; like I was drugged. Sometimes, people didn't recognise me – like my own doctor.

But I kept going.

I'd go for coffee with my friends and kept my 'social calendar' active.

My birthday was coming up, on 27 August. I thought it was great because it wasn't a chemo day so I could enjoy the day. It also happened to be the day my kids were at daycare.

On the morning of my birthday, I dropped them off, went to church and then had lunch. My family had given me a massage voucher, so after lunch I had a two-hour massage.

In the afternoon, I'd invited my friends who were moving back to Canberra from Sydney to my house. I'd said, "Can you come to my house today? It's my birthday and my father-in-law will have a cake ready." I asked my friends if they could pick me up from my massage.

When I got in the car, they looked at me. I said, "FYI, I've got cancer."

They didn't know. It was a surprise to them – a shocking one.

My birthday was a small celebration at my house. I'd had such a wonderful day, but around nine o'clock that night, I started to shiver – even though it wasn't cold inside.

I remember being told that when you're in the middle of chemo treatment, if you have a temperature you must go straight to Emergency. I didn't have a fever; I had the chills. I couldn't stop shaking.

"I think we have to go to Emergency," Kai said.

We arrived not long before midnight and within fifteen minutes, I was covered in tubes. Always trying to make light of things, I said to Kai, "They have good service here. Look, I have special treatment – I have my own private room." I was in the isolation room to stop me from picking up every infection in the hospital.

In reality, it was serious. I had UTI symptoms. I was coughing and couldn't stop. My body was so beaten up. To add to this, I wasn't able to sleep because the nurses had to keep coming in to check on me, poke me with things and take my temperature. And my 'special' room was like a freezer. It had to be that way to keep all the germs out because I couldn't risk getting sick; I was completely immunocompromised. Anyone who came in had to be in full personal protective equipment (PPE). It was full on.

---

*Later that night, they found out I had pneumonia.*

---

I was scheduled for an X-ray first thing in the morning.

Of course, I was starving but I wasn't allowed to have anything to eat before the X-ray. I was tired. I felt sick. And I was hungry. All I wanted to do was eat rice. In the Philippines, this is what we eat when we're sick.

"We'll try and find you some plain sandwiches for after your X-ray," one of the nurses said to me. It made me cry more. I wanted rice, not sandwiches. "We don't have any rice," the nurse said. She was so apologetic.

I was desperate. I ended up calling a good friend of mine who owns a restaurant. It was early in the morning but I knew she'd be awake. She couldn't come until after seven o'clock because she had to prepare her daughter for school but she came. I was crying. I couldn't stop.

Even when they came to take me to the X-ray, I was sobbing. The guy wheeling my trolley said, "Are you okay?"

"I'm hungry," I said. Being in hospital was like the little cherry on top of the last few weeks; feeling sick, not being able to eat much. I needed something comforting and familiar.

Anyway, my friend came. She had rice and she'd also cooked me some scrambled eggs. It was so simple, but when something is made with love and care, it's very special. I could only eat a couple of tablespoons at a time. My friend spoon-fed me. She'd feed me one tablespoon and then we'd chat for a bit. Then she'd feed me another. She stayed with me for a couple of hours in that cold room. Her kindness is something I'll never forget.

I had neutropenia – a very low white blood cell count.

It's quite common with people who are having chemotherapy but my ability to fight off infections was particularly bad. The doctor told me I had to be more careful from that point on. They were even saying things like, 'wear a mask at home' and 'avoid your kids as much as possible'. It was funny. How do you avoid your kids when they're so little and all they want is a cuddle from mummy?

My oncologist was more realistic. "There's nothing you can do. Even if you live on your own, you're going to get sick at some point."

I found it hard to put good nourishment into my body. I just wanted comfort food. My life then was all about finding happiness through food or 'finding my way' through food. It became quite costly, especially when we ate out because I could only handle a couple of tablespoons of food. But I wanted to try. I needed to know my taste buds were still there and I could remember what food tasted like.

It felt like my tongue was damaged. I was always parched too, but couldn't even enjoy water. It didn't taste nice. I'd have a variety of things to try. I'd drink coconut water. Soft drinks were tolerable. I don't normally drink soft drinks but their fizziness sort of helped. I even braved the drive-thru (for the first time) to get a milkshake at McDonald's. The drive-thru scared me a little – what if I scratched the car or the person couldn't understand me because of my accent or because I was wearing a mask? But I did it because I was that thirsty and so hoping a milkshake would help.

> *My boys knew what was going on.*
> *They would say, "Mummy's sick".*
> *But they didn't understand why I was sick for so long.*

It was hard when they couldn't come and visit me in the hospital. And when I couldn't play with them as much or go for walks outside. Kaleb was getting really confident with his walking and he wanted me to walk everywhere with him.

We had video calls, and because their granddad was with us, it was a novelty for them and they weren't so focused on missing me.

Both the boys, but particularly Keiran, seemed to realise that if I was in bed, I was really tired and sick. They would come in with water for me and then stay and rub lotion on me.

After a while, I'd move out into the living room and cover myself with a blanket. I liked being there with them. I'd try to play when I could – you still have to be a mum, even when you're sick.

Once I started feeling a bit better, I was able to cook again. Keiran had grown up seeing me in the kitchen, making food, so when I was back there, he seemed so content. He stopped asking for attention all the time. He'd watch me cook. I guess he might have been tired of eating frozen meals.

I finished chemo on 9 December so we were able to go to the Philippines as I'd planned, although we had to come back sooner than I'd hoped because of my surgery. It was booked for late January.

While we were away, Mt Taal in the Philippines erupted and we became concerned we wouldn't be able to get back to Australia because of flights being affected. So, we made the decision to come back even earlier. Back in Australia, there was chaos with the bushfires. Because of all the smoke, even though I was staying inside, I ended up with a throat and chest infection – which meant my surgery had to be postponed.

The smoke from the fires was particularly bad in Canberra and my throat infection wasn't clearing. I was determined not to postpone the surgery any further because I'd already prepared myself mentally so I was drinking lots of honey lemon tea. At least I'd be hydrated.

I had my surgery on 14 February. It was hard on Kai because it outshone his fortieth birthday on 15 February. We had his birthday in my hospital room. A little cake and just us.

It's the timing again! Always the timing.

On a positive note, the surgery went well. When I was in recovery, I could half hear Kai talking to the nurse who was looking after me. "Oh, you're Filipino," he said. "My wife is Filipino." I could hear them but couldn't open my eyes.

I was really groggy but I remember being told, "If you feel pain, click this." I did exactly what I was told – click, click, click. I loved those drugs. I'd sleep, wake up, click and sleep some more. It was like a reward for me after the last year.

> *Six weeks after my surgery, I was booked to start radiotherapy. Of course, Covid had arrived in Australia by then. I was finally rid of the drain from the surgery and I wasn't allowed to go out anywhere – except to radiotherapy.*

Timing, again.

Lockdown was hard. It was hard for everyone. I'd already been in isolation, but now everyone was. When the news came through about the lockdown, I was at a playgroup with the boys. On the way home, I'd planned to go to the shops, but after the lockdown announcement, it was crazy. People were everywhere. The car parks were full and cars were parked on the grass. It was stressful. We had to go home with no groceries.

With the radiotherapy, I supposed I was at least able to go out every day. For six weeks. Many people tell me now how hard radiotherapy was for them. Driving to and from the hospital every day, trying to find a park. For me, there was no traffic. It was easy to find a park at the hospital.

I was so used to the routine that one day – a day I didn't have to go – I got in the car and went to the hospital. It wasn't until I arrived that I realised and thought, 'Why am I here?' But it was an outing.

When I think about it, that lockdown was a blessing for me. My brain was still foggy and I was still feeling really weak. The lockdown forced me to slow down. There were no demands of going out, attending birthday parties on the weekends or catching up with people. We were also able to access free daycare for the boys, because my radiotherapy appointments were considered essential. For them it was good to have the routine; for me it forced me to give myself time to heal properly.

At the end of my radiotherapy treatment, the nurses said, "Ring the bell." Everyone clapped. Yay, it's finished.

> *But I felt empty.*

I was used to the routine. I had some purpose each day; somewhere to go. Then suddenly, it's gone. The free childcare finished, too. I loved having the boys back with me during the day but at the same time, I was still healing. And my emotions were all over the place.

It was probably the lowest I'd felt since I was diagnosed.

My hormone treatment started right then too. Tamoxifen. It was bad timing. The medication affected my brain and my mindset. The first day I had the treatment, I felt so sad afterwards. I was awake, crying, at 2 am. The following day, I woke up crying at 4 am. It grew worse. I couldn't sleep.

And I was so cranky. I was always in pain. At night, after a day of looking after my boys, my joints were terrible. At night, when I needed to rest, I was in so much pain, I couldn't sleep. I'd get up the next morning and take them to daycare. I was cranky at myself for sending them away so I could have a rest. But they were kids; of course, they'd push my buttons.

I'd have these outbursts; the boys were only little but I wanted them to grow up. Have their own life. It was a difficult time for our family. Our relationship was really challenged. I tried to manage it myself. If I felt uptight, I'd go for a walk for an hour or so. I'd feel a little better after the exercise but not for long. I still felt sad, ninety per cent of the day.

Eventually, I went to my doctor, crying. I felt it was the medication that was making me depressed. Explosions of crankiness weren't me; no matter what happened in my life, I'd always been strong and happy. "I'm not me," I said. "I went through chemo and I was still smiling and laughing – that's me. This one little tablet is killing me emotionally."

If I'd lived alone, I believed I would have been able to handle it. I told the oncologist that. "But I have a family to think about," I said. "Do I really need to be on this medication – for five years?"

My oncologist listened. I was taken off the hormone treatment, but I will be regularly monitored for any signs of recurrence.

---

*I was off the medication but the effects lingered longer.*

It was around the same time that I saw a brochure at the hospital for dragon boating – Dragons Abreast were planning a 'Come and Try' day but not until July at least. It was too long to wait; I was desperate for some exercise to help with my depression. I contacted the coordinator of the team and she said I could come on a Wednesday, which was a social paddle, so it was a little easier than normal training. It was my own 'Come and Try'.

I forced myself to go, apparently the weather that day wasn't good for paddling so it ended up being cancelled. I did meet a couple of the ladies though. That was good.

I contacted the coordinator again and I was invited to go on a Saturday. It was nice because everyone was just coming out of lockdown and starting more gently than their normal routine.

I loved it.

Every time I went out, I could feel the endorphins afterwards. I was still coming off the hormone medication at that time and I really noticed how happy I felt after paddling. My elevated mood wouldn't last long, but it helped.

At first, though, I admit I considered not going back. I was so sore. I'd never done exercise like this before and my body wasn't used to it. The coordinator emailed me: *It takes a couple of weeks or so before your body will bounce back,* she wrote. *So keep coming.*

I'm glad I listened.

I'd spent so long worrying about other people and trying to be everything for everyone ... dragon boating was my chance to do something for me. It was refreshing.

I would describe my entire experience with breast cancer as an awakening. I'd forgotten about myself and breast cancer forced me to see myself again. It forced me to accept my limitations and work within my capabilities. I am usually easily content with what I have in my life, but this experience made me accept me – as a whole person.

Most of all, I think it made me realise that I can't be there for everyone if I'm not there for myself.

You can't give love if you don't have enough for yourself.

# Bench 9 – Left

Twenty-two women catching their breath after race practice is quite the sound – but we're all pleased. That race felt good.

Jenny confirms it. "Good race. Great timing everyone. Only the tiniest dip in the middle but you all responded well to the lift."

"Yay us," Natalie cheers.

Drink bottles rattle and we all sit silently, getting our breath back. Waiting to hear what's next.

"We swapping, Nat?" Lyndall asks.

"You bet," Nat says.

Paddles sit flat on the water, steadying the boat while Nat swaps from Bench 9 to take Lyndall's position up the back as our sweep. It's quite the manoeuvre – a full boat, in the middle of the lake, not much room – but they do it in style.

"How do you not fall in?" Gillian asks.

"Been there. Done that." Nat laughs. "Sort of goes with the territory. Living dangerously." She laughs again, her bright upbeat voice sailing down the length of the boat, making every one of us smile.

Kellie Nissen

**Name:** Natalie

**Initial diagnosis:** 2016, ER/PR positive, but HER2 joined the party during chemo

**Further diagnosis:** 2018, metastatic

**Age at diagnosis:** 47

**Job at diagnosis:** psychologist

**Job now:** counsellor and health coach

**Joined DAC:** 2017

**Favourite boat position:** sweep or paddler

**Most memorable DAC moment:** the oar sweeping ME off the boat when I was learning how to sweep

**What I've learned:** how to really love life

## Nat's Story: If You Didn't Laugh, You'd Cry

*After I turned forty-seven, I decided that I was going to have to do something about my cysty boobs because they were starting to hurt. At the doctor's, I went through my usual laundry list of issues and completely forgot to talk about my sore boobs. And then I went off to Bali.*

I've had cysty boobs ever since I was in my thirties. At thirty-five, the doctor sent me for an ultrasound, to reassure everyone they were just cysty, dense boobs. And that's what they were but still, over the years, I was a good girl and went to the doctor every couple of years to do our girly checks.

We'd check boobs and we'd check bloods and we'd check all the things.

I'd say, "Oh, it's a bit lumpy and sore here."

"Ah, that's just your cysty boobs," she'd say.

This continued throughout my early forties – but by the time I was forty-six, those cysty boobs were painful and it felt like one of the cysts was quite large. So, I went back to the doctor.

"You know," I said, "it's feeling a bit sore."

"No, no," she said, having a bit of a feel, "it's just the cysts."

Anyway, around that point I started getting crankier because they were so painful. It was across the Christmas period, around the time I turned forty-seven that I decided to do something and made another appointment to see my doctor.

Going to the doctor, for me, always involved a long list of things to discuss because of my various other health issues. The painful boobs were firmly on that list but, I don't know what happened – maybe my head was full of my upcoming trip to Bali – but I walked out of the appointment having mentioned everything on my list except the boobs!

I tried to put it to the back of my mind to enjoy my time in Bali and, as it happens, while I was there, one of the ladies in my group started talking about her breast cancer and how she'd had a lumpectomy and whatever. That piqued my interest.

"Can you notice where I had it?" she asked.

"No, I can't notice it at all," I said.

Later, I was standing under the shower and having to put a washcloth over my breast because it was a powerful shower and was causing quite a bit of pain. I thought: 'My doctor is never going to do something about these cysty boobs.' So, when I returned home, I made an appointment with a different doctor at the surgery.

I said to her, "We need to do something about these cysty boobs. I can't bear this anymore. There must be something we can do. This is painful."

By that stage, I'd noticed that my nipple was starting to invert. I said this to the doctor. "And now my breast is starting to swell, and there's this massive lump here. You know, I'm just done with it."

Her eyes popped open. "Oh my, you need a mammogram, an ultrasound and a biopsy."

I was horrified. "I what? A mammogram? You want to squash this in between a couple of plastic things. You're kidding – I can't even let the shower run on it."

She was very matter-of-fact. "Well, you're going to have to." She gave me the referral sheet. "Make an appointment. Make it this week."

She even ran out to the car park after me and said, "I'm serious. Make sure you make that appointment. Don't ignore this." She knew.

For some reason, the first centre on the list couldn't do it. So, the doctor made the appointment for me with someone else, and made sure I got in within the week.

They rang me later to confirm. "You're booked in for a mammogram, an ultrasound and a biopsy. You're happy with that?"

I said, "Well, that's what the doctor ordered."

"There'll be a separate charge for each of those procedures, even if we don't have to go through to a biopsy."

That surprised me. "Oh? How much are they?"

When I found out how much I'd be up for, I told them not book in a biopsy straight away.

*As it turned out, I did have the biopsy — six of them.
And they found two tumours.*

I saw the blood flow.

"Cysts don't normally get blood flow, do they?" I said to the radiologist.

"No. But cancerous tumours do. We're going to get as many biopsies of that as we can, and then we'll see what the surgeon would like to do," he replied.

I went home after this, still telling myself they wouldn't know for sure until they tested the cells. I even said that to my kids when I told them that night. "Well, you know, I had this thing and it doesn't look good. But we'll wait and see." They were upset, of course, but we all had to wait.

I got the call the next morning.

"I'm just calling to confirm that the cells have all tested positive," he said. "I've done a report and I'll send it through to you ..." Blah, blah, blah.

All I could think was: Oh, shit. Let the journey begin.

Both my daughters were at home — Courtney was at university and Matilda was just finishing Year 12 — and my son Wesley, who was in Year 10, had headed to school just before the phone rang.

Courtney vomited when I told her. It was pretty horrible. I had to leave them there because I went straight up to the school and got Wesley pulled out of class. I told him right there because I knew he needed to know. I sat with him in a room and we both cried. Initially he was angry with me, for not telling him. I had gone straight to him. He was just scared.

When I got the report from the radiologist, I noticed that he'd named the wrong breast throughout the report. It was my left breast but the report said it was my right breast. I rang him and said, "You've got to change this. I don't want anyone confused about which breast it is."

In the end, I don't think there was much confusion but I was particular about it. I reminded everybody. "Now it does say there that it's the left, doesn't it?" I double-checked everything – my health, my life. And it's their job and we all know that in our jobs, sometimes, we're not as focused as we could or should be. I think I was made more aware of this from the word go when the radiologist mixed up the right and left.

*I was like, wow, man!*
*You've got to get fundamental things like this right.*

He was actually very good, despite this.

The real fun began when my doctor rang me – she'd received the report at the same time I did. Two tumours. I went back to see her that morning and she put me on to a breast surgeon who was fairly new to Canberra; actually, fairly new to being a breast surgeon as well, but my doctor said at least I'd get in quick to see her.

The doctor was right about that. I saw that breast surgeon on the Monday. "You're inoperable," she said. "It's too locally advanced. I can't do surgery on that breast." The bigger tumour was just too big. It was long and skinny and went from my breast right up into my lymph nodes. As for the second one, it wasn't exactly small either and was near the bottom of my breasts. It was everywhere.

The breast surgeon rang an oncologist who got me in the following Thursday. Then she booked me in for all of the scans – the bone scans and the CT scans – to see if the tumours had metastasised. They were pretty sure they had because they'd aspirated a lymph node – so knew it was in the lymph nodes – plus the blood flow.

Courtney came with me and we went from scan to scan to scan. So many hours of scanning.

*Surprisingly, when the scans came back, they showed*
*the tumours hadn't metastasised at that point in time.*

I think the breast surgeon and oncologist were shocked they hadn't, but we were all absolutely relieved at that news. Obviously, though, we were still devastated about the tumours.

On the Thursday, I saw the oncologist and was set up to attend a chemo education session the following Wednesday. Less than two weeks after the mammogram, I was having my first chemo infusion of AC (Adriamycin and Cyclophosphamide). They said, "We have to be quick. We've got to kill this before it metastasises."

I'd always known, if I'm honest, that it wasn't good. Being me, of course it wasn't the easy cancer. It wasn't the simple one. It wasn't the one that ninety-six per cent of women supposedly 'survive'. But I knew there were lots of treatments. And it was a well-known cancer. I think that was probably one of the things I was going with – you dig around for anything to hang onto.

I went through six months of chemo and never vomited. I still laugh about that because I'm phobic about vomiting. I'd look at Courtney and say, "Thanks for doing the vomiting for me, honey." She vomits when she's anxious so she did all the vomiting, which was great – for me.

I was a single mum and so my kids were fairly close by me the whole time. I went through four rounds of AC. Lost my hair. All the ups and downs of chemo and life. And in the middle of all that, we had an unbelievable stuff-up fixing post-storm water damage in my roof.

My bathroom and part of my loungeroom were wrecked. I had water in my roof and the mould was settling in. The electrician they finally sent out cut the power off completely – leaving us cold and in the dark. All he said was, "This is what's happened. I'm sorry." By the time he came back, friends had loaned me lamps and strings of lights – and then he wanted to check my wall sockets. I sent him packing, figuring I'd just turn everything back on.

He'd cut through the wires.

That's when I really lost it. I rang the insurance company and when they tried to tell me it was my problem, I told them exactly what I was having to deal with – cold and sick with chemo. "How do you think *A Current Affair* or *Today Tonight* will feel about that?"

## *It was fixed the next day.*

I'd had a scan partway through the four rounds of chemo and my large tumour had halved in size and my other tumour had supposedly disappeared. We were cheering about that; obviously, the AC was doing a good job.

Three weeks after my last AC chemo, I went for my first weekly dose of Paclitaxel, also known as Taxol. I was supposed to have this for twelve weeks. The first dose seemed to go fine. I went home afterwards and it was quite a blessing after the AC because I felt reasonably well. Not too horrible. I thought I could probably manage this one.

The night before I was due to go for my second Paclitaxel, Matilda, who'd been absolutely wonderful and caring the whole way through, made burgers. She had buns and some salad, all fresh food. After dinner, Wesley looked at me and said, "Mum, you're swelling."

I was like, "I'm what?"

He was right, my face was swelling up. My lips, my eyes – swelling.

I ended up being Courtney's first patient. She'd been studying to be a nurse at uni. She took one look at me and said, "Oh, my goodness."

I took some antihistamine and it looked like the swelling had stopped but we decided we'd better go to the hospital anyway. So off we went.

I had the golden ticket – the card that said I was undergoing chemo. That golden ticket gets you straight through to a private area, a little spot in a corner that wasn't a sealed-up stuffy room and had a single bed, away from the noise of the waiting room.

They did some tests and couldn't work out what it was. I didn't seem to be swelling any more but they gave me more antihistamines, just in case. They spoke to my doctors and then sent me home.

The next day, I told the chemo nurses the story and they rang my oncologist. He told them to put the next dose off for a week because I was far too reactive at the moment with everything that had gone on. Plus, my histamines were up.

So, I had a week off.

The following week, they tried the Paclitaxel again. I felt pretty good and hoped there'd be no problems. They started pumping it through but after about fifteen millilitres, I started getting this weird shooting pain up my spine. It felt like someone was punching me in the side and working their way up my spine. There were spasms, too, really strong spasms up my spine and they were basically making me dance. I'd get a spasm to one side and I'd jump, then a spasm to the other side.

The nurses came rushing over and stopped the infusion. It had moved up to my neck and my throat and my chest – my lungs were spasming too. The nurses were all saying, "You're fine, you're fine." But my eyes were popping out of my head and I was terrified I was going to vomit.

It was frightening. They gave me a whole bunch of stuff and it stopped and started to settle. They kept giving me stuff – who knows what it was? Then they said, "We're going to try running it again, more slowly. We're here with you. We're watching you."

They started running it slowly, but as soon as they began, I broke out in hives. "No," they said. "We're going to stop for today. We'll get you to see your oncologist."

My oncologist decided he'd put loads more steroids on board, and more antihistamines, and we'd have another go the following week.

So, back I went. I wasn't exactly excited about it. Seven millilitres in, I started getting all of the spasms again so they sent me home.

I was allergic to the chemo. I rang my surgeon in tears and said, "Get this thing off me. Get rid of it. Get it off me. It's reduced so get it off before it spreads again."

Of course, the surgeon wanted to talk to the oncologist first at one of those group meetings they have – they decided they'd start me on the Docetaxel. Three-weekly doses.

So, by that stage, I was three weeks post AC. I'd had one dose of Paclitaxel, then I'd had a week off because of the reaction I'd had. After that, I'd only received fifteen millilitres before they had to stop. And then only seven millilitres.

Essentially, I'd had about seven weeks of no real chemo.

At my next oncologist appointment, he was doing the breast check and said, "Have you noticed this?"

I said, "No. You do all the feeling, I don't go near it. I just want it gone."

Anyway, he'd found a new tumour – the size of a ten-cent piece.

My oncologist said, "Okay, so we'll do Docetaxel. We're not going to change anything. We're going to move forward."

I wanted the thing off me but he disagreed and said it would be better to do the Docetaxel. Try to reduce the size of the tumours. Less risk at surgery. So, that's what we did – four rounds. The treatment took from June 28 through to just after Christmas.

In that period, a few nice things happened. My birthday, for example.

Well, both my girls were away. Wesley was around but he was probably going to be with his girlfriend.

When I realised it was going to be just me on my birthday, I put a message up on Facebook – I'd do that every so often just to keep people across what was going on with me. I'd had people who'd sat and cried with me at the start. The support was amazing.

---

*Hey, it's my birthday. I'm going to go up to Snapper on the lake. The weather's supposed to be beautiful so I'm going to have some fish and chips. Nothing exciting, but I need to get out of the house and do something for my birthday. Please feel free to come along and get some fish and chips and sit with me.*

---

Seriously, probably twenty or more people showed up. One of my friends turned up dressed as a clown with balloons. There were so many people there; just thinking about all the support, I get teary.

It was so good. It was absolutely insane.

I rode motorbikes, too. The girls even got me out on my motorbike while I was in the middle of chemo. They took me down the coast. They put up with me snoring and if I was unwell, they supported me to get home. They did pink ribbon rides.

Finally, I got to the end of chemo. My surgeon knew how keen I was for the surgery and she knew I had the new tumour. So, ten days out of chemo, I finally had my mastectomy.

During my second lot of chemo, I'd picked up an infection and it landed me in hospital for a week, which was a blur because I was quite sick. So, with the mastectomy, I was half looking forward to a lovely, restful week in hospital, getting all the good juice to feel amazing again. But as much as I wanted the thing off me, I was so exhausted I bawled my eyes out the whole time I was there. I cried and cried because I felt so awful and so tired. It was also the unknown.

A couple of days after the operation, my surgeon said, "You can go home."

"You know," I said, "I've got three children. Well, they're not children, they're young adults but it's not their job to look after their mum. It's not their job to feed me or dry me after a shower."

I was too exhausted and in too much pain, and I kind of refused to leave hospital. I ended up being in hospital for a good week after my mastectomy.

Courtney was about to start one of her placements at that same hospital while I was there. She said to them, "I'm starting a placement here tomorrow. Mum's going to be here until Tuesday."

They sent her in to put the meds up and to do a bit of my care. I have a photo of my nurse daughter taking care of me after my mastectomy. It was really lovely.

And because she was at the very end of her training, she was at that point where she was taking on patients to do their full care. So, there she was, my daughter, picking up my towels – and, as it turned out, helping me dry the bits I couldn't reach – and everything... seriously, though, it was great.

My surgeon had been checking in on me every day, then one day she popped in and said, "Oh, by the way, your cancer is now HER2-positive." Then she practically danced away.

What?

I was ER positive and PR positive before – that much I knew. But now I was also HER2 positive? I was triple positive.

I couldn't believe it!

Kellie Nissen

---

*I knew what being HER2-positive meant.
I'd done my research. It meant aggressive.
It meant deadly.*

---

When I saw my oncologist, he turned to me and said, "No, this is good news."

Hearing him say that, all these thoughts starting running through my head. I wasn't sure what was good about it. I'm glad they found it but why didn't they biopsy that new tumour that turned up halfway through chemo? Why did we do this? Why didn't we do that? Three months with no Herceptin and I had this HER2 tumour sitting there, growing.

What a waste of three months of my fabulous life!

But, it was done now.

"We'll apply for you to get Herceptin," the oncologist said. "It'll be a few weeks, though."

After that, I went downstairs and made an appointment to get my first Herceptin dose.

They told me, "We'll have to get you to sign this because it's worth five-and-a-half thousand dollars and if the government says no, they won't cover it, you'll have to pay for it."

"Sign me up," I said. I was about to lose my house anyway, so whatever! If the government says no, I say yes.

The whole timeline up to this point had been crazy. From mid-June 2016 when I was first diagnosed, first chemo at the end of June, last chemo at the end of December that year – then the mastectomy in early January 2017.

I should have had that bloody mastectomy the minute they found that tumour – chopped that beast off before it got a hold. Okay, so it was too big for surgery at the start, but half way through it had shrunk. Should we have bothered with the Docetaxel? It hadn't made any real changes. These questions will always be there. What if I hadn't had that 'chemo break'? Would the new tumours have still grown? What if I'd had the mastectomy earlier? What if?

The fact was, though, I'd grown more tumours. Too late for wondering now. One of them was quite small – the other two hadn't blinked. They also found another tumour, a vascular tumour, so it was in a blood vessel. Kind of makes you wonder why you have all your lymph nodes taken when tumours set up blood flow and settle in!

The ones they knew about hadn't grown, but they hadn't shrunk either. The surgeon basically tore everything out – lymph nodes included.

The recovery was hard. I was tired. I was wasted. Six months of chemo and I could barely walk fifty metres without being out of breath.

---

*Everything was broken – physically and financially.*

---

I'd set up a GoFundMe to pay for my surgery. I was completely broke. Being partially self-employed at the time, the taxman was also unhappy I hadn't made my PAYG payment, even though I'd sent through all my medical records. I'd even spoken with them and said, "Look, I'm barely working so no, I won't be making this payment. I don't know what it is I need to do. But you know, I've barely earned anything and I can't pay you."

They chose to ignore me and sent the debt collectors in. I think I was going through radiation at the time the letter arrived. I spoke with the debt collectors and said, "They know I have cancer. They know I've had chemo. They know I've barely been working. They've got letters from my doctor." I was feeling bitter and twisted. "Take me to court if you want. We're going to have a joyful little conversation. Go for it. You can't get blood from a stone. Tell the tax man to go for it."

Centrelink weren't going to help me out either. "Oh, no, you won't be sick enough for long enough," they said. "No, you'll be fine. You'll be right."

I ran up about $50,000 worth of credit card debt. I had bills from my own practice and ended up losing my contract position with another employer because I had to miss work for treatment. Wesley and Matilda were in Year 10 and Year 12 – expensive years with formals and a life to live. I wasn't about to deny them that. And, in the middle of it all, I had to sell my house because I couldn't afford the mortgage repayments.

Not everyone was an arsehole though. Wesley's school was amazing. They bought his suit for him and paid for his Year 10 formal ticket.

*And friends. Good friends are absolute gold.*

One wonderful friend – a really beautiful, caring woman – came over and packed my house when I was moving. She helped me set up my house for the photos. I didn't ask her, she just did it.

I had crowds come and do my garden. The motorbike crew and the scouting crew – they all came over and got my gardens up to scratch.

The generosity was unbelievable. I was so tired and people stepped up.

Another lovely couple, who I'd known for many years, came over and cleaned the rooms as they were emptied. Other people were filling trailers and taking stuff to my new house.

I had to do the exchange on the same day because I couldn't afford for them to look into my finances. My financial loan guy was across that – we asked the seller for early access. It all worked out. I even moved everything in and lived in the new house early because they knew my story. They did rip off my arms and legs with the price, but I guess that's what that's all about. Financially, things were not so dramatic anymore.

Three weeks after my surgery, I went in for my first Herceptin. We still had no idea if the government were going to cover it through the PBS at that stage so they told me they wouldn't make me pay for it upfront. "But if they don't approve it ..."

"That's fine," I said, again. "Whatever. I have three kids who need me so I'm not going anywhere."

Luckily, though, the government did cover it. I met whatever the particular PBS guidelines were for that medication.

Twelve months of Herceptin was the deal but it was pretty pain free. I also had to do twenty-five rounds of radiation at the same time.

It was while I was at radiation that I came across the Dragons Abreast dragon boating club. I'd considered dragon boating about ten years earlier. I'd even gone out for a trial with another club. At the time, though, my children were extremely young and it was too hard for me to leave them at home while I went to paddling training. I loved it, though.

I was still working through all of this, obviously, so I had made all my radiation appointments late – after I'd finished work. This one day, I'd came straight from work and was rushing into the radiation rooms when I saw a Dragons Abreast stall in the foyer. I was running late but thought: 'Oh my gosh, I'm going to go and talk to them when I'm finished here.'

When I came back out, they'd packed up and gone.

The lady at the reception desk must have noticed the look on my face. She called me over and handed me a flyer. "They have a Come and Try. Take this."

I was determined to go to that Come and Try day. The date was just after I'd be finishing my radiation. It was winter – a late season Come and Try – but I didn't care. I was going.

On the morning of the trial session, I arrived late. My dog was elderly and unwell and was leaving me little messages all over the house, waiting for me to get up each morning. It was one of those mornings – the story of my life, really – and I was running late. It wasn't a good start, it seems, turning up late. You miss the debrief. Miss the warm-up. But I was there.

The trial session itself was hard, possibly because I was still reeling from the after-effects of the treatment and the year I'd had. I was tired and broken and possibly more sensitive to comments than I might otherwise be. But the joy of paddling trumped all of that. I loved it. Right from the first time I dipped that paddle into the water.

There were a few hiccups with joining after that Come and Try session – miscommunication and misunderstandings about times and location, the usual stuff. It was a bit hard – everything was hard at that point. But I was so determined, plus, I had the golden ticket needed to join the club. It didn't need to be hard. I just wanted to be a part of it all.

The upshot is that I paid my money and joined the club.

I was in.

"Are you coming to Italy?" one of the ladies said at the end of my first session.

"Italy?" I said.

"Yes – you should definitely come. It's a huge regatta."

It didn't take me long to decide. Just before I'd started chemo, my parents had been planning a trip to the UK. We'd all been born in the UK and my parents were heading over in October to visit family. I was at the point of saying, "You know, I could really do with a holiday. I might book a ticket and come with you all."

Of course, then I got sick so it was a case of: looks like I'm not going to the UK after all. It was one of my driving forces throughout treatment, though; when I get through this and I'm out the other end, I'm going to the UK and I'm going to visit all my relatives. I hadn't seen them since I was eighteen. It was a physical and financial goal that I'd set myself.

When Italy was mentioned, straight away I thought: 'Italy. Europe. Close to the UK. Sign me up, Scotty.'

They found someone I could share a hotel room with and I was all set, then my room buddy hurt her back and had to pull out of the trip. I now had this hotel room on my own – $2500 for six nights.

My room buddy said, "No, that's not fair. I'll still pay my half."

And I'm said, "Well, that's not fair. You're not even going." I was hoping she'd at least consider still coming to Italy to watch, but no, she wasn't going at all.

There was no way I could afford to stay in the team hotel, now. Cancer had sent me broke but I wasn't going to let that stop me. I was going to Italy no matter what.

I look back now and think, 'Oh my God, what were you doing?' I was still working. I had the kids. I was dragon boating. I was still having radiation. In my head, I had the energy and the ability but in reality, I didn't. I had no energy. I had no ability. It was awful. I have no idea how I did it – but I did.

I finished with the Herceptin on Valentine's Day, 2018. I'd paddled right through the summer with Dragons Abreast and was loving it even though I was getting in trouble at every turn. I'm destined to always be in trouble. I'm not one to shy away from it and I won't let anyone rain on my party.

Because we were coming up to the Italy regatta, it was on for young and old at paddling. We wanted to be competitive. I joined in with everything I could – fundraisers, extra training, the lot. I really enjoyed being around women who were overcoming similar things to me –

some many years beforehand and some more recent than me. They just got it. They understood if I wasn't feeling well or if I was tired or trying to work the issues out with my shoulder. If I needed to talk, I could, without people saying, "Are you ever going to stop talking about your cancer?" It ruled my life at that time so, yes, I needed to let it out. No-one on the team gave a shit. It was great.

Things were starting to look up.

> *Financially, I was starting to recover. My active treatment had wound down. I was starting to work more. And I had this great big holiday planned – I was going to Italy, Paris and the UK.*

I flew into Venice. It wasn't all smooth sailing. Being on the aromatase inhibitors, you have issues with your joints and I'd been having a real problem with my foot. It was absolute agony and walking around Venice was nearly killing me. I had to stop at nearly every pub on the way to have a cool drink and put some ice on my foot.

Then I spent a couple of days in Verona. I wanted to see Juliet's balcony and do the Shakespeare thing. I chose not to pay ten euros to see the fictional grave of fictional characters but I did like the fictional balcony; it was quite lovely. And, I wanted to see the place that was brought to life in Shakespeare's work.

From there, I headed down to Florence to join the team for the regatta. Not staying in the team hotel was a bit difficult but I managed. By then, my foot was so bad I was lucky there were bikes you could hire. So, I scooted around on those to meet people at the different locations. On our non-paddling days, there were all sorts of walking tours organised but I couldn't do those so I decided I'd go on a Vespa tour instead. I toured around the wineries and out the back of Florence. I'd pass 'dragons' on the way, doing my maximum speed of forty kilometres an hour. It was so much fun. The whole time in Florence was amazing – the regatta, the social events with hundreds of people from all over the world who'd had breast cancer. The regatta itself was only two days but boy did we pack a lot into that weekend!

In Rome, I used the 'hop on, hop off' buses a lot. Then, in Paris, I jumped on the Segways. I did the Segway tour of Paris for one day and then, the next day, I went to Disneyland.

In my usual style, there were a few ups and downs. I'd bought what I thought was a five-day five-zone pass but the little Frenchman only gave me a five-day three-zone pass. At Disneyland, my ticket didn't cover it and I was hit with a massive fine for having the wrong pass. I had to buy a whole new, extremely expensive ticket.

*I took some deep breaths, wrote a Facebook post and told myself: you're at Disneyland – enjoy it.*

I had every intention to go on all the rides. My foot wasn't any better and I was literally hobbling everywhere. Standing in long queues didn't exactly help. I found myself wishing I'd gone for the disability angle – at least so I didn't have to stand in the queues with my very broken foot.

Nevertheless, I stood in the queues and I went on all the rides – all of them. There were a couple of sneaky rides; ones that looked tame but actually weren't. I went on one ride that I thought would be lovely and gentle. So, the carriage started moving and the next thing I knew, it was dark. We'd gone under the water and come out inside this mountain. From there, I thought it would be a nice little trip around the mountain where we could see lots of lovely scenes but no – there was a very cheeky loop-the-loop or two. And it was pitch black. That's my sort of ride!

I was staying in a nice little Airbnb in the main street of the town. It didn't have an air conditioner, though; I'd forgotten to check that. Damn, it was hot. I had to have all the windows open but there was no fly screen so all the mosquitoes were coming in, plus, it was Bastille Day so there was a party going on. At one in the morning, they were still blasting and I had this terrible headache. It was really sharp. My mind went off on all sorts of tangents: 'Maybe I didn't drink enough water; maybe it was the loop-the-loops; maybe my brain was shrinking.' Whatever it was, something was bashing against the side of my head. It was awful.

I'd planned to go back to Disneyland early the next morning – there's always more to see and I wanted to make the most of it. I changed my mind. Decided to take it slowly because of this terrible headache. It was coming and going and at times the pain was so sharp it would make me close my eyes. Just in the same spot.

Eventually, I made it to Disneyland at around 11 o'clock. My headache seemed a bit better so I took a little walk around the other parts and then I went on a few rides. I didn't last long – I was done. I was tired. I was headachy. I'd worn myself out so I decided to go back to my accommodation and take it easy. I was heading to the UK to see family the next day anyway.

My train wasn't until later in the afternoon but I wanted to get up early to go and see the Notre Dame. I hadn't seen it since I was eighteen and it was one of my favourite places. I love all the statues; it's an amazing and beautiful place. I don't know, maybe I'm a *Ghostbusters* fan – when all the statues come to life. Anyway, I loved the place so I had to go and see it again; I wanted to go inside this time, too.

I headed off into Paris and when I came out of the railway station, I just stopped. Oh my! Not only had it just been the Bastille Day celebrations but they'd just won the Soccer World Cup. The atmosphere was electric. People were dancing around the streets with the French flag and whatever else. It was intense. To be honest, the atmosphere didn't feel right. I couldn't go out into that so I found myself a corner in the train station, bought a cup of tea and pulled out my book. Another long story short, I was also duped by a seemingly kindly Armenian 'gentleman' who was 'helping' me find my train! He grabbed my large suitcase and off 'we' trotted, where he proceeded to demand money from me (kind of lucky I didn't carry cash). Thank goodness for the train station staff who got me back to my safe corner where I was left alone, other than kindly conductors who came to check on me, occasionally.

When I got on the train, I realised I was glad to get out of Paris.

Trust your gut, you know. It wasn't until I arrived in the UK that I found out there had been riots that night. Joyful riots but riots all the same.

I visited with family, down south and up in Scotland.

*Throughout that whole time, the headache kept coming back. A zappy headache – and it was getting worse.*

I was staying with my cousin at her place when the zap hit me really bad – made me physically cringe.

My cousin looked at me. "You okay?"

"Yeah, I've had this headache. It comes and goes of its own accord," I said. "Just turns up. I can't put my finger on whether it's lack of sleep, whether I've been doing too much or whether it's more sinister."

I knew what it was.

I put up with it until I went home. I contacted my oncologist straight away. I spoke to his receptionist first. She said, "Have you seen your GP?"

"Why would I see my GP if it was just a headache?" I didn't know what she was thinking and it confused me that she'd even ask that question. You don't see your GP if you have a headache. "Just take down the description of what's been happening and let him know." If I'd gone to my GP, I would've been sent straight to my oncologist anyway.

She rang me later. "He's written you up an MRI request."

No surprises there.

Courtney, who was nursing at the hospital by that stage, popped over and picked it up for me.

It was a week-and-a-half until I had the MRI. That was a Tuesday night and I was at work on Wednesday morning when the oncologist's receptionist called and said, "He'd like to see you."

I started howling.

I knew.

I knew I had brain metastases.

My appointment wasn't until the next day, which was too long to wait to find out for sure so I rang my GP straight away. I had to know.

"I think I've got brain mets," I said when I got put through. "Oncologist can't see me until tomorrow but I need to know now. I want to come in. I want to see the report. I have to know what's going on or I'm not going to sleep tonight so you might as well tell me."

I cancelled my clients for the rest of the day and rang Courtney, sobbing. My business partner came into the office and she started crying too. Then Courtney turned up so we all sat and cried together for a while until we'd cried ourselves out. Only then did Courtney and I head off to the GP.

While we were there, my oncologist rang back and said he could fit me in later that afternoon. "Let's go see what the plan is," I said to Courtney. Of course, I hadn't given him time to make a plan but knew he'd have a better idea than I did.

Turns out he did have a plan. "I'm going to put you in touch with a neurosurgeon," he said. This was a private neurosurgeon who, it turns out, was about to go away for a couple of weeks.

The neurosurgeon rang me that night. At home. "It'll be okay," he said. "We've got you booked in. It's all been handed over and you're booked in." He gave me the dates. Gamma Knife radiosurgery.

They'd found two mets – one in the frontal lobe and a sneaky one at the back. The frontal lobe one was the one causing the headaches. Going on all the rides at Disneyland had inflamed it and made it build up a lot of oedema.

---

*If you look at it one way, it was there anyway. Going to Disneyland and going on all the rides helped me find it quickly. I didn't have to have any seizures or anything else nasty. Plus, I got to go on all the fun rides instead of having a seizure. I was pretty pleased with that.*

---

I had the Gamma Knife. It wasn't that bad because I was on a big dose of Dexamethasone. I was euphoric. I was full of beans and I found everything quite funny!

I'd had to pull money out of my super to pay for the Gamma Knife upfront. After Medicare paid me back most of it, I ended up with a wad of money in my account, which I initially thought I'd pop away for future costs!

Then I saw this trip to Canada and Alaska.

I went with a friend for a month.

We did the Rocky Mountaineer and went on a cruise up to Alaska. We went to Denali. We saw bears and moose and loved every moment! All this time, I knew this thing in my brain was growing. It had shrunk after the Gamma Knife and grown back a bit, which we'd assumed was necrosis. But now, it was growing again.

I already had an appointment with my neurosurgeon for another MRI after I got back. That MRI showed massive growth. It was pushing on what they call the midline.

The neurologist just said, "Right, you're having a craniotomy. In three days."

"I'm what?"

I Googled it later, like I Google everything, and saw it could cause some kind of brain damage. Having something pushing on your midline apparently isn't good.

The idea of having a craniotomy was scary. As it turned out, and to my surprise, the craniotomy was pretty easy. Little pain, a night in ICU and another day in hospital and then a few weeks off at home, supported by friends and family as I wasn't allowed to drive for a few weeks.

Interestingly, he did an MRI right before the craniotomy and saw that things had started shrinking again. It may have been the long flights and lack of oxygen on those flights. It was confirmed post-surgery, as suspected, it wasn't new cancer but necrosis. Courtney, now an ICU nurse, was by my side the entire time and even took out my staples! As always seems to be the case a small hiccup occurred in my drama-filled life, and I developed an infection in the wound and once the neurosurgeon finally looked at it I had another operation to clean up the wound to prevent dreadful brain infections from occurring.

Around twenty-one months after those first brain metastases were found, they discovered something strange. We watched it as it kept growing. By April 2021, the neurosurgeon decided it was time to do another Gamma Knife radiation treatment as it appeared to be another new met. It shrunk and then started growing again, just like what had happened with the previous mets, and it's only recently that the growth has started to slow. It appears it's not unusual for my brain to develop necrosis, which brings forward my MRIs to every six weeks for growth monitoring.

My life now is a series of MRIs, every six weeks to three months, watching to see what's going on. It feels like a game of whack-a-mole at times! I live my life only knowing what the next few weeks or months will bring – long-term plans are harder but I keep planning a long life! I'm still dodging the next craniotomy!

---

*People say they don't know how I keep going.*
*I don't know how not to.*
*Maybe I'm too scared of dying to let that happen.*

---

I don't want to die. I don't want to leave my children. I want a wonderful life. I deserve a wonderful life.

I try not to live in the land of regrets – like 'I wish' and 'why me'! I live in a space of gratitude because I've come across so many amazing people who've picked me up when I was down. People who've saved my bacon.

I wouldn't wish this on anyone but what a ride, right?

What a journey I've been on and am still on.

Seriously, you can't make this shit up.

Kellie Nissen

# Bench 9 – Right

"Welcome to Bench 9," Joanne says as Lyndall settles in.

"Why, thank you," Lyndall replies. "It's nice to be here."

A number of us, like Lyndall, have multiple roles – drummer, sweep, coach – but we all started out as paddlers.

The wind picks up, slowly gaining momentum throughout the session as is typical for this time of year. It's not unsafe but not pleasant either – especially for the strokes who tend to wear the spray as the water hits the front of the boat at speed.

"Let's take her up the river for the last bit," Jenny says. "Bit of endurance, then a few games to finish off."

Nat angles the boat, pointing it towards the Molonglo River and calls the team to start.

"Endurance is basically code for non-stop paddling, isn't it?" Joanne says to Sugar, who's sitting in front of her.

"I think it might be," Sugar replies over her shoulder.

"Well," Joanne says, reaching forward that extra inch, "looks like I'll have to show them that us oldies can hang in there with the young ones."

"But I'm only forty-two," Sugar says.

"And I'm twenty-one," Joanne says. "Well, young at heart anyway." She laughs her deep laugh and starts to sing an Olivia Newton-John song.

Before long, we've all joined in.

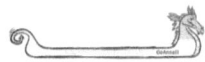

*Bench 9 – Right*

**Name:** Joanne Widdup

**Initial diagnosis:** 2019 – a Christmas present

**Age at diagnosis:** 70

**Job at diagnosis:** natural fertility teacher – part-time

**Job now:** natural fertility

**Joined DAC:** 2021

**Favourite boat position:** behind the strokes, on the left

**Most memorable DAC moment:** receiving my first ever sporting trophy in 2022 – the Rookie Award

**Favourite time to paddle:** winter at sunrise

**Little-known fact:** the letter 'B' seems to be an important part of my life – born in Bellingen, fell in love with Bach, Beethoven and Brahms, owning two beehives, breast cancer and dragon boating

**What I love:** my six amazing children

Kellie Nissen

# Joanne's Story: Let the Games Begin

*When the doctor told me, I didn't burst into tears or get flustered or anything like that. I've not cried – not even once.*

I didn't find the lump myself – it was one of the nurses who found something. She was doing a routine check and said, "Oh, this looks a bit suspicious."

That was the first I knew of it.

I'd be going for general mammograms for years. I have six children, breastfed all of them for nearly two years each – I'd always thought that was a good thing. Something that helps fix your body and protects you. Originally, they found a lump in my left breast during one of these checks. They asked me to come back for further checks, a few days later – a biopsy and scans. When I heard what they wanted to do, I remember thinking it might be a bit serious – but it turned out to be negative.

When I went back for the follow-up six months later, a nurse did the check. "We're not only going to check your left breast each time," she said when I queried her. "We have to look at both." The right one was where she found it. The lump.

Off I went for another fine needle biopsy.

This one came back positive.

It was funny, when the doctor told me, I didn't really feel anything. It was very different to when my friend told me earlier that she'd been diagnosed with breast cancer – I burst into tears and gave her a big cuddle, I felt so sorry for her.

With my diagnosis I was calm. "Okay. What's the process?"

Before I knew it, I was in hospital having an operation and then I was having chemo.

That year, my daughter said, "Christmas is not going to be at your place. It's going to be down here in Wodonga." I was pleased. We all made the big trip down there and it was nice, not having to do anything and sitting around, waiting for things to happen. It was different and new, and very much appreciated.

Before I started the chemo, they told me my hair would fall out by Christmas and sure enough, right on Christmas Day, I put my hand up to brush through my hair and out came a huge chunk of it. 'Oh well, that's it then,' I thought. But it put the heavies up my kids and my husband Doug as I pulled out huge clumps of hair. I didn't shave it, my daughter was a hairdresser and she cut it short for me., One day, I woke up and it was just skin on my scalp.

Amazingly, to my great surprise, I liked having no hair. In a way, it was very liberating. It's such a bother, having to wash it and deal with it every day.

I did buy a wig. I was advised to see a most supportive lady at her business in Holt – Heads Up – which is where I had it fitted. It was a returned wig, so quite cheap. I wore it once and somebody said, "Oh, wow, your hair looks great." All I thought was, 'Urgh.' I didn't want people to talk to me just because my hair looked nice. I also wore it once to a function. It was all nice and everything – not a hair out of place – but it wasn't me. I always wore something on my head, but not those horrible beanies. I liked scarves and wanted to make sure it looked good and represented me. I'd have all these little tassels on my scarf, hanging down – I owned it. It made me feel I could deal with everything and that I was making the best of it.

I became a bit theatrical with the head gear. I had the most beautiful scarves and I'd wear them with boldness. I'd wear great big earrings and big bright tops and bright yellow pants. The way I saw it was that I didn't want to lock myself away, saying, 'Oh, poor me.'

---

*I wanted to be out there. Bold.*
*This is me. Take me or leave me.*

---

Back then, I had a beautiful black top with big white spots, these bright yellow pants and a black-and-white spotted scarf. I loved them, but I can't wear them now. I don't want to. It's not like they bring back bad memories or anything – that time of my life was a very loving time because it brought Doug and me much closer together. I don't need them now.

Prior to my diagnosis, I was teaching sex ed at schools part-time and also teaching natural fertility awareness – but I was out of the classroom at the time of the operation. I'd let my teacher accreditation lapse a while back because my mother-in-law was living with us and I was her official carer.

I thought I'd be okay but once I started chemo, I found I couldn't deal with the computer work – saving documents and rejigging them and doing corrections online, and all the other admin stuff that comes with teaching. My supervisor was patient with me; she must have thought I was such an idiot. Looking back, my brain was really mushy. I tried to tell myself I could do it, that I was on top of it all. Yeah?

No – I wasn't. You hear people talk about chemo brain and chemo fog – it's absolutely a thing, but you never 'get it' until you've been through it.

During chemo, apart from the brain fog, I was also sick. Some days I couldn't get out of bed. We've never been people who have a cup of tea in bed but sometimes it was nice and I really needed it. I'd have my Vegemite on toast and a cup of tea or just tea – it was lovely.

Friends came with meals. We had the most beautiful meals and people were so kind. I couldn't believe it, but I suppose I wasn't shy. If people asked, I'd say things like, "Oh, look, a meal would be great. Yes. Nothing fancy. Just something simple."

I think people were thankful for that because it was something they could do – knowing they could help. I think if you say, "Oh no, I'm alright," they don't know what to do, so they bring you flowers or something.

Thinking about it now, it brought me much closer to people who then became very good friends. Before this, they were acquaintances. I remembering thinking, 'Wow! People are lovely.' And now, I'm finding I'm able to do the same thing for some of them. With one particular couple, the husband's been diagnosed with cancer. It's interesting because men don't tend to talk much about these things and how they're feeling – but he'll talk to me about it. Sometimes, all I have to say is, "Oh, isn't it a bugger!" And he knows I understand.

Of course, this was all happening in conjunction with the lead-up to the Covid explosion. By the time Covid hit the shores of Australia, I was in the middle of radiation, so my major treatment had been done. The thing was, though, because Covid was raging overseas and the focus here was on preparing for it, I was f left on my own for the majority of my treatment.

I didn't see the breast care nurses at all. Didn't get the *My Journey* journal and the other associated material. I didn't have contact with anybody apart from the medical professionals like my surgeon and oncologist. It was just Doug and I, doing it together.

> *Everyone was in isolation and lockdown so, apart from going to chemo, we couldn't go to anyone for the support sessions and nobody could come to us.*

I really didn't know what to expect and, in a way, the ignorance was bliss.

After a while, I talked to my friend who had recently been through treatment. She said, "Oh, what about diarrhoea? What about constipation?"

All I could think was, 'Oh, my God.'

I took all those things in my stride. My attitude was: 'This is what you're dealing with'. Every day, I woke up and thought, 'Just do it.'

So, the chemo eventually finished and then I was on to radiation treatment.

Doug looks back on that time with tenderness, which is interesting because I dragged him down to the radiation clinic at Canberra Hospital with me every day. I could have driven myself, I suppose, but honestly – finding a park … That's when it's great having a supportive partner. He'd drop me at the door, go and park and then come in and do the whole hand sanitation ritual and all the other documentation. Then, we'd sit isolated in our little sections, waiting for my turn.

Even though all the radiation patients were isolated from each other, there was still camaraderie in that we were all in the same boat. We were all wearing the same paper shoes; all wearing the same gowns and all in the same isolated situation.

The whole getting dressed and undressed and dressed again thing drove me nuts. Every day – clothes on, clothes off, gown on, gown off … I needed a quick way to deal with it. A wonderful, stretchy, sleeveless black top came to my rescue. I'd flip it down over my shoulders, have my radiation and then flip it back up again. The only other thing to do was put a coat on. I had it down pat!

Of course, there was the bra issue, too – so I stopped wearing them for a while.

Traipsing off to the hospital for radiation every day for weeks was a pain, so Doug and I decided we wanted to turn it into something positive. We thought about it and I said, "Okay, this is our date." We're not normally 'go out for coffee' people, so this was going to be special. "We've got to find a new café every day after radiation," I added – just for a challenge.

The café challenge was tougher than I'd anticipated, thanks to Covid, so we relaxed the rules and went back to some of our favourite places a number of times.

In the cafes, people had to sit spaced apart and then you'd see the police going past and checking we were all doing the right thing. But we found some lovely coffee shops, which made that pain in the neck something joyous and good instead. We'd have a slice of decadent cake and a beverage and watch people and chat.

Doug and I did something else that was unique, for us. We have a big block of land – a big house – and we had a whole lot of wooden sleepers containing the gardens. They were all falling down; rotting, as wooden things do, and one day I said, "We need to restore all this." They'd been there for forty-odd years so it was about time. We got a quote to replace the sleepers with stonework – $64,000. Ha! Not happening.

I'm not sure what I was thinking, but after one of my radiation sessions, I looked at Doug. "Come on. We're going to do the sleepers ourselves."

Doug said there was a fellow he knew from golf who lived on a farm. His farm had a river running through it that had changed its course over many, many years – so, there were lots of river stones scattered through the paddocks. This very generous man told us we could come and get what we needed for free.

What a bonus! Our plan was to do a little bit, day-by-day, until it was done – for however long it took.

We did it!

Our kids were absolutely astounded because Doug isn't exactly a hands-on, Mr Fix-it type of person – he'll mow the grass and that's about it. We knew nothing about concrete, nothing about laying stones, certainly nothing about the engineering behind doing the stonework – but we did it.

---

*It was quite an achievement and it gave us something to do every day. And now, we sit back and look at this wall and think, 'We did that!'*

---

The radiation ended and I went back for my next tests and check-up. That's when I found out I had thyroid cancer.

I was like, "Holy smoke – what does that mean?"

Apparently, it meant another operation. All I could think was 'What now?' I also wondered how long it was all going to last and would it go anywhere else?

I'm a musician. My background is with the Conservatorium of Music and I love singing. When I asked about that, they said, "Well, this thyroid operation may affect your vocal cords and your voice may change."

It was another thing I had to think about and deal with. There wasn't much I could do about it, though.

I had half my thyroid taken out. I've got a big scar on my neck now but I decided I'd have to go and buy myself some Paspaley pearls to cover it up. I figured I deserved that.

Chemo, radiation and everything else – like the bonus thyroid cancer – aside, the worst part about the breast cancer for me was the lymphoedema. They'd taken out masses of nodes. I ended up having to go to the lymphoedema clinic to get measured up for a sleeve and glove.

Covid was still an issue. I remember going in to the clinic one day and I had a dry throat and had to cough. Well, the lady sitting beside me got up and went off. "Please ask that lady to move. I feel compromised."

All of us in the clinic were compromised with our depleted immunity, but I suppose it was the fear and panic at that time.

I wore that sleeve diligently for a whole year. And the glove that goes with it. So annoying. The glove was always getting filthy because I love being in the garden. I only had two gloves and they were both always revoltingly dirty; we'd go out to dinner to someone's place and I'd be so embarrassed.

One day I thought, 'Why can't I empower myself and take it off?'

That's what I did. The sleeve and glove were restrictive and hot, especially in summer. Plus, I play piano and trying to play with the thing on my hand and restricting my arm was just annoying.

I'm still supposed to wear a sleeve and glove but I quite often don't. I got sick of it. I suppose I should do something about it but, honestly, compared to a friend of mine who has lymphoedema in her leg, my arm's not looking too bad. I can wear long sleeves and, let's be realistic, I'm so old it's not a vanity thing for me.

It took me a while to get into dragon boating. I've never been a sporty person. I tried tennis for a bit, but it wasn't me. I used to ski too. It scares me now, although, I'd like to get back into it.

A friend of mine, the friend who had breast cancer before me – much younger – asked me to come along to a Come and Try with Dragons Abreast.

*If she'd asked me a year earlier, I would've said, "No way."*
*I wasn't in the right headspace then, but she picked her time right and I surprised myself by saying, "Sure. I'll give it a go."*

Dragon boating wasn't totally new to me. My daughter had paddled when she was in high school. Her team once went to Darling Harbour to compete. I remember thinking it looked like a lot of fun but I never thought I'd be the person sitting in the boat with the paddle one day.

Anyway, I went along to the Come and Try.

The thing I like the most about Dragons Abreast is there's no expectation that you'll be a great athlete. I love that. When we're training, if I have to pull my paddle in – which you do – I don't feel like a real dope.

You could say I was 'enthusiastic' – and maybe a bit naive. I did the Come and Try and then, four weeks later, I put my name down for a regatta. "You can do the two-kilometre race," they said. Two kilometres – seriously? I'd barely been paddling.

I'll tell you what, though. I did it. And I didn't pull my paddle in because there was no way I was going to let my team down.

I'm getting much better. Much stronger. It's amazing what this sport can do for your mindset.

I have to say that this breast cancer diagnosis, in hindsight, was not the end of the world.

It was like coming to a T-intersection, but the left turn is blocked off and you have to go right. It's not the end of the world; you deal with whatever happens after you go right. When you have no choice, you try to make the most of it.

The experience makes you reflective. It made me more appreciative. I think I've become more patient. I was always busy, busy, busy – get this done, now do this. You can get cranky sometimes, frustrated. But what's the point of carrying on with that? There's too much to do. Too much to see and feel and enjoy. Don't take anybody for granted. Every day is important. Remember to smile and feel joy.

Of course, because I was relatively older when I was diagnosed, I already had aches and pains. I've had a lot of kids, so there were all those associated worries as well. I saw breast cancer as just something else to deal with. I'd tell myself not to be precious. I didn't have the time for that, and I've never been a precious person.

---

*Mind you, in the dragon boat the other day, someone said to me, "Oh, it's all about you, isn't it?" They were joking, of course, but I thought, 'Yes. Yes, it is.'*

---

It is amazing the things you forget once it's all over. There are so many things I'd forgotten about.

Fortunately, I started keeping a diary for the first time ever when my treatments began. Not a journal full of my thoughts, but more of a diary to help me remember to take things and when my appointments were. Before this, I was never an ill person. I was never on a regime of tablets. Now, I've got a whole new routine in my life. I need that diary or I'd never remember anything – in fact, I think I've forgotten today's lot of tablets, so there you go.

# Bench 10 – Left

Every training session is a mixed bag. Something for each of us – for our strengths, our preferences and our goals. It's what we love. This, and the social chit-chat.

Endurance paddles – the seemingly never-ending ones where the stroke rate is even and steady, with the occasional call for a lift or to correct our timing – are excellent for social chat. You either chat, or get too much in your head with that annoying little voice suggesting that you're tired or your arms are sore.

The boat enters the river. Clare Holland House sits on the corner and, out of respect, we are silent as we glide past the hospice. Once we're fully past, the chatting resumes.

"How do you all paddle and talk at the same time without getting out of breath?" Gillian asks.

Che laughs. "I don't know, to be honest. Some people just have that skill. Maybe chatting is like an on-switch for energy."

"It doesn't exactly help the timing though," Nat says. Then calls to the team, "Timing, DA. Watch the strokes."

Effective dragon boating requires all of our paddles to be reaching, driving and pulling back past the boat's side at the same time. Every stroke in sync with the rest of the crew. The last thing you want is for the boat to look like a drunken caterpillar, with legs moving at different speeds. It takes time and focus to perfect, but it's not difficult. Lose your focus though, and you'll likely hear that sharp crack as your blade hits the paddle in front or behind.

Further and further down the river we travel. Some of us pulling our paddles in briefly to reset, others continuing with dogged determination.

"It's good practice for the Ord," Che says, reaching forward a little more. "I'm really looking forward to heading up to Kununurra for that challenge. It's going to be epic."

Kellie Nissen

**Name:** Che Mortimer
**Initial diagnosis:** 2017, invasive ductal carcinoma, ER/PR+
**Age at diagnosis:** 42
**Job at diagnosis:** criminal investigator (detective), NSW Police
**Job now:** public servant
**Joined DAC:** 2018
**Favourite boat position:** sweep (in training), stroke
**Most memorable DAC moment:** competing with DAC at Lake Karapiro, New Zealand, in 2023 – so many amazing experiences with my family by my side cheering me on, and my husband paddling in the supporters' boat
**What I love:** the ACT Brumbies

# Che's Story: Always Go Forwards

*My story is probably different from others in that
I had cancer, a lymphoma, when I was sixteen.
After chemotherapy, a relapse and more treatment –
I was finally finished when I was about eighteen.
For twenty years after that, I had no issues ...*

After a long journey on the IVF road, I had my son Roan. He was fourteen months old when my husband Shawn and I decided to try for baby number two. It was September 2017.

I was fit and healthy. Tired, naturally, because I had a young child, but other than that, I was good. Part of the routine was to go to my doctor to get a prescription for the Pill, which sounds odd because we were trying to fall pregnant but being on the Pill helps the medical team schedule the different IVF stages. It can also reduce the side effects of IVF.

I was already in menopause and using the Pill as HRT. Whenever I went to get the prescription, my doctor always did a breast check at the same time. Intermittently, I would do the checks too.

I'd made the appointment with my doctor and just thought I'd do a bit of a check first myself.

I found a lump.

The lump was small, but obviously it started a panic. Luckily, I was in to see my doctor the next day.

She went through the usual spiel. "Eighty per cent of lumps are benign ..." Then she sent me off for a mammogram and fine needle biopsy if needed – which it was.

You sort of know without being told. The ultrasound pathologist who came in said straight out that "it looks a bit suss" – not a great bedside manner. And then the look on my doctor's face the day I went back for the results – you know it's bad news.

So, that was it. I saw my GP on the Tuesday, had the mammogram on the Wednesday, and had the results by the Friday.

Friday – the same day Australian philanthropist Connie Johnson died, 17 September 2017.

If it was fast up to that point, from then on it was a whirlwind.

Panic obviously wasn't going to achieve anything. Roan was a little over a year old, and I didn't know how extensive this cancer was going to be; it was hard not to panic.

As a teenager, my time with cancer was different – your sense of mortality is enhanced when you're older.

---

*Dr Google was not my friend.*
*There's a lesson for everyone; don't do it to yourself.*

---

A bit of knowledge is not necessarily a good thing. I had a science degree and my background meant I knew all sorts of medical stuff other people might not. Plus, I'd worked in the melanoma unit in Sydney for a while. And now, I had all this new information from Dr Google.

It was a messy time.

Shawn didn't know me during my earlier treatment, so he didn't know what was going on or what to ask. I was trying to tell him we didn't know what was happening. Had it spread? Had it progressed? What was I looking at in terms of treatment – my future? Neither of us knew a lot of people with breast cancer, so 'early stage' didn't mean much. Did I have a long time? Was it possible to achieve no evidence of disease and possible remission?

I was panicking. I wasn't sleeping. I wasn't eating. I was worried about my job. And my son – what about Roan?

"Book in to see one of these surgeons," I was told.

A surgeon?

I'd been with my oncologist for twenty-odd years and I didn't understand why I was being told to see a surgeon. It didn't make much sense to me, to be honest; when you have cancer, why you don't see an oncologist first? I must have argued this because I was told, "No, no. This is the way you do it. You see a surgeon first."

I said, "But what about tests? Don't I have to have tests to find out how far it's gone?" I knew I needed to find out if it had spread.

Luckily, I got in to see my surgeon really fast, but I'd also made a call to my oncologist. "Look, just so you know, this has happened," I said.

My oncologist was away at the time but the secretary asked who I was seeing. I told her and also gave her the name of another who'd been recommended.

She told me to go with the one recommended and she'd let my oncologist know the diagnosis. I also managed to get in quickly to see this surgeon. Basically, I walked into that appointment wanting to take control. "Don't leave it in," I said. "Let's get it out." That's who I was, a 'cut-it-out' sort of girl – because of my previous cancer experience.

"You're eligible for a lumpectomy and radiation," she replied.

"I've already had radiation," I said. "I can't have any more." It would need to be a mastectomy.

The surgeon gave me a whole lot of other information – different options – things to 'help me with my frame of mind.'

---

*Too much information can be dangerous. It sends my mind into overdrive. But I didn't have time for that because, the next thing I knew, I was booked in for surgery the following week and being bustled off to get all the scans.*

---

Personally, I would have preferred to have all the scans well beforehand, but it all happened so quickly I had to have them in the week leading up to my surgery. I was really unsettled on the day of the surgery because the scan results hadn't come back – I hadn't seen them, anyway. I was literally in the waiting area, laying on the bed and they're about to wheel me in to the operating theatre.

"All set?" my surgeon said. "We're going in. I'll see you in surgery."

"Wait," I said, "did you get the results back?"

She nodded. "There was no sign of any spread or anything like that."

That was great but I would have liked to have known earlier; at least so I could tell my husband. So we knew it would be straightforward with no other auxiliary extraction and so on.

My recovery post-surgery was easy. Easy peasy. I'd decided to have a nipple-sparing mastectomy with immediate reconstruction. I had no issues. Having a fourteen-month-old son kept me forward-focused anyway. It just had to be one day at a time.

I was lucky Mum happened to be in town at the time I was diagnosed and after the surgery. It was school holidays and she was here from Queensland, helping out my brother. Of course, Shawn's work gave him whatever time he needed off, but having Mum around was wonderful. She'd been with me through all of my earlier stuff, and I knew I could talk to her.

It was hard because Roan, being so young, didn't understand. After the surgery especially, why couldn't I pick him up when he wanted me to? That sort of thing. He was so little; he needed everybody to help him and he'd barely started to walk.

We were looking at baby number two when I got that diagnosis. I was looking at starting hormones again – going on that whole journey. The sense of relief was huge. Thank God I didn't. Thank God I wasn't already pregnant with number two. This was going to be our last try – we'd already decided that before the diagnosis. My doctor suggested that maybe we could try again after a year, after all the treatment.

"No," I said. This was it. It was either going to happen or it wasn't going to happen; it would've worked or it wouldn't have. We were never going to try again next year or the one after, anyway. I would have been another year older, and I was already in my early forties. Yes, there was disappointment that we wouldn't have another baby – after years of going through it all, but we saw ourselves as fortunate that we had the one we did get.

I saw my oncologist barely a week after my surgery. He'd been my oncologist for many years.

"This is shit," he said. "It's just so unfair."

I couldn't disagree with that.

"You had radiation before," he said. "Well, that put you in the high-risk zone."

Hang on, what?

> *No-one ever told me that. No-one ever said that the radiation I had when I was eighteen was going to put me at a higher risk of getting breast cancer.*

Of course, my lymphoma treatment was twenty-five years earlier. The treatment I had then – radiation from the neck to the midriff and across both shoulders – they don't do that for lymphoma anymore. These days, they do a more targeted treatment. These days, those possible side effects are commonly known.

In fact, I saw one of the nurses who used to give me chemo all those years ago and when I told her I had breast cancer, she nodded. "Yep. That's no surprise."

I also recently spoke to someone else who had lymphoma around the same time as me; we were in CanTeen together. She said she'd been told it wasn't a matter of 'if' but 'when'.

It was like a ticking time bomb, except I hadn't known it was ticking.

The other thing I have is a leaky heart valve – also caused by the radiation. The only reason they knew this was because, a few months before my breast cancer diagnosis, around the time my son was turning one, I became dehydrated and ended up in Emergency where they subsequently discovered I'd been born with this thing called Wolff-Parkinson-White Syndrome. This led to me needing to have a cardiac ablation, which is when they discovered the leaky valve.

Radiation!

> *Now-a-days, they block areas off and do all sorts of things to try and protect your heart. But back then, it was a case of wham! Take that!*

When I saw my oncologist, he said, "You know, we can just give you a pill. We've got this cancer … there's just a tiny bit left in one of the nodes. But we're pretty confident. We took six nodes; there was nothing in the rest of them. Obviously no more radiation, but we think you could get away with hormone blockers."

He mentioned something about being on the blockers for five years and that would be it. Then he added, "Look, you could have chemo but given your history with the lymphoma and the bone marrow transplant – we wouldn't like to do that."

I asked him about the numbers. He knew I would.

"Right now," he said, "you're around eighty per cent chance of no recurrence. If you take the blockers, that'll bring you to eighty-five. Chemo would maybe bring it to ninety-two."

I had a fourteen-month-old child who I wanted to be around for. "I think I'm a ninety per cent sort of girl," I said. "I'm a high achiever. I would like the chemo."

I knew what I was getting into. I'd been there before.

He wanted to go and have a chat with the medical 'brains trust' first – to be sure. So, I left but was back the following week. "We can do it," he said. "We'll give you the Neulasta and maybe drop down the first dose …"

I wanted to make sure he understood where I was coming from. "For my mental wellbeing, I want chemo," I said. "Just do it. I'm different to others in this situation; I know exactly what I'm signing up for."

He nodded. No argument.

I wanted to make sure I was well prepared. That first time, when I was younger and had the bone marrow transplant, I was sick for such a long time. I'd had eight days of solid chemotherapy and then three weeks in hospital. It wasn't great. When I came home, I had no energy and was so sick. All these weird viruses kept putting me in hospital. I remember being so depressed about things back then. It's tough as an eighteen-year-old who just wants to get on with her life. I had to delay uni and it took ages for my immune system to get back up to scratch.

I don't think I ever got as bad as that the second time around. I kept going to work during the chemo. I'd force myself to work for a week in every three-week cycle, to prove my brain was capable and keep it functioning. The brain fog from the chemicals was something else – I called it chemical drunkenness.

Work gave me something other than myself to focus on as well.

> *Sometimes you get over the fact that everything's about you and your health. Everyone's focused on you and your health. You're focused on you and your health. You worry about you and your health and all the side effects you're suffering.*

My work was great with it. They didn't expect me to come in but understood that I needed to – mentally. At home, I was alone because my son was in childcare most of the time.

I'd treat each day as a new day. I became entirely forward-focused. Being in the Defence Forces, Shawn was away a lot, so I couldn't allow myself the luxury of not looking forward. I had to be organised. I had to be disciplined. I had to have things in place. If I was caught at work, if Roan was sick, I had to have everything sorted. There was no time to crash and burn.

I started the chemo in October and finished just after Christmas 2017. I was lucky; I only had four doses of the TC treatment – Taxol and Cyclophosphamide. Then I was put on those horrible aromatase inhibitors – Exemestane in my case.

A while after I'd finished chemo, I found a lump in my other breast. Despite my pre-existing history, it was hard to get in for a mammogram and ultrasound, let alone a fine needle biopsy if needed. I persevered and, luckily, it turned out to be glandular tissue.

Two months later, I had my scheduled check-up with my surgeon and I took the scans in to show her. "This confirms it," I said. "I really want that breast off as a precautionary." I knew it wouldn't stop me from getting cancer again, but it would give me peace of mind.

Thankfully, she agreed and the airbags got balanced almost a year-and-a-half after diagnosis.

Roan coped so well throughout all of this. Although he was too young to remember that first treatment – the surgery and the chemo – he does sort of recall that second mastectomy a year after the chemo. He doesn't talk much to me about it all but he talks to other family members and close family friends. He talks about the time 'Mummy was sick' and 'she had the ouchies'. He remembers not being able to touch Mummy's chest.

He's also seen photos of me with no hair. When it was falling out he didn't even blink. I went around the house with nothing on my head – he didn't care. He still knew who I was; never shied away.

What makes it more real for him now is that his aunty has breast cancer and she's going through treatment at the moment.

He knows. He doesn't understand, but he knows. And he's such a snuggle-bug; he has such a great attitude.

---

*On reflection, they give you all this information but the one thing they never really talk about is the cost. It's like a big secret – being sick is really expensive.*

---

When you get diagnosed, it's scan after scan after scan after scan. They're not cheap. Most of us aren't on pension cards. I had private health – I've never let it lapse – but I still had thousands of dollars of out-of-pocket expenses. Not everyone is that lucky.

Those people who have done, and are doing, those medical trials – they make it good for the rest of us. They've gone before us and put us in good stead. Honestly, if we had to pay full freight for those things, I don't know where we'd be.

And then, there's dragon boating.

It was one of those things I'd always wanted to try. Having had cancer as a young person, I used to do the Relay for Life with my friend. I did it for ten years. Every year, we'd see the Dragons Abreast Canberra ladies walking around the track and think, 'Yeah, one day'. It was good to know there was a team in Canberra and I guess it was always at the back of my mind.

As a teenager I was part of CanTeen; I actually became the president of the ACT division. But you had to retire by twenty-four. I wanted something similar to that. It's nice to be with people who'd also 'been there and done that'.

## Bench 10 – Left

I can't remember where I saw a Come and Try sign, but I did. It wasn't that long after the team had been to Florence for the big IBCPC Dragon Boat Festival in 2018. I thought I'd give it a go.

It was great. I was hooked on my first go, although I don't think I was particularly good. I needed a lot of work – I still think I need a lot of work – but I loved it.

I love everything about it, actually. The support. The team spirit. If you want to chat to somebody about something, you can. If you don't want to talk, you don't have to. The team is a bunch of people who love the same thing and have that one little other thing in common.

People in the team have a whole range of experiences. Everyone is different. My experience was different from the next person and the next person. Sure, I went in with my eyes wide open, but there was also a lot I didn't know and that scared me.

A friend of mine recently got diagnosed with bowel cancer and she said to me, "Oh, it's so scary. I'm reading all of these things."

I wanted to tell her to stop reading, to say, "Your journey will be different to everyone else's journey." That's the advice I have to give.

Also – advocating for yourself is so important.

It's something I'm far more forceful about now. I've always been a proactive person when it comes to my own health and I don't hide from things. I've never been a hider. The minute I find something, I say to get rid of it. You want to take a biopsy? Nah. Do you think it's skin cancer? Take it away then. None of this take a bite now and then come back and take another bite. Let's just do it. It might be, or it might not – just get rid of it.

---

*That's me – my perspective is different because of my past experiences but I think you've got to be your own advocate. You've got to push yourself.*

---

In September 2023, I reached five years post-diagnosis.

That five-year mark. There's something about it that people focus on but I don't believe, with breast cancer particularly, the five-year mark means much. Look at Olivia Newton-John – twenty-five years later and it came back. But five years is when things start changing.

The 'crash and burn' that I mentioned avoiding earlier … it happened this year instead. The five years.

Mentally, for me, I think it was the culmination of the last six years. From my son being born, the diagnosis, the treatment, more treatment, my husband being away and coming back then being away again …

I reached the point where I thought, 'What am I doing? I've been on this roller-coaster for the last six years.' I'd always been able to push it aside – just move forward. Just deal with it. But at some stage you've got to stop.

That was this year, 2023. I needed to take a break and see where I was at.

Those aromatase inhibitors. In February 2024 I reached the five-year mark on those and I had to decide whether to continue. I couldn't wait to stop but at the same time didn't know how I was going to be. Would I be more worried that it's going to come back?

At some point, I think you need to accept when there's nothing more you can do. I mean, I could take more drugs, which could damage my bones more and make it harder for me to function. It's my choice. But they tell me I don't need them so I'm not going to continue if my medical team thinks I don't need them. You have to trust them.

I think I've done as much as I can do. I have regular scans; I have chest X-rays. If something is going to show up, I want to know about it early. The whole thing is almost natural for us now – for me, anyway.

I don't lose sleep over it. It does cross my mind, though. It's always there but I refuse to dwell on it.

I push.

I advocate.

I get things checked.

There's no more waiting until we're in our sixties and retired to do what we want to do. I don't know what my health will be like. I don't want to miss out. We do things we want to do now.

I might not be here for a long time, but I intend to have a good time while I can.

# Bench 10 – Right

*GoAnna II* continues down the river. Past tall reeds and overhanging branches; the morning traffic from the road above a distant rumble, muffled by nature. It's much calmer here. The water flat. Glassy. Almost untouched before the paddles slice through, the slightest of plonks then a satisfying swoosh – it's hypnotic. Meditative.

"What's the Ord?" Gillian asks. "Sounds a bit ominous."

Nat angles the boat out to the right, giving the canoe polo team a wide berth as a few keen ones engage in some extra training.

We start heading towards the Malcolm Fraser Bridge.

"It is – sort of," Che says.

"Fifty-five kilometres of ominous," Nat quips.

Gillian stops paddling. "What? You dragon boat for fifty-five kilometres?"

"In one day," Che adds.

"And you do this for fun?" Gillian says.

Che nods.

"You've got to live, right?" Nat says.

June 2024 will be the third time our team from Canberra will be participating in The Ord River Challenge. It's not a 'Pink' event – any team can enter – but this time, five out of the nine boats will be Pink. It's a massive undertaking, but everyone participating is keen to rise to the challenge.

"You lot are unbelievable," Gillian says. "I take my hat off to you all."

Kellie Nissen

**Name:** Gillian Horton
**Initial diagnosis:** 2008, lobular cancer
**Age at diagnosis:** 48
**Job at diagnosis:** public servant
**Job now:** owner Colleen's Lingerie and Swimwear
**Surprising fact:** has never paddled but supports DAC with all fundraising (one day, we'll get her in the boat for real)
**Why we love her:** Gillian is all about supporting women and making them feel good about their bodies and boobs – no matter how many there are, what size or what shape. Plus, she's funny – very funny
**Little-known fact:** after her cancer treatment, she went to a little village in France for some R&R; she bought a house there and now offers it to other women who've had breast cancer

# Gillian's Story: Not Without Me ...

*I didn't notice anything different. I should have, though, because there was a lump. I was getting regular checkups, but with how busy I was moving house and other things, I hadn't been checking my breasts myself. Obviously, I now understand the importance of that; all I can say is thank goodness I was still doing my regular breast screening. It saved my life.*

I was diagnosed in 2008. I have a family history of breast cancer, so I'd been having an annual mammogram since the age of forty.

At the end of 2007 we moved to Canberra from New South Wales. I was due to have my mammogram but didn't have it on time because we were moving. Once I'd settled in and started my new job, I took myself off to BreastScreen ACT for my regular check-up – just a little later than normal.

Interestingly, and I don't know if this is related or not, but my hair felt different after we'd moved. I actually said to someone, "Oh, the water here must be different." It was one of those throwaway lines, yet I do wonder.

A few days after the check-up, I was called back.

I thought, 'Oh yeah,' and went in by myself. Honestly, I didn't think I needed to take my husband with me.

Sitting in the waiting room with all the other women who'd been called back was a little odd. We're all sitting there in our gowns, looking at each other. Nobody was doing the jigsaw puzzle laid out on the table.

Eventually, I was called in for my second mammogram and ultrasound. It was fine – at least, I thought it was – but they came back in and said, "We need to do a biopsy." That was the point I started to think that, possibly, things weren't looking good. Ever the optimist, though, I told myself to wait and see what happened.

That biopsy was extremely painful. They gave me some ice to stick in my bra when I left. It was surprisingly nice. As I was leaving, one of the nurses said, "When you come back for your results, bring somebody with you."

'Well,' I thought, 'that's obviously part of the process.' I didn't really want to go there, though. There was going to be about five days to wait so I tried not to think about it at all.

When I went back to BreastScreen – with my husband this time – I remember seeing the doctor and the nurse sitting in the room, all serious.

"Unfortunately, it's cancer."

This was April 2008.

I'm pretty sure my husband was more shocked than I was – but I was shocked too. All the little alarm bells had been there – the callback, the need for the biopsy, being asked if I had a GP.

On the GP issue, I'd answered, "No, I've just arrived in Canberra."

They recommended a GP for me in the city, near where I worked. I went in to discover they weren't taking any more patients – their books were full. "Oh," I said, "but BreastScreen sent me."

They gave me an appointment straight away.

Still, alarm bells and all, in my mind, it wasn't going to happen to me. I'd had regular mammograms. I was only forty-eight – still young.

Yet, here I was.

---

*Even when you have a family history,*
*"You've got breast cancer," are not words you expect to hear.*

---

"What's next?" I said.

The breast care nurse was phenomenal. She explained things really clearly. There was a lot to take in, though, so afterwards my husband and I went and sat in a park for a while, to try and digest everything.

Telling the kids was hard. We have three children – a blended family – they were all mid to late teens at this point. Even though, being a blended family, we're quite good at talking things through, this was different. Just sitting them down and saying what was happening and trying to reassure them that everyone was going to be okay. It's what you say, isn't it? Even if you don't believe it. I believed it, but my focus was much more on the immediate – what's next for me?

My new GP gave me a referral to a surgeon and I got in pretty quickly.

"We'll remove the lump," he said.

"No," I said, maybe like most women. "Just take the whole breast. I'm happy to have a mastectomy."

"No, we'll be okay," he said. "We'll get the margins; we'll just remove the lump."

So, that's what it was – straight into surgery for a lumpectomy. The surgeon fitted me in for one of his last surgery appointments before he was due to go on holidays.

It wasn't until a bit later on that I received a phone call from his receptionist. "We've got your results," she said. "We need you to make an appointment."

I was confused about the need for an appointment as the surgeon had been confident it would be all okay. Obviously, the receptionist couldn't give me the results herself, although she did say they "weren't what they'd expected".

What does that mean?

"How long before I can get in?" I asked.

"Well, he's away at the moment," the receptionist said, "so it will need to be for when he gets back."

The whole situation wasn't handled particularly well and I recall being really, really upset. "I can't wait for however long it's going take him to get back from holidays," I said. "What's the process here?"

As it turned out, the process was 'wait'.

Mentally and emotionally, I couldn't wait. I needed to know, so I contacted my breast care nurse. "Can you please find out the results?" I asked. "And then can you please talk to me because I can't wait for the surgeon; I have to see these results for myself."

Again, my breast care nurse was great. She rang around for me, trying to find out what was going on.

She found out.

It was lobular cancer, right through the breast.

> *It didn't get picked up on the ultrasound.*
> *It didn't get picked up on the biopsy.*
> *In fact, it wasn't picked up until I went for the surgery.*

Unfortunately, lobular cancer is one that's hard to detect. It can appear is a bit of shadow but you need to be able to compare your screening results against each other – another reason regular screening is important.

Once the breast care nurse had explained all the ins and out, she said, "You're going to have to go back and have the breast removed."

I was fine with that. I'd said I was happy to have a mastectomy in the first place. The issue was that my surgeon was still away. My GP offered to send me to another surgeon, which I took her up on.

"Look," the new surgeon said when I went in for the consultation, "you can wait. There's no rush. I could do it for you now but you may as well go back to your surgeon."

'Fabulous,' I thought – and it was. We had a trip booked to Malaysia and the 'no rush' meant I could go. I'd look at doing the surgery when I got back.

As I was packing, I pulled out a dress and thought, 'I'm going to wear this dress because I'm possibly not going to be able to wear this dress after surgery.'

We were going over for an event – an Air Force anniversary – because we'd lived in Malaysia for a period of time. Friends we hadn't seen for a long time were coming as well. I knew lots of the people there, but I chose not to tell them because I didn't want the focus to be on me. I didn't want to have people being upset for me and saying, "Oh my gosh, what are you going to do?" The focus was on enjoying ourselves and celebrating.

Taking that dress and wearing it was kind of my little smile to me; I've got two breasts now but not for long. That was as much as I thought about it – the cancer. It wasn't something I was worried about or nervous about; I was matter-of-fact – I was having a mastectomy after our holiday. It was going to happen.

Anyway, we really enjoyed ourselves; I'm glad I made the decision not to say anything. However, I knew I was going to have to – and soon. I'd only recently moved to Canberra so didn't really have any friends there, so waiting to tell people before they accidentally found out wasn't such an issue. I knew I'd have to tell my family though.

The thing is, my family – I have four brothers and four sisters – are all over in Europe and technology in 2008 wasn't as savvy as it is now, so it wasn't like I could get them all together on a Zoom call.

*In the end, I picked up the phone and rang one of my sisters. "Guess what?" Then I told her. "Can you tell everybody else?"*

The mastectomy went well. So well, I went to the movies the day I left hospital. My family were going to see *Mamma Mia*, and I said, "You're not going without me."

They protested, of course, but I failed to see why I couldn't go. I was fine. There'd been no complications and I wasn't in pain. Sure, I had a drain in, but that was it.

"I'm coming," I said and that was it. We all went to the movies together.

*That little inconvenience was not going to stop my way of life.*

After surgery, I had chemo. It was my choice.

I was in the grey area. There were no nodes involved bar a microscopic bit of cancer in one of them. My oncologist, as oncologists are inclined to do, threw all these statistics and figures at me: if you do that, there's a 2% chance … this gives you 90% success … blah blah blah.

I'm sitting there, listening and thinking, 'I've got no idea what you're saying.'

"What should I do?" I said, eventually.

"Well," he said, "it's your choice."

That wasn't the answer I was after. I wanted him to say, "In my professional opinion …" but he didn't. He told me to take some time to think about it.

This was getting serious! I had no idea what to expect in terms of chemotherapy or what would happen with alternatives. That's when I finally contacted Bosom Buddies – the breast cancer support group. It was the first time I'd felt the need for help. You hear all these stories about chemotherapy – they're all different – and I had no idea. I wanted to talk to somebody who'd been through it and could answer some of my questions.

"I'll have the chemo," I said to my oncologist when I went back. So, he went ahead and booked me in.'

It's not easy being away from family at times like this – but my family, over in Europe, are the most amazing group of people. On the day of my first chemo, I was sitting there on the couch, waiting. I did a lot of waiting. I didn't know what to expect. You do all the information sessions but still, you don't know how you're going to feel when it finally gets started.

So, I was sort of in my own little world and the next thing I know, my daughter's produced this photo album. Inside, there are photos of every single person in my family – immediate family, distant relations, my dog – from overseas and from Australia. And, in every photo, the person in it is wearing this pink hat. There was a short poem, too, which still makes me emotional every time I think about it. The poem was about the hat being filled with love.

Then, of course, the hat itself appeared.

I call it my 'happy hat' because that's the effect it has; and I wore it to every single chemo session I had plus any time I was feeling a bit down. I'd put my pink hat on and instantly feel the love of my family.

It was all my sister's doing. She's amazing like that.

The chemo itself wasn't too bad; everyone reacts differently. I didn't feel nauseous, as such, but the drugs kept me awake. For about three days after a chemo session, I was absolutely wide awake.

*Fortunately, I didn't feel like doing the housework, so that was good.*

What I did feel like, though, was writing. I wrote and I wrote and I wrote. Journal, journal, journal – for three days straight. Then I'd sleep for twenty-four hours or so and I'd be right to go. I'd head out and have coffee and do whatever I wanted to do.

I stopped working. That was my choice. Being immunocompromised and having to travel on buses and work in an air-conditioned environment didn't take my fancy; I was fortunate that I didn't have to work and I could choose not to.

By this stage, I'd told a lot of my friends – or they'd randomly found out ... One particular friend had been with us on that trip to Malaysia – where I didn't tell anybody – and I bumped into her; at a rugby match, I think. By this stage, I had no hair. I saw her looking at me and just said, "Oh, I probably need to tell you something."

She said, "What?" even though she could see 'what'. She understood why I hadn't told her, though. "No, you did the right thing," she said. And it was all okay.

Many of my friends came and sat with me for my chemo sessions. They travelled – from Queensland, from New South Wales – which was just beautiful.

Being so far away, my family couldn't sit with me during my sessions but I'd get these random photos all the time through the mail. One was a photograph of three of my brothers wearing pink ties. That was it. Nothing written. No caption. Just my brothers together, wearing pink ties. Another one was a photo of hearts drawn in the sand. Just that. It was all I needed to know, though. They were thinking of me. It was so beautiful to receive them.

In addition to the photos, they'd send me pink things all the time. I'd turn up to chemo with pink feather boas or pink thongs on my feet or the longest, brightest pink wig you've ever seen. Every time I went to chemo, the nurses had no idea what I was going to turn up in.

---

*Each time, I had a completely different, crazy pink outfit on and that was my way of coping.*

---

Everything for me was a party. I had a hair-cutting party. I had a wig-choosing party. In my head, if I added 'party' to whatever I was doing, I could cope with it. A great sense of humour will get you through anything. My humour probably became quite out there – weird, even – more so than usual.

One of my chemo sessions was scheduled for Halloween. "Oh, we used to dress up in Scotland," I said to the nurses before my Halloween chemo. "I'll think of an outfit and come in that."

Naturally, bald head and all, I was perfect to be Uncle Fester from the Addams Family. I went all-out for this one. I put the make-up on and gave myself really big black eyes.

My husband said, "You can't do that."

"Yes, I can."

When I walked in, though, it didn't quite have the effect I'd intended. People thought I was really, really, really sick.

Maybe my husband was right but, I thought, this is my way and I'm going to keep on doing things my way. I'd bought a pumpkin full of lollies for everyone, so I got up and went around to everyone and said, "Here, have a lolly from the pumpkin."

I used chemo as an excuse for everything then. "The chemo made me do it," I'd say. Or, "The chemo made me say that." Or "It's the chemo talking, it's not me." It was a way to get through things.

Three of my friends turned up for my final chemo session. One of them had shaved her head for a fundraiser. She was completely bald. We all had pink wigs on for the last chemo, then, when we were driving home afterwards, we were routinely stopped by the police. Me and my friends are all sitting there, in our pink wigs, and the police officer says, "Oh, a hen's night?"

I took my wig off.

The police officer said, "Oh!"

Then my friend took her wig off, so there's the two of us, sitting in the car, bald as.

The poor guy. He just gaped at us.

> *"You want to try it, don't you?" I said.*
> *"You want to try this pink wig on."*
> *"If my boss wasn't here," he said, pointing back at his police car, "I would." He ended up letting us go without doing the routine vehicle check.*

Having a joke with people kept me grounded. I was doing it all the time.

I'd had a bit of a heart flutter every now and then as a result of the chemo drugs. Never anything major, but when it's your heart, they like to take every precaution. I had this friend, who I'd met in the chemo ward. She was having her last chemo and I'd gone in to sit with her. At one point, she's all hooked up and I said, "Ooh, my heart's doing something funny."

Immediately, the nurse jumps up and says, "You're going to Emergency."

I'd only just finished chemo myself and was in no real position to argue so off I went to Emergency – fully escorted.

When I got there – priority treatment – they said, "You'll need an angiogram."

Fine. Whatever. So, I'm sitting in the room and a nurse comes in with a razor. "I'm really sorry," she said, "but I have to use this to shave your groin for the catheter."

"No, you're not," I said.

"No, no," she said. "For the angiogram – we have to make sure there's no hair there."

"No," I said. "No shaving."

I'm sitting there – completely bald and she still hasn't twigged. I could see she was a bit upset, wondering what she was going to do with this difficult patient.

"I think it'll be the cleanest, neatest area the surgeon's ever seen," I said.

She looked at me, confused, and then finally realised. Thankfully, she burst out laughing.

"I'm so sorry," I said. "I just had to …"

Luckily, she shared my sense of humour. "That was really, really funny," she said.

Afterwards, when the ambulance guys came to take me back to the other hospital, the two of them walked in – both bald as well.

"Thanks, guys," I said. "Thanks for coming out in sympathy with me."

You had to laugh, or you'd cry. Having no hair anywhere on your body was weird. You don't realise until it's not there. The constantly dripping nose was the worst – no hair up your nostrils, nothing to slow the flow or absorb it.

The day after my final chemo was also the day of the first ever Handmade Market – 22 November 2018 – at the Albert Hall. Two of my friends, who were from Queensland, decided they'd go.

"Not without me," I said.

So, there I was, the day after my last chemo, wandering around all those wonderful market stalls. I was as tired as all get-go, but all I was thinking was 'I'm doing this. I'm doing this. I don't care how tired I am.' No way was I missing out on one minute of being with my friends and going to these markets.

Many people, who haven't been through this themselves, believe that the end of chemotherapy – or the end of radiation, which I didn't have to have – is 'the end'. You're finished. It's conquered and you can just get back to life. I tried. I did go back to work but something wasn't quite right.

---

*The period after I'd 'finished' treatment was the hardest time in the whole process.*

---

I didn't know what was going on. Chemo had thrown me into early menopause, but the way I was feeling was more than that. Nobody knew what I 'had'. It was like having a really bad stomach. The GP sent me for lots of various procedures to try and find out what was going on. Then my oncologist said, "I'm sending you to a psychiatrist."

"What? You think I'm mad?"

However, it was the best thing because within about two minutes of seeing me, the psychiatrist said, "You've got anxiety."

It wasn't just anxiety. I had panic attacks. I had insomnia. I had no energy whatsoever. I could hardly get up for work in the mornings. My whole immune system – my entire body – was out of whack. So, I went to see a naturopath.

It turns out my body wasn't making any cortisol.

"I'm surprised you can even get out of bed," she said to me. "Let's fix that."

The supplements she gave me really helped in terms of my energy but there were still the emotions to deal with. It was like a downward spiral. One thing after another – it was horrendous. It wasn't until I went to a coffee morning and a lady gave me an article to read that I started to see that what I was feeling was normal.

Normal!

---

*Why don't we talk about this?*
*The end of treatment is certainly not the end of it at all.*

---

For me, surgery was okay. Chemo was okay. But it was afterwards – after all the treatment – that things went downhill. I couldn't be myself because I didn't know what I had control over in terms of what the chemo had done to my body and what the hormone drugs were doing. Horrendous, is the only way to describe it.

Looking back at what was happening, I have no doubt in my mind that it was PTSD. Trauma.

As it turned out – and this will sound odd but it's not – I was fortunate that my husband was being deployed overseas. I had six months up my sleeve while he was away and I said to him, "I'm going to go to France."

"Okay," he said.

It was the right time – that was the fortunate bit. My husband would be tied up with work, our children were independent.

"I need to do this," I said, "because I can't see a way forward here. I need to focus on myself."

I headed off to France and found a small village in the Loire Valley and settled in there. I had no idea what I was doing there or why I was there, but I was determined to figure it out.

Interestingly, my oncologist had told me to go off the Tamoxifen six weeks before I travelled because of the risk of DVT. I did what he said, of course, and lo and behold, I started to feel better. So, very naughtily – and I'm not recommending others do this – because I was feeling so much better, once I was in France, I decided I'd stop taking the drugs and try to figure myself out.

It was the right time to do it.

If I didn't sleep, it didn't matter. If I wanted to have a snooze in the afternoon, I could do that.

---

*There were markets nearby, so I'd go to the markets and buy what my body told me to buy. Fortunately, that meant lots of cheese.*

---

I did a lot of walking. I joined a gym and did water aerobics there and strength classes, but the walking was the best. There was so much to see, I'd go out walking pretty much all the time.

By complete chance, the lady I rented my apartment from had also had breast cancer. She was English-French and had all these books. "You can read them, if you like," she said.

When I wasn't walking, I'd sit in the garden and read these books. A lot of them were for mindfulness. I read about the practices and did many of them – instinctively actually, looking back.

I ate well. I exercised. I did the mindfulness. I wrote a lot. I was also doing a lot of processing – what is my new normal? What does that look like? What does this mean? What am I going to do with this experience? What changes should I make?

All those questions I think we all tend to have are conversations going on in our heads. I was lucky I was able to process them because I didn't have any distractions. I could focus exactly on what my body was telling me it needed.

---

*Bit by bit, it was like coming out of a fog.*

---

I'd been in that fog for three years. It was a long time.

After my six months in France, I did some more travelling. It was like seeing the world through different eyes – there was a heightened sense of everything. I was in Norway, which is spectacular on an ordinary day, but I had this appreciation of every single little thing I saw. I ended up writing lots of poetry and I celebrated life. Yes, well, and, you know, so the midnight sun on the back of the *Hurtigruten* ship. At three o'clock in the morning, on the *Hurtigruten* ship, after having seen the midnight sun, I was the only one still dancing and singing. Everybody else had gone to bed – but I was on the deck, watching the sun and dancing until five o'clock. There was no way I was missing a second of any of that.

I've always been a *Carpe Diem* kind of person. Always one to 'seize the day'. But I think that mentality has been heightened – my appreciation of life, the appreciation of the little things and the people around me. I want to make the most of everything I see and where I'm at.

---

*Being able to go overseas – live in France for six months – was an incredible opportunity. It was a real healing experience and I'm so grateful I was able to do that. If I hadn't, I truly believe I wouldn't be doing what I'm doing now.*

---

Once I came back to Canberra, and was back at work in my public service job, I remember one day looking out the window and thinking, 'I'll never get this minute back in my life. What am I doing?'

I literally walked out and never went back. I didn't know what I was going to do but that didn't stop me. Again, I was fortunate I was in a position to be able to do this. After I left my job, I took myself through a process of all the pros and the cons. What could I do? What were the advantages? The disadvantages? In the interim, my husband and I had bought a house in that village in France and I took some time back there, working on some renovations.

When I returned to Canberra, I mentioned to my husband that I needed to make an appointment at Colleen's – the lingerie shop where I bought my bras.

He said, "Well, she's going to be closing down. It was in the newsletter."

"What?" I said. "Why?"

"She's retiring."

Immediately, I felt this big smile filling my face.

My husband looked at me. "I knew that's what you were going to say."

I hadn't even said anything! But we both knew what I was going to do. What I needed to do.

I had no idea what I was doing but I was committed. I didn't want other ladies to have the experience I had. I wanted them to have a greater choice than I'd had. Not having control over your treatment and the way your body reacts is bad enough, but to not have control or choice over the bras we can wear – that's the cherry on top at a time when you're feeling vulnerable and wondering what your life is going to look like. The last thing you want to do is worry about your underwear.

It seems such a simple thing, but it can have a profound effect on you emotionally. I love being able to say to women, "Okay, let's see what's there that's perfect for you." And then finding something that is – something that makes them smile.

---

*Things are changing and I'm pleased to be a part of it.*

---

It's not just bras that are changing, though. My diagnosis in 2008 was a long time ago. I've learned a lot and understand a lot more now than I did then and, with that in mind, I still think there needs to be more patient advocacy. Patients need to understand their choices – not necessarily to override the professionals but to know they have choices and what they are. It's all part of a much larger process and there's definitely a phase, or more than one, where you feel like you're a rabbit in the headlights. It's like: 'What's next? Now, what's next?' But there are times when you can pause; where you can say, 'What information is there? Do I have other choices?' It's extremely difficult when you're going through it and I understand that, but choice is important. I'm a huge patient advocate in terms of 'other choices'.

It's a double-edged sword, though. We want choices but we also want the doctors to just tell us what to do.

When people tell me they've got cancer, as a person who's had a lived experience, I feel it's about seeing that their experience is unique. Every experience is unique. But if I can help in any way, I'm there. I'm always there to listen, to share my story if it's going to be helpful or just to sit in the puddles with them until the sun comes out. It's not about giving them information that isn't going to be helpful or they don't need. People let you know if they want information, others don't want to talk about it. In every case, I feel privileged to be able to support women, however they need it.

> *Nobody expects to get cancer. Even if you have a family history of cancer, nobody expects it.*

And cancer affects everybody in some way. It's not only the person with the cancer but your family, friends – even your community. I think that's something we, as a society, are recognising more.

There's the survivor's angle but also the carer's angle. We have to think in terms of what the person with cancer needs but also what do other people who are affected by your diagnosis need? It's that feeling of helplessness; people want to fix things. They want to help.

A lot of the time, for those of us with the diagnosis, we get frustrated. We say, "Stop asking me what I need – I don't know what I need." That can upset people because they want to help but they can't help.

That's one thing I say to women now – the greatest gift that you can give yourself and give to others is to accept the offer of help. Women often have this mentality of having to be the carer. I'm looking after my children. I'm looking after my parents. I have to do this and do that. But we don't need to do everything, and we certainly don't need to rush back to doing everything afterwards. There are others around who can do this instead.

Having cancer is life changing. It doesn't matter how you look at it – the good, the bad or the ugly – you don't come out of this experience unchanged in some way.

You just don't.

# The Sweep

"Okay, easy," Nat calls.

We've reached 'the bridge' with its sign warning watercraft not to proceed because beyond the bridge lies the power boat and waterskiing area. It's an 'at your own risk' situation, but also one of courtesy and common sense.

Nat works the sweep oar, turning the boat while we have a drink, stretching our arms and arching our backs.

"Paddles flat while we swap sweeps again," Nat calls.

The transition is smooth. There's barely a wobble as Lyndall moves back to take the oar and Nat slips back into Bench 9.

"Anybody need to swap sides again?" Jenny asks. She sits up taller, eyes flicking from side to side as she checks for hands raised. "No? Great. Let's take *GoAnna II* home with a few games."

"Sounds good to me," echoes down the boat – a chorus of agreement.

"I smell coffee," Deb adds.

"Twenty to get the boat up and running, then I'll start," Jenny says. She nods down the boat at Lyndall. "Right …" Jenny grins at the team as the boat starts moving again. "Keep paddling if you've been at training any time in the last fortnight."

A deliberate call, trying to give those of us who are back for the first time in a while a slightly longer break.

After thirty or so strokes, Jenny looks down at Elly, "Your turn," she says.

"Keep paddling if …" Elly pauses to think. "… you're wearing sunglasses."

The game continues down the boat with everyone having a turn. Lots of laughter, groans, cries of 'not fair, you said that on purpose'.

Then it's Gillian's turn, "Keep paddling if you have a complete pair."

Everyone laughs. We all know what she means. Most of us stop but a couple keep going. And that's just it – we're Pink Ladies and we can laugh at ourselves. At our common element. Most DAA Pink Paddlers can; after all, it's what brought us together.

"Nice one, Gillian," Lyndall says. "Do I get a turn?"

Jenny nods.

Lyndall waits a few more strokes but not too long as there's only a couple of us still paddling. "Everyone – keep paddling if you want coffee and brekky."

The whole crew cheers. Paddles go up. We're on our way home.

*The Sweep*

**Name:** Lyndall Milward-Bason

**Initial diagnosis:** 2015, Stage 2 Hormone Receptor

**Age at diagnosis:** 51

**Job at diagnosis:** manager in the Commonwealth Public Service Industry Department

**Job now:** retired (2024)

**Joined DAC:** 2016

**Favourite boat position:** sweep

**Most memorable DAC moments:** winning our last heat at the IBCPC regatta in Florence in 2018; paddling 55 km in the Ord River marathon in 2019 and again in 2024; holding hands with counterparts while drummer for DAC in the Flowers on the Water ceremony at Nipples on Ripples regatta in Tasmania in 2020

**What I love:** catching up with friends over a glass of bubbles at Veducci clothing parties; bushwalking

Kellie Nissen

# Lyndall's Story: It Was Tough But I Was Tougher

---

*I've got to book in. I'm fifty-one and I've missed two appointments. I've got to go.*

---

I started going to BreastScreen ACT because of the history with my mum and my two aunts, Barb and Sue. I saw Sue at a family gathering. She'd been going through chemo – that's what prompted me.

As soon as I came back from Sydney after that gathering, I made my appointment and went to have the mammogram. Tick. Done.

Then I got the callback.

It surprised me. So, I went to have a look in the mirror.

Even though I'd been doing the testing in the shower or at night – a bit ad hoc – it was actually visible, now, in the mirror. It was up high, where I couldn't see it by just looking down. And it was soft, not hard. It wasn't in the places where you'd normally check, when you're told how to do a self-check.

They wanted me to come in for a biopsy. Then I had to go back later for the results; I took my sister Jenny with me for that. I'm glad I did. It was fairly confronting, but because we'd had the experience with Mum, I don't recall having that great sense of fear that some people talk about.

My mother, the least fit person on earth, got through it all. She was sixty-eight. Barb was also sixty-eight and got through it. And Sue was around sixty-six when she was diagnosed – and she was getting through it. Sue experienced a tougher road, I think, than the other two.

I was much younger; I was confident I'd be fine.

I had private health insurance but it turned out that my 'cover' covered not much at all – choice of your own doctor in a public hospital. That was it. My GP gave me a list of private specialists who took public patients in public hospitals and I went with the one whose rooms were the closest to where I lived. I hadn't heard of any of them because Mum was in Melbourne, not here in Canberra, so my choice was just a guess.

He was really good.

Because I had the 'dense breasts' thing, my surgeon wanted to make sure there wasn't anything else lurking. He needed to know as much as possible about the size of the tumour so he'd know whether he could do a lumpectomy rather than a full mastectomy. He wanted to be confident there, and I appreciated that.

He sent me off for a number of tests. They were expensive and with my 'non' private health coverage, I had to pay full price. Luckily, as a public servant earning a reasonable salary, I could afford this. I also thought, 'What's an extra bit of money at this point?' I was also happy to pay because I wanted that certainty. Mum suffered psychologically from having her full breast removed so I definitely preferred the partial option.

Mind you, I had seen some awful pictures in a few of those books they give out sometimes. It's frightening, wondering whether that's what you're going to look like at the end.

All of this was happening in the lead-up to Christmas so my big panic was trying to get all the tests done and then secure a surgery slot before Christmas. I didn't want to have to wait until January. I didn't want to go through Christmas with it hanging over me.

I made it. I managed to be the last patient that my surgeon saw that year.

> *The surgery before mine went over, so I ended up going in quite late. By that stage, the people who do the testing of the tumour had gone home so I had to wait another week for the for the results to come back anyway.*

I took leave over Christmas – three weeks in total although some of that was Christmas shutdown. My job at the time was intense – working on a high priority government initiative to bring in the new food labelling protocols.

When the results did come back, they discovered that the tumour had been more aggressive and bigger than they'd thought. There was one speck that wasn't contained – everything else was fine – just this one speck, quite a distance back.

My surgeon wasn't worried. "I'm pretty sure we've got it all," he said.

But you never know. What does 'pretty sure' actually mean?

When I went to see the oncologist, I had a plan because chemo is confronting. If he said that having chemo would give me a ten per cent chance of surviving beyond twenty years, I would definitely do the chemo. If there was only a two per cent chance, I wouldn't do it.

Of course, the numbers came out at six to seven per cent, didn't they? I had to make a decision.

I thought about Mum and how terrible it was for her, being so unfit and already having a lot of other issues. She'd had a fall, many years ago, where she'd lost her spleen and ruptured her pancreas, so she really struggled to fight infection and absorb nutrients. When she was going through chemo, it was really an issue for her to try and maintain her nutrition. By the time she finished, she looked like she was ninety. But she got through it and I knew I could too.

Then I realised that another twenty years added to my life would only get me to seventy-one. I wanted to live longer than that. Mum was seventy-two when she passed. I wanted to get to more than seventy-one.

I also thought about what the surgeon had said and the words 'pretty sure'. That's what finally convinced me to definitely go ahead with the chemo and radiotherapy. Just to be safe.

---

*It was an option for me and I took it.*

---

My oncologist booked me in for the start of February. That night, I had a weep in the shower for five or ten minutes, but that was all.

Three weeks after surgery, I was back at work. I received an Australia Day award that year for the work I'd done the previous year on a major project. I had the high of the award at the end of January, then into chemo at the start of February. The first Tuesday of the month.

There was never any question in my mind that I wouldn't continue working throughout the treatment. I was open about everything that was happening right from the start – so everyone knew. I didn't see any point in not being open. I discovered at a young age that trying to keep things private ends up being too much hard work. It gives you too much stress. In this case, it was my health. There was nothing I could do about it.

My husband John was really supportive throughout the whole thing. So was Jenny. My kids were twenty and eighteen, so I didn't have to worry about looking after them. There were a whole lot of other things that don't seem to worry you as much when you're my age with this sort of diagnosis, like the threat of going into menopause. If I did, then I did.

I tried to do this thing where you keep your hair by wearing a skull cap. It was like a swimming cap, but neoprene. And very cold. It's not only your head that gets cold but your whole body. The first time you have chemo, it takes a lot longer. They do it more slowly because of the ice cap. I kept laughing at myself when I saw my reflection.

I wanted to give it a go because my younger sister Cathy was getting married later in the year, so I thought it would be nicer in the photos if I still had my hair.

It did stop the hair from falling out but my head was too small for the cap, so there was a large section at the back that wasn't in contact. I was quickly going bald in that section after the second chemo treatment so I decided to give up on the ice cap.

Once I'd stopped the ice treatment, the rest of my hair came out in alarming clumps. I went to HeadsUp in Kippax – the store where they sell scarves and hats and wigs for people who are experiencing hair loss.

Sue Owen, who runs the shop, is fantastic. "Don't wait for it all to fall out," she said. "I can shave your head for you." And she did – right there, on the spot. I bought a few bamboo hats and that was it. She was great.

I did end up getting a wig, too. Mainly because I was going to Parliament House a lot and I needed the wig so I looked like the photo on my security pass. I wore it to work a few times, always on the days I had to go Parliament House. Otherwise, I didn't bother and just wore a hat. I looked alright bald. It wasn't too hard to bear. I didn't mind; so much so that I ended up doing 'Shave for a Cure' the following year.

The wig I ended up with was very seventies – a Jane Fonda sort of haircut. I tried a lot on when I went to the Look Good, Feel Better place – where you can go and do the make-up classes and so on. One of the wigs I tried on was blonde; it made me look like Cathy. I'd never thought about that before, but it made me realise that if I were actually blonde we'd look quite alike – like sisters!

> *For me, the chemo and the recovery period did get progressively worse.*

I'd have chemo on the Tuesday. By Friday afternoon, I'd be starting to feel it and over the weekend, I'd be really bad. After the first treatment, I started feeling better on the Monday. The second one took longer, maybe the Tuesday, and so on. Recovering after each time took that little bit longer.

My brain wasn't in the right place some of the time. I helped a colleague interview someone to help us out with the task force. When I was sitting there, my stomach started to do that whole rumbling, rolling thing, like it was telling me to get the interview over with quickly – but in reality, it was just digestion issues the chemo was causing. All I could think was that I needed to get out of there because things were going to go terribly wrong very soon. You could say I was distracted. I was trying to hide it but was clearly not successful because, afterwards, he said, "I thought you were really weird."

I lost a lot of weight, partly because I had almost instant loss of taste, so trying to find something that was worthwhile eating was nearly impossible. Plus, my stomach wasn't able to digest food very well.

Trying to stay healthy and put weight back on or not lose so much was a constant struggle. I couldn't taste any salt. All the takeaway foods in the world were pretty much useless to me. Chips. Pizza. Bleurgh – I couldn't eat any of that. I could taste sweetness, though, and that's what I settled on in the end. I had read something about it as well – sweetness with carbs – things like rice puddings and tapioca puddings. They were much more palatable when I was trying to get carbs into my system. With protein, I could eat lamb and prawns.

> *Prawns. John didn't understand how much I wanted prawns. "Just get me prawns," I'd say. I could taste them because they were on the sweeter side of the spectrum.*

Fruit and vegetables, particularly veggies, tasted really nice.

Wine tasted terrible! As a red wine drinker, it was the saddest thing about the whole experience. And balsamic vinegar – I love balsamic vinegar but it tasted atrocious. I love food because of the way it tastes so that loss of taste was the most tragic thing about it all.

The support from everyone around me was wonderful. My close friends – brilliant. Bushwalkers – brilliant. Clothing party ladies – brilliant. Family – brilliant.

I do remember thinking that it was harder for everyone else than it was for me. Particularly my family. I knew what that was like because I'd been through it with my mum.

It was hard when Mum was sick. I couldn't be myself with her because I was so worried. I was not coping; not as well as I wanted to. I recall her fourth treatment being really difficult. At the time, John didn't understand; he couldn't – he was used to me being the rock. The person that others leaned on.

Then, with me, I think he finally understood how I'd been feeling with Mum. He was there all the time. He was so attentive. Very protective. Jenny would try to visit and John would say, "No. She's not seeing anyone today."

He had to let me go to work though. And the people at work were brilliant too. They had to be. I was there, in front of them, confronting them. They had to work out what to say and what to do. Sometimes, I'd come in with my hat. Sometimes with the scarves. Sometimes wearing nothing at all on my head. I'd be different, depending on what I felt like on the day.

Work had been crazy for months but by the time I was due to start radiation, it had calmed down a little so I asked for some time off. "Would it be alright if I took every afternoon off after two or three o'clock, depending on when my radiation appointment is?"

"Yeah, sure. Whatever you need," my boss said. "You could take more if you need it."

I told him a couple of hours was all I'd probably need and I was right. I was barely affected by the radiation, until the last week. I think they do a double-down or something. I went from being okay, having managed not to be burned to a crisp the whole time, then suddenly that last week brought it all. Crispy skin and everything.

That was the worst of it though. I wasn't tired like a lot of people are. Probably the way I timed it helped because I was able to go to work, go to radiation then go home. There was no backtracking or anything. No going out of my way.

Anyway, radiation finished and then it was the drug therapy. They put me on Tamoxifen first – to make sure the menopause the chemo had thrown me into wasn't going to reverse itself. There's not supposed to be side effects with that drug, apart from the hot flushes, but I struggled not to put on weight. It was the complete opposite of when I was having chemo and couldn't put on weight – now, I only had to look at food.

Once they'd confirmed the menopause was there to stay, they changed me to Letrozole, which was better. By then, John had been diagnosed with metastasised prostate cancer. His drugs also gave him hot flushes – much worse than mine. He'd be talking and suddenly sweat would appear on his face.

> *I had no idea there was a dragon boating team for people who'd had breast cancer. In fact, I'd never given any thought to learning how to dragon boat in the first place.*

I did, in the past, have a colleague who was into dragon boating. She was on another team. And my boss was also into dragon boating – he kept trying to get all of us to join his team, Canberra Griffins. "Come on. Join dragon boating," he'd say to all of us. "You'll love it."

I didn't think being on a team with my boss was a particularly good idea.

Then, my boss told me about Dragons Abreast. I had heard about them when I was still having chemo. John used to come with me to chemo, but while I was sitting there, he'd wander off and visit other people he knew. One day, he came back with some information about the team. At the time, I was disappointed I'd have to wait until I finished treatment, but it had been in the back of my mind ever since.

"How do they go?" I asked. "Are they very competitive?"

"They're up there," he said. "But competition's not the main game for them."

*The Sweep*

The team had a 'Come and Try' in September and I was going to go, but it was terrible weather that day and I knew if I went when the weather was horrible, I'd hate it and wouldn't go back. I decided to give the September one a miss and go to the next one in November.

I loved it. I loved it so much I went to the regatta in December and bought pants and a paddle and gloves. I hadn't joined at that stage but I'd loved that 'Come and Try' session so much, I wanted all the gear.

Every year, the team does a Christmas paddle and I was invited to go along.

---

*That was the first time I realised you can't be late for training. I missed the boat. Five minutes is too late. The ship has sailed.*

---

They were already on the other side of the lake by the time I'd parked and run to the shore.

I watched them for a minute, then turned to head back to my car and tripped over the copper's logs. Fell flat on my face. Another team was warming up and they all saw me. "Are you alright?" they called.

"I'm fine. I'm fine," I said.

I certainly learned my lesson.

Despite that, I did get invited to their Christmas party – and I went along. One of the paddlers had a farm and the party was out there, which was really nice.

When the regattas started up again in January, the team was short of people. I had all the gear now – a paddle and special sticky pants, as well as a PFD, DAC shirts and a jacket, thanks to Jenny and her ex. I'd only had two trial sessions but I just joined and went straight into the regattas. I didn't even think about it; I just did it.

I was hooked. I loved paddling. I had a go at drumming later as well, and loved that. Then decided I wanted to try sweeping. There's nothing quite like standing at the back of the boat with the sweep oar in your hands – it's my favourite thing to do.

About a year after I'd completed all my active treatment, during Breast Cancer Awareness Week, I was asked to speak about my experience.

I talked about the roller-coaster ride and some of the tough times. I also talked about the surgery, making the point that, a year after surgery, my breast didn't look too different to how it looked before. I could see people were surprised at that, but they shouldn't be. These days, it's not only the surgical techniques that have improved but the surgeons as well. If you're having a partial, they do so much to try and preserve as much as they can.

The other huge improvement has been the research. Although, I do have a theory – if you get one of the common cancers, like breast cancer or prostate cancer, in some ways, you're fortunate. They are so prevalent that somebody with money, or one of their loved ones, is going to have that cancer, and that's where they're going to put their money. It's these common cancers that attract the private research foundations. So, if you are going to get one, get a 'popular' one rather than a rare one. There will be more information and more support. In this country, we rely so much on research that's done by private foundations, publicly-funded research organisations and private foundations.

It's been a long trek. I don't think I've changed particularly – but maybe I have. The way I view things. My opinions and so on.

---

*I guess, right from when I was diagnosed and knew what my treatment path would consist of, I viewed all of this as a journey – or a detour, if you like. One where I'd veer off on another pathway for a bit but then come back onto my usual track.*

---

It was never going to be the case.

Although you're still the person you were before breast cancer, you've detoured a bit. You never really get back on the exact same track that you left.

# End of Session

The boat rounds the corner, back past Clare Holland House and out into the Lake Burley Griffin.

Small white caps greet the crew.

"Where did that spring from?" Anita says.

The boat cuts through the water, which sprays the ladies on the first couple of benches.

"It's surprising how sheltered it is down the river," Amanda says.

It's not the roughest weather we've been out in, but it's a stark contrast to the stillness of the Molonglo.

"Keep paddling," Lyndall calls. "Dig deep. Lean out."

We respond, doing everything she asks as she keeps us upright and safe.

"How often do dragon boats capsize?" Gillian asks.

"Very, very rarely," Che says. She's right. It happens, but they're heavy boats. It takes a lot to tip them over, even more to tip the crew into the water. As long as all the paddlers are responsive.

Paddling is tough now, particularly at the end of a long session, but we all dig in and work together. The boat rises and dips. We're all copping the spray but it's nothing we haven't seen before.

Jenny drums, keeping us in time. Motivating us to keep going, she's wearing a huge grin, but then she's sitting higher than the choppy spray.

Lyndall angles the boat out into the lake so she can turn and head straight in for shore, aiming for the tyres right next to the pontoon. "Slow the boat," she calls and we all respond.

She parks the boat perfectly.

"Well, that was fun," Jenny says. Exhilaration dances on her face.

"That was hairy," Nadine says.

"Nah," Jenny replies. "Remember Jindabyne?"

Some of us nod. The Jindy regatta, day two. The wind came up early. We sat in the boat, ready to head out to the start of the 200 metre race, for around twenty minutes while officials waited for the wind to drop. When they finally got the go-ahead, the wind waited just long enough for us to be half way to the start before picking up again. The race was like a roller-coaster, but with Susan on the sweep oar and Jenny on the drum, we had a ball. Albeit a wet and challenging one.

"I remember you gripping the drummer seat with one butt cheek," Anita said.

"My thigh muscles were burning, that's for sure," Jenny said. "But it was so much fun." Jenny stays put behind the drum while Clare and Elly climb out and sit on the sides of the boat at the front, weighing it down so we can all disembark safely.

Bench by bench, we unload. Slowly, carefully. Thanking Jenny, and Clare and Elly, for a good session. Once the boat is empty, we work as a team under Lyndall's instruction to get *GoAnna II* onto the purpose-built trolley and we roll her up alongside the other boats, give her a good clean and cover her up.

Jenny calls us over to stretch. Standing in a circle in the shade, some light chatter fills the air as we ease potential aches and stiffness from our limbs. "Great session," she says, in debrief. "You all worked hard, particularly in that last bit. And, well done to Gillian – stellar effort for your first time out."

Everyone claps and Gillian shakes her head. "Now, I understand what it's all about."

Jenny reaches her hand into the middle of the circle as the rest of us close in and follow suit.

"Three, two, one …" Lyndall counts it down.

The Pink Ladies chime in, "Go—oooo …" We lower our hands, then sharp and swift, raise them as one high in the air. "Anna."

"Coffee?" Deb says.

"Table's booked," Marion adds. "Usual place."

And off we go. The Pink Ladies. Dragons Abreast Canberra.

*GoAnna.*

# Epilogue

The bright sun sparkles off the blue-tinted lake – mist, fog and frost burned off, the day has become another beautiful early spring day.

*GoAnna II* – resting on her tyre bed – looks a little lonely. Almost all the other boats are out somewhere on Canberra's beautiful lake – dancing on the water, pushing hard towards an invisible goal. But, she's happy to rest. We worked her hard today – as well we might.

Until next time. She sees us in her mind's eye.

She is proud of us.

Kellie Nissen

# Appreciation

I've said it before and I'll say it again – at the risk of cliché, it takes a village to write a book. Although, in the case of *A Blink in Time*, it took a dragon boating community – and an amazing support crew.

First and foremost, to all of the strong women whose stories you have read in this book – thank you for your willingness to open up and share your personal stories with me. Your trust in my ability to retell your journeys, and your growing excitement has kept me going. Each and every one of your stories humbled me. I hope I have done you all the justice you deserve.

The family and friends of the Pink Ladies – thank you for supporting these women and allowing yourselves to be acknowledged in their stories.

Kaaren Sutcliffe – author coach and editor extraordinaire, and fellow author paddler – a mere 'thank you' is not enough. Your expertise, enthusiasm and, above all, your friendship while I have been writing this book have been invaluable.

James Knight, although you may not realise it, the structure of this book came about because of several coffee conversations I had with you. Your love of sport storytelling and the ideas you brainstormed with me sowed the first seeds.

Kerrie Griffin OAM – I was thrilled when you agreed to write the foreword. Thank you too for checking all the little details and gently correcting my woeful lack of knowledge in many areas.

Thank you to Susan Pitt and Jeannie Cotterell (along with Lyndall and Natalie) for your advice on all matters 'sweeping'. To our drummers, Kathy, Jenny and Janet, for your attention to detail. And to Julie Kesby for fact-checking a number of details for me.

Patsy Sheales, Marion Leiba and Katherine Davis – thank you for taking the time to sit with me and answer my questions about the early days of DAC.

*Appreciation*

Claire McGregor – thank you for your advice regarding the layout of the book and your beautiful work on the cover and the internals.

Mel Thornberry – you take the most wonderful, true-to-life photos. I love working with you.

Dani Vittz – what would I do without you? So talented, so creative and so much fun. Your caricatures, map and dragon boat images have brought this book to life.

To Dragons Abreast Australia, Dragon Boat ACT and most of all, Dragons Abreast Canberra – where would we be without the best sport in the world?

And finally, to my husband Karl and my children Ashlea and Geordie – always supporting me in doing the things I love. Thank you.

Kellie Nissen

# A Little Bit of History

For me, history equals story. And it is the stories and anecdotes from happenings in the past that interest me. Once you get talking to people who were 'around back then', it's amazing what they remember and how long you can spend listening enthralled.

In the interest of providing a glimpse into the 'backstory', and also keeping this book under 100,000 words, I have selected only a few of the stories told to me by Patsy Sheales, Katherine Davis Kralikas and Marion Leiba.

## Dragons Abreast Australia (DAA)

In October 1998, the National Breast Cancer Conference for Women was held in Canberra, and BCNA was founded. Among attendees from all over Australia sat Michelle Hanton and Anna Wellings-Booth OAM.

Listening to a Canadian journalist, Sharon Batt, talk about the dragon boat teams for breast cancer survivors in Canada – an initiative that grew off the back of Dr Don McKenzie's 1996 research – Michelle thought, 'We need to bring this to Australia'.

Back in Darwin after the conference, Michelle went to work and by December had started a dragon boating team of breast cancer survivors, Northern Territory Breast Cancer Voice, who paddled on the Fannie Bay foreshore.

Along with a number of other conference delegates, Michelle was also the founder of our national organisation, Dragons Abreast Australia, which celebrated its 25th anniversary in 2023.

## Dragons Abreast Canberra (DAC)

DAC commenced paddling early in 1999 after the hard work and dedicated lobbying and advocacy of founder Anna Wellings-Booth OAM. The club commenced with six paddlers, including Anna and June

McMahon. Without a qualified sweep, they relied for several months on a sweep from another club, Les Williams, who took the team out on the waters of Lake Burley Griffin whenever they wanted to go.

Before long, however, a couple of the paddlers – Sylvia and Maggie – had qualified as sweeps and the team was able to go out on its own.

In 2000, seven of the DA Canberra members – including Marion Leiba – competed in the Australian National Dragon Boat titles in Penrith, joining a composite DAA boat.

DAC was the second breast cancer survivor team to form in Australia, and is now the oldest, still-running club in the country. We're celebrating our 25th anniversary in 2024.

## Paddling with Anna

Anna never took no for an answer. Over her time as a paddler, Anna Wellings-Booth OAM was instrumental in the organisation of events, such as DAC's annual corporate fundraising regatta, and was a foundation and board member of BCNA. Anna was also a key figurehead for the promotion of the club and breast cancer awareness in general, organising the first BCNA Field of Women, which featured the now iconic Pink Lady silhouettes, along with a number of white silhouettes to represent the high number of deaths at that time.

Awarded an OAM on Australia Day in 2012, nothing was too hard, too big or too much trouble for 'our Anna'.

In October 2013, a representative from Telstra rang Kerrie Griffin at work, asking for Anna's phone number. Telstra wanted to have a photo of Anna on the front cover of the 2013-14 telephone directory for Canberra, Yass and Queanbeyan. Anna insisted the photo should include the whole team – not just her.

It wasn't all serious business for Anna, particularly when it came to paddling. She loved to have fun and was not afraid to dress up and laugh at herself. Together with her bestie, Sylvia Flaxman, Anna made sure training sessions were not all hard work and no fun. With Anna's encouragement, Sylvia would often give the crew unusual instructions. "Keep going for another 67-and-a-half strokes," she'd say, much to the confusion – and then the laughter – of the crew as they froze their paddles halfway through stroke number 68.

The team trained four days a week – Saturday, Sunday, Tuesday and Thursday – always early morning, except for Sunday when they were allowed a little sleep-in. Even though Anna set the training start time and insisted that paddlers be prompt, there was a slight problem in that she liked to listen to the 8 am radio news. Never mind, because it was only a 5-minute broadcast, she could hide behind the cars with Katherine, listen to the news, then sprint for the boats 'just in time' – although the mock frown from Sylvia may have suggested otherwise to the unknowing bystander.

Loyal to a fault, Anna always put the paddlers first.

"Brace yourselves for a long one," she said one morning as people arrived. "We're heading to Clare Holland House."

Nobody batted an eyelid. Sylvia was in Clare Holland House – 'the hospice' or palliative care unit situated on the shores of Lake Burley Griffin, in the East Basin area, some five kilometres from the home of the dragon boats in Lotus Bay.

When the team arrived outside Clare Holland House, there was Sylvia. Wearing a bright pink tracksuit and surrounded by balloons, she was sitting in the garden, out in the sunshine, smiling and waving.

Feisty, fit and funny people die too soon.

Anna's motto was 'whatever is said on the boat, stays on the boat'. She made the dragon boat a safe space – where paddlers could vent, rant, cry, support and laugh.

That's who she was and her spirit and legacy stay with the team today.

# Where to Find Info

It is difficult to provide all the information readers may want here, not only because of global book distribution but also because websites tend to change.

In general, if you want to find out about dragon boating clubs (not only breast cancer survivor teams) in your area, I would be inclined to check your local community or government directory, or use your trusted web browser. The same applies to people wanting more information about breast cancer and support groups, including dragon boating teams for survivors.

What I can provide, though, is a point of contact for people who live in Canberra, and Australia in general. You can get in touch with the organisations listed below through their information pages and someone is sure to guide you in the right direction. Do bear in mind, however, that most are volunteers.

In a pinch, please feel free to contact me directly at kellie@justrightwords.com.au

## Breast cancer support

Bosom Buddies Canberra https://bosombuddies.org.au/

BreastScreen Australia https://www.health.gov.au/our-work/breastscreen-australia-program

Breast Cancer Network Australia https://www.bcna.org.au/

Colleen's Lingerie and Swimwear, Garran ACT https://www.colleens.com.au/

Heads Up Kippax https://headsup.net.au/

McGrath Foundation https://www.mcgrathfoundation.com.au/

National Breast Cancer Foundation https://nbcf.org.au/

## Dragons Abreast (dragon boating for breast cancer survivors and supporters)

Dragons Abreast (2007), *A Dragon's Tale*, Australia

Dragons Abreast Australia https://dragonsabreast.com.au/

Dragons Abreast Canberra https://www.revolutionise.com.au/dacanberra/

International Breast Cancer Paddlers Commission (IBCPC) https://www.ibcpc.com

## Dragon Boating (in general)

Australian Dragon Boat Federation https://www.ausdbf.com.au/home/

Dragon Boat ACT https://www.dbact.com.au/home/

International Dragon Boat Federation https://www.dragonboat.sport/

## Other references

(Podcast) What You Don't Know Until You Do, with Dr Charlotte Tottman

(Podcast) What You Don't Know Until You Do: Unlimited, with Dr Charlotte Tottman

https://www.bcna.org.au/resource-hub/podcasts/season-2-episode-0-charlotte-tottman-podcast-series/

www.ingramcontent.com/pod-product-compliance
Lightning Source LLC
Chambersburg PA
CBHW022032290426
44109CB00014B/833